OXFORD READINGS IN PHILOSOPHY

ETHICAL THEORY 1

Other volumes are in preparation

ETHICAL THEORY 1

The Question of Objectivity

Edited by

JAMES RACHELS

OXFORD UNIVERSITY PRESS
1998

Oxford University Press, Great Clarendon Street, Oxford OX2 6DP

Oxford New York

Athens Auckland Bangkok Bogota Bombay Buenos Aires
Calcutta Cape Town Dar es Salaam Delhi Florence Hong Kong Istanbul
Karachi Kuala Lumpur Madras Madrid Melbourne Mexico City
Nairobi Paris Singapore Taipei Tokyo Toronto Warsaw

and associated companies in
Berlin Ibadan

Oxford is a trade mark of Oxford University Press

Published in the United States by
Oxford University Press Inc., New York

Introduction and selection © Oxford University Press 1998

British Library Cataloguing in Publication Data

Data available

Library of Congress Cataloging in Publication Data
Ethical theory / edited by James Rachels.
(Oxford readings in philosophy)
Includes bibliographical references and index.
Contents: 1. The question of objectivity—2. Theories about how we should live.
1. Ethics. I. Rachels, James, 1941– . II. Series.
BJ1012.E88345 1998 170—dc21 97-42646
ISBN 0-19-875192-3

1 3 5 7 9 10 8 6 4 2

Typeset by Best-set Typesetter Ltd., Hong Kong
Printed in Great Britain by
Biddles Ltd., Guildford and King's Lynn

CONTENTS

INTRODUCTION

JAMES RACHELS

The question of ethical objectivity is as old as philosophy itself. In the ancient world, sceptics were attracted to the idea that morality is nothing more than a set of social conventions. Herodotus, after reviewing the moral beliefs of various cultures, declared that 'Custom is king o'er all,' and said that anyone who thinks otherwise is merely naïve: 'Everyone without exception believes his own native customs, and the religion he was brought up in, to be the best.'[1] In Plato's *Republic* Socrates encountered Thrasymachus, who gave the idea a sinister twist. Right and wrong, said Thrasymachus, are inventions of the strong that help them dominate the weak:

Each ruling class makes laws that are in its own interest, a democracy democratic laws, a tyranny tyrannical ones and so on; and in making these laws they define as 'right' for their subjects what is in the interests of themselves, the rulers, and if anyone breaks their laws he is punished as a 'wrongdoer'. That is what I mean when I say that 'right' is the same thing in all states, namely the interest of the established ruling class.[2]

The partisans of such views assume that there are no such things as *moral facts*—there is nothing in the nature of things that makes one sort of action right and another wrong. Pyrrho made this assumption explicit. According to Diogenes, Pyrrho taught that 'Nothing was honourable or dishonourable, just or unjust. And so, universally, he held that there is nothing really existent, but custom and convention govern human action; for no single thing is any more this than that.'[3]

Modern sceptics, while agreeing that there are no moral facts, have been attracted to the idea that morality originates in the desires and emotions of the individual. Thomas Hobbes observed that

---

[1] Herodotus, *The Histories*, tr. Aubrey de Selincourt, rev. A. R. Burn (Harmondsworth: Penguin, 1972), 220.

[2] Plato, *Republic*, 338e; tr. H. D. P. Lee (Baltimore: Penguin, 1956), 66.

[3] Diogenes Laertius, *Lives of Eminent Philosophers*, ii, Loeb Classical Library (Cambridge, Mass.: Harvard University Press, 1955), 475.

Whatever is the object of any man's appetite or desire, that is it which he for his part calleth *good*; and the object of his hate and aversion, *evil*; and of his contempt, *vile* and *inconsiderable*. For these words of good, evil, and contemptible are ever used with relation to the person that useth them, there being nothing simply and absolutely so, nor any common rule of good and evil to be taken from the nature of the objects themselves . . .[4]

But it is David Hume, more than any other figure in modern thought, who is associated with this idea: 'when you pronounce any action or character to be vicious,' wrote Hume, 'you mean nothing, but that from the constitution of your nature you have a feeling or sentiment of blame from the contemplation of it'.[5]

I

Such ideas seem to contradict our ordinary understanding of ethics. When we judge something to be good or bad, we do not understand ourselves merely to be venting our emotions—if we wanted to do that, we could just say that we like it or dislike it. Nor do we understand ourselves merely to be applying the standards of our society—after all, we know that our society's standards could be misguided. Instead, we mean to be saying something that is objectively true, independently of our feelings and social conventions. One way of expressing our ordinary understanding is to say we assume there are moral facts. We think it is a fact, for example, that slavery is unjust and that anyone who thinks otherwise must be mistaken.

But this common-sense view is not easy to defend. We may begin by noting three problems, all identified by Hume. First, there is the *ontological problem*. Do 'moral facts' really exist? If we take an inventory of the world, we find plants and animals and rocks and atoms and stars. We find that Antarctica is bigger than England, that dinosaurs lived 65 million years ago, and that smoking causes cancer. But do we find good and evil? Suppose we examine an act that is undoubtedly evil—a murder, for example. We see a man with a knife; we see him strike; we see the victim fall; we see blood and then a lifeless body. But where, among these facts, is the moral fact? This was Hume's argument: 'Take any action allow'd to be vicious: Wilful murder, for instance. Examine it in all lights, and see if you can find that matter of fact, or real existence, which you call *vice*. In which-

[4] Thomas Hobbes, *Leviathan* (1651), ed. Edwin Curley (Indianapolis: Hackett, 1994), I. vi. 28–9.
[5] David Hume, *A Treatise of Human Nature* (1739–40), ed. L. A. Selby-Bigge (Oxford: Clarendon Press, 1888), III. i. 1, p. 469.

ever way you take it, you find only certain passions, motives, volitions and thoughts. There is no other matter of fact in the case.'[6]

Closely related to this is the *epistemological problem*: how do we know moral facts? In science we discern the existence of things by observation and experiment, or perhaps by inference from observations and experiments. In mathematics there are proofs. In ordinary life we rely on ordinary perception. But moral facts are not accessible by any of these familiar methods. If the existence of moral facts is to be defended, we need to be able to say how they are discerned.

Thirdly, there is the *motivation problem*. Moral beliefs seem to be necessarily motivating. That is, when a person has a moral belief—a belief that a certain way of behaving is right or wrong, or that something should or should not be done—this necessarily involves the person's having at least some motivation to act accordingly. Suppose, for example, I say that gambling is wrong. You would expect me to avoid gambling. But what if you discover that I play in a high-stakes poker game every Friday night? My behaviour contradicts my pronouncement. What is to be made of this?

There are several possibilities. (1) Perhaps I lied; I do not really believe that gambling is wrong. I may have been teasing you or speaking sarcastically. (2) Another possibility is that I was only reporting what other people say—I only meant something like 'Most people think gambling is wrong'. I did not mean to be expressing any view of my own. (3) Or it may be that I am morally weak. Although I think it is wrong, and I resolve not to gamble, when Friday comes around I am overcome by temptation. Afterwards I reproach myself for having succumbed.

Or perhaps some other explanation might be tried. But the point is that my conduct requires some such explanation. I cannot gamble happily, without hesitation, and reflect on my conduct with no sense of self-recrimination, if it is true that I believe gambling is wrong. It is not necessary, of course, that I always do what I think is right, but it is necessary that I have at least some motivation to do it. This motivation need not be so powerful that it cannot be overcome by other desires. But it must supply some inclination, however slight, so that there is something there for the other desires to overcome.

We may sum this up by saying that there is an internal connection between moral belief and motivation. Why is this important? For one thing, it poses a problem for the idea that there are moral facts. There is no internal connection between ordinary factual belief and motivation. If I say that Antarctica is bigger than England, this leads to no expectations

[6] Ibid. 468.

about how I will behave. It is just a fact, towards which I might be utterly indifferent. Of course, if my statement is considered alongside other information about me, such as that I desperately want to visit somewhere bigger than England, then you might conclude I have some motivation to visit Antarctica. But it is the added information about my desires that supplies the motivating power. With moral belief, the motivating power seems to be built into the belief itself.

The upshot is that moral beliefs seem different from ordinary factual beliefs, in a way that is discouraging to the idea of moral facts and congenial to the theory that moral beliefs are fundamentally matters of 'feeling or sentiment'. Hume again:

Scince morals, therefore, have an influence on the actions and affections, it follows, that they cannot be deriv'd from reason; and that because reason alone, as we have already prov'd, can never have any such influence. Morals excite passions, and produce or prevent actions. Reason of itself is utterly impotent in this particular. The rules of morality, therefore, are not conclusions of our reason.[7]

II

Sceptics have argued that morality is an area where disagreement reigns. In science, they say, there is widespread agreement on fundamental matters; and when there are disputes, there are established methods of settling them. But in ethics there is endless disagreement about even the simplest points, and the disagreements are impossible to resolve rationally. Therefore, the argument goes, we should acknowledge that ethics is unlike science. Ethics is just a matter of opinion, and that's the end of it.

Although this is a popular argument, both its premisses appear to be false. In the first place, the pattern of agreement and disagreement in ethics is about the same as in science. In ethics, as in science, we agree about a great many basic things: that murder, theft, and rape are wrong; that children should be protected; that promises should be kept; that honesty, courage, and generosity are virtues; and a great deal more. If anyone objects that there are lots of people who don't accept all this, we can remind them of an equal number of people who do not accept science. And in both ethics and science there are a smaller number of disputed questions about which agreement has not been reached. If there is no general agreement about the morality of abortion, neither is there general agreement about some issues in quantum mechanics. The illusion that disagreements in ethics are more widespread than in science may be due to

[7] Hume, *A Treatise of Human Nature*, 457.

nothing more than our tendency to cite certain sorts of examples: when we think about ethics, we tend to think automatically of the most difficult unresolved issues; whereas, when we think of science, we think of the matters about which there is consensus.

Moreover, it is not true that there are no rational means for resolving ethical disputes. Such methods are easy to find. They are not identical with 'scientific' methods, but they are no worse for that. Ethical disputes are settled by appeal to reasons and principles. If you say that Jones is a bad man, and I deny it, you can prove you are right by showing that he is a chronic liar and cheat, that he is needlessly cruel to other people, and so on. Once again, the illusion that there is no 'proof' in ethics may be due only to our inattention to the facts of real-life moral reasoning.

The existence of ethical disagreement provides no special support for subjectivist theories of ethics. On the contrary, the fact that such disagreement exists has been used as an argument *against* some forms of ethical subjectivism. 'These words of good, evil, and contemptible', said Hobbes, 'are ever used with relation to the person that useth them.' Suppose we interpret this to mean that, whenever someone says that something is good, this means nothing but that he or she has a positive attitude towards it (and similarly, the statement that something is bad means that the speaker has a negative attitude). We may call this *simple subjectivism*. This is a natural way to understand the subjectivist view. But, as G. E. Moore demonstrated, if this is what subjectivism says, then it can't possibly be right, because it leaves us unable to explain ethical disagreement. Suppose I say that something is good, and you say it is bad. If simple subjectivism were correct, then I would be describing my feelings and you would be describing yours; therefore, there would be no disagreement between us. (I will agree that you have a negative attitude, and you should likewise concede that I have a positive attitude.) But this is absurd; of course we disagree. For this reason, and others like it, Moore concluded that ethical subjectivism is not tenable and that we must look elsewhere for an adequate theory of ethics.

But such criticisms only prompted an improved version of subjectivism. *Emotivism*, which became the most influential theory of ethics in the mid-twentieth century, was developed by the Logical Positivists—most notably Moritz Schlick and A. J. Ayer—and the American philosopher Charles L. Stevenson. It was a more subtle and sophisticated theory than simple subjectivism because it incorporated a more sophisticated view of moral language. Emotivism began with the observation that language is used in a variety of ways. One of its principal uses is in stating facts, or at least what we take to be facts. Thus we may say that Mars is the fourth planet from the sun and that penguins cannot fly. In each case, we are saying something that is either true or false, and the purpose of saying such things is, typically, to convey information to the listener.

There are, however, other purposes for which language may be used. Suppose I say to someone who is thinking of suicide: 'No, don't do it'. This utterance is neither true nor false. It is not a statement of any kind; it is a request, or an entreaty, which is something altogether different. Its purpose is not to convey information. Rather, its purpose is to influence behaviour. Again, consider utterances such as 'Hurrah!' and 'Alas!', which are neither statements of fact nor requests. Their purpose is to express (not report) attitudes. The difference between reporting an attitude and expressing it is of paramount importance. If I say 'I like *Little Dorrit*', I am reporting the fact that I have a positive attitude towards Dickens's novel. My statement is a statement of fact that is true or false. On the other hand, if I shout 'Hurrah for Dickens!' I am not stating any sort of fact. I am expressing an attitude, but I am not reporting that I have it.

According to emotivism, moral language is not used to state facts, not even facts about the speaker's attitudes. It is used, first, as a means of influencing people's behaviour: if someone says 'You ought not to do that', she is trying to stop you from doing it. Thus, the utterance is more like a request than a statement of fact; it is as though she had said 'Don't do it!' And, secondly, moral language is used to express (not report) attitudes. Saying 'Racism is wrong' is not like saying 'I disapprove of racism', but it is like saying 'Racism—yech!'

By interpreting moral judgements in a new way, emotivism made a place for ethical disagreement and made possible a new and more illuminating understanding of it. Stevenson emphasized that there is more than one way in which people may disagree. If I believe that Lee Harvey Oswald acted alone in assassinating John Kennedy, and you believe there was a conspiracy, it is a disagreement over the facts—I believe something to be true that you believe to be false. But suppose, on the other hand, I favour gun-control legislation, while you are against it. Here we disagree, but in a different sense. It is not our beliefs that are in conflict, but our desires. (You and I may agree about all the facts concerning guns and gun-control, and yet still want different things to happen.) In the first kind of disagreement, we believe different things, both of which cannot be true. In the second, we want different things, both of which cannot happen. Stevenson calls this a disagreement *in* attitude, and contrasts it with disagreement *about* attitudes. Moral disagreements are disagreements in attitude.

In the mid-twentieth century many philosophers believed that the truth about ethics had finally been found. Emotivism, they thought, had solved all the problems. The epistemological problem was easy: there was no need for an account of how we know moral truths, for there are no moral truths to be known. Emotivism also had a simple explanation of the internal relation between moral belief and motivation: to have a moral belief is to have a certain sort of attitude, and attitudes are dispositions to act.

Obviously, the emotivists denied that there are moral facts, and so the ontological problem was side-stepped too. But at the same time the emotivists were able to offer an explanation of why the belief in moral facts seems so natural. Facts are the counterparts of true statements: the fact that Buster Keaton made movies is what makes the statement 'Buster Keaton made movies' true. We think there are moral facts because we mistakenly assume that moral 'statements' are the kinds of utterance that could be true. If in saying that Hitler is wicked we are saying something true, there must be a corresponding fact, Hitler's being wicked, that makes it true. However, once we understand that moral 'statements' are not really statements at all, and indeed are not even the sorts of utterance that could be true, the temptation to think there are moral facts disappears. Thus, the belief in moral facts could now be seen not only as the legacy of discarded scientific and religious views but as the symptom of a mistaken assumption about moral language as well.

III

Moral judgements must be founded on good reasons. If I tell you that such-and-such action is wrong, you are entitled to ask why it is wrong; and if I have no good reply, you may reject my advice as unfounded. This is what separates moral judgements from mere statements of preference. If I say that I like cottage cheese, I do not need a reason: it may just be a fact about me that I like cottage cheese, and that's all there is to it. But if I say that you ought to eat cottage cheese, I need to have some reason to back up my statement. An adequate theory of the nature of ethics must, therefore, provide a plausible account of the way that reasons support moral judgements. A chief weakness of emotivism was that it could not do this.

What could the emotivists say about the nature of moral reasoning? Remember that, on their view, if I tell you that such-and-such action is wrong, I am not trying to alter your beliefs; I am trying to influence your attitudes. Therefore, if you challenge me to explain why it is wrong, I will want to cite considerations that will influence your attitudes in the desired way. The business of giving reasons therefore turns out to be an exercise in psychological manipulation.

This might strike us as a realistic, if somewhat cynical, account of moral reasoning. What is wrong with it? The problem is that, if this view is correct, then *any* fact that influences attitudes can count as a reason for the attitude produced. If the thought that Smith is an Oxford professor causes someone to distrust him, then 'Smith is an Oxford professor' would become a reason in support of the judgement that he is untrustworthy. Can this possibly be right? Stevenson embraced this consequence of his view without flinching: 'Any statement', he said, 'about any fact which any speaker considers likely to alter attitudes may be adduced as a reason for or against an ethical judgment.'[8] But, in the end, this account of reasons proved to be the most troubling aspect of emotivism.

Is there any way that the basic idea of emotivism can be recast to provide a better account of moral reasoning? In 1952 R. M. Hare did this in his book *The Language of Morals*.[9] The emotivists had been right, Hare argued, in thinking that moral language is prescriptive rather than descriptive. But, according to Hare, the emotivists erred by overlooking an important logical feature of words such as 'right' and 'ought.' When we use such words to make moral judgements, we implicitly commit ourselves to universal principles. If, for example, we say on a particular occasion that someone ought not to lie, we are committing ourselves to the general principle that lying is wrong. This, in turn, commits us to similar judgements on other occasions. This is a matter of logic: if we are to be consistent, we may not appeal to a principle at one time that we would not be willing to accept at other times. Hare dubbed this feature of moral judgement 'universalizability' and he called his view 'Universal Prescriptivism'.

The requirement of universalizability imposed the needed constraints on what could count as a moral reason. Universalizability meant, for example, that we must apply to ourselves the same principles we use in judging others. As one writer put it, I can't say you're wrong to drink my beer when I am aiming to drink yours.[10] Or consider the story about King David recounted in 2 Samuel:

David had fallen in love with Bathsheba, the wife of Uriah, a soldier in his army. After a visit to the palace, Bathsheba was found to be carrying

[8] C. L. Stevenson, *Ethics and Language* (New Haven: Yale University Press, 1944), 114.

[9] R. M. Hare, *The Language of Morals* (Oxford: Oxford University Press, 1952).

[10] Brian Medlin, 'Ultimate Principles and Ethical Egoism', *Australasian Journal of Philosophy*, 35 (1957), 111–18.

David's child, and to cover up what he had done David arranged for Uriah to be killed in battle. Bathsheba then became David's wife. But the prophet Nathan knew what had happened, and he confronted David on a day when the king was dispensing justice. Nathan presented David with this case for his judgement:

There were two men in a certain city, the one rich and the other poor. The rich man had very many flocks and herds; but the poor man had nothing but one little ewe lamb, which he had bought. And he brought it up, and it grew up with him and his children; it used to eat of his morsel, and drink from his cup, and lie in his bosom, and it was like a daughter to him. Now there came a traveller to the rich man, and he was unwilling to take one of his own flock or herd to prepare for the wayfarer who had come to him, but he took the poor man's lamb, and prepared it for the man who had come to him.[11]

When David heard this, he was indignant and declared that 'The man who has done this deserves to die'; whereupon Nathan told him: 'You are the man.' Then David realized that he was, indeed, guilty of the very offence he had just condemned.

Nathan had induced David to reason in a certain way. First he elicited the principles to which David was already committed, by presenting him the fictitious case. Then he brought David to realize that these principles, when applied to his own behaviour, would lead to its condemnation. So David was bound to judge his own conduct wrong, not because there were 'moral facts' that he was forced to acknowledge, but because consistency required it. Hare contends that all moral reasoning is, in the end, like this.

IV

We may distinguish two senses in which ethics might be 'objective':

(1) Ethics could be objective in the sense that moral problems can be solved by rational methods. These methods would show that some moral views are acceptable while others are not.

On Hare's theory, ethics is objective in this sense. Morality is not merely a 'matter of opinion'. Whether an act is right depends, instead, on whether it is justifiable by sound methods of reasoning.

Social contract theorists also see ethics as objective in this sense. On their view, moral rules are rules that rational people will agree to establish for their mutual benefit. Each of us, for example, will be better off in a

---

[11] 2 Samuel 12: 1–4 (RSV).

society in which murder is prohibited and promises are kept. So each of us has good reason to accept such rules, provided that other people will accept them as well. (Our own compliance with the rules is the fair price we pay to secure the compliance of others.) By such reasoning it may be shown that the prohibitions on murder and promise-breaking, and many other such rules, are rationally defensible.

These theories make morality out to be objective in at least this first sense. But the problem we mentioned at the outset remains: these views still seem radically incompatible with our ordinary sense of what we are doing when we make moral judgements. This is the problem of moral phenomenology: our theory of what morality is should be compatible with our sense of what it is like to make a moral judgement or to engage in moral thinking. When judged by this standard, any theory that sees morality as essentially connected with feelings or social conventions is bound to fall short. Moral judgement seems to have an absolute character that is missed by such theories. Thus, we may want a theory that makes morality out to be objective in a second, stronger sense:

(2) Ethics could be objective in the sense that moral predicates—'good', 'right', and so on—refer to real properties of things. Moral facts are part of the fabric of the world.

Moral realism is the view that ethics is objective in this sense. But exactly what does this come to? What would it be like for there to be 'real' moral properties of things? What do such properties consist in? We may distinguish three approaches.

1. One view is that moral properties are distinctive properties that are separate from an object's other qualities. When, after recounting all the other facts about a murder, including the facts about emotional reactions, prevailing social norms, and the like, we say that the murder was evil, we are mentioning a new and additional fact.

But this is exactly the kind of moral fact that Hume thought did not exist, and others have shared Hume's scepticism. J. L. Mackie argued that, if there were such properties, they would be utterly strange, unlike anything else in nature. They would have to tell us what to do and then motivate us to do it—and what sort of 'property' could do that? Moreover, to detect such properties we would need cognitive capacities unlike any with which we are familiar. None the less, Mackie suggests, it is easy to understand why people believe so easily that there are such properties. Our ordinary way of thinking and talking about morality assumes that such properties exist. This led Mackie to propose an 'error theory' of ethics: our ordinary thought and speech about ethics involves us in a systematic error about the nature of reality.

A different sort of sceptical argument is suggested by Gilbert Harman. Harman points out that facts figure into how we explain observations. If someone observes that there is a wooden horse at the gate, and we ask ourselves why he observes this, our explanation will inevitably refer at some point to the horse and the gate. The explanation will go something like this: the observer has a certain sort of perceptual apparatus (eyes, ears, brain) that interacts with the external world in certain complicated ways. The external world contains a wooden horse juxtaposed with a gate; and so, on this occasion, the result of the interaction between the observer's perceptual apparatus and the environment is the observation that there is a wooden horse at the gate. The point to be noticed is that our best explanation of the observation involves the fact of what is being observed.

But when we turn to moral observations, things are different. Suppose somebody sees a murderer in action and observes that what he does is wicked. We can explain this observation without referring to the fact of wickedness at all. There is a killer, a victim, and an act that causes death; the observer sees all this in the usual way and then has a negative reaction to what he sees. To explain his 'observation' we need only refer to the observer's psychology and perhaps to the social norms and training that helped to shape that psychology. The 'fact' of the murderer's conduct really being wicked need not enter the picture at all. Thus, moral facts turn out to be metaphysical danglers that do no work.

Finally, there is a more general reason to doubt that moral facts of this sort exist: it is hard to fit such 'facts' into the picture of the world presented by modern science. There are, of course, other ways of understanding what the world is like that are more congenial to moral facts. Consider, for example, Aristotle's view. Aristotle believed that the world is a rational, orderly system with values and purposes built into its very nature. He taught that everything has a purpose—just as the purpose of a knife is to cut, and the purpose of the heart is to pump blood, so the purpose of the rain is to provide water for plants. And the plants have a purpose, too:

> we must believe, first that plants exist for the sake of animals, second that all other animals exist for the sake of man, tame animals for the use he can make of them as well as for the food they provide; and as for wild animals, most though not all of these can be used for food or are useful in other ways; clothing and instruments can be made out of them. If then we are right in believing that nature makes nothing without some end in view, nothing to no purpose, it must be that nature has made all things specifically for the sake of man.[12]

[12] Aristotle, *The Politics*, book 1, ch. 8; tr. T. A. Sinclair (Harmondsworth: Penguin, 1962), 40.

It is a neat hierarchical arrangement, with everything having its own place and purpose—and, not coincidentally, an arrangement quite favourable to human beings. Now suppose this combination of ideas formed the core of our best theory of what the world is like. It would then be natural to regard 'moral facts' as part of the overall scheme of things.

At one time the Aristotelian world-view may have been the best available. But it has now been displaced by modern science, and science gives us a very different picture. The rain does not fall so that plants can grow; if it appears so, that is only because plants have evolved, by natural selection, to take advantage of the rainy climate. Nor were the animals made 'for the sake of man'; nor do human beings have any privileged place in the scheme of things. Hume was one of the first to note this implication of the new world-view when he commented that 'The life of a man is of no greater importance to the universe than that of an oyster.'[13] The reason moral facts seem so 'queer', and the reason they do not figure into our best explanations of moral observations, is that we now view the world in the way set out by modern science. Science provides the best general understanding of the world that we now have, and no part of philosophy, including ethics, may be inconsistent with it.

2. A second possibility is that moral properties are not special, peculiar properties but are identical with ordinary properties. For example, the property of being good might be identical with the property of being pleasurable. This approach has the great virtue of making moral properties non-mysterious. There is nothing strange about something's being pleasurable; we know exactly what that is and how to discern it. And there will be nothing in such a view at odds with scientific understanding.

But which ordinary properties are identical to the moral properties? It all depends on which substantive ethical theory is correct. If egoistic hedonism is the best such theory, then 'good' is the same as 'pleasurable'. If the divine command theory is correct, 'good' is identical with 'approved by God'. And if classical utilitarianism turns out to be the best theory, the relevant property is 'produces the greatest happiness for the greatest number'. Of course, philosophers do not agree about which substantive theory (if any) is correct, but that does not matter here. If moral philosophy has not yet progressed to the point at which we know what theory is best, all that means is that we do not yet know which ordinary properties are identical with the moral properties.

For a long time after the publication of Moore's *Principia Ethica* in 1903 it was thought that this approach is untenable. Moore had argued that any

[13] David Hume, *Essays Moral Political and Literary* (1741–2; Oxford: Oxford University Press, 1963), 590.

such view commits the 'naturalistic fallacy'. First, he said, if we focus our attention on what we mean by 'good' and what we mean by (for example) 'pleasurable', we will clearly see that they are not the same. Moreover, there is an argument—the 'open-question argument', as it came to be known—that seems to show that goodness cannot be identical with anything other than itself. The question 'Are pleasurable things good?' is an open question, and to say that pleasurable things *are* good is a significant affirmation. But, the argument goes, if goodness and pleasurableness were the same thing, this would be like asking 'Are pleasurable things pleasurable?' An analogous argument can be given with respect to any other ordinary property with which goodness is identified.

Moore had made a fundamental mistake. His argument, if it were sound, would also show that the Morning Star cannot be identical with the Evening Star. If we focus our attention on what we mean by these terms, we will clearly see that they are not the same—the first is a star seen in the morning, while the second is a star seen in the evening. And the question 'Is the Morning Star the Evening Star?' was an open question the answer to which was unknown for many centuries. But in fact the two are identical. Today we would say that Moore went wrong because he did not distinguish necessary identity from contingent identity. Moore is hardly to be blamed; the importance of this distinction did not become apparent until long after his career was over.

Another idea of Moore's has proven to have more lasting value. Moore discovered the *supervenience* of moral properties (or, if there are no moral properties, of moral concepts). Whether something is good or bad is always determined entirely by what its other properties are. For example, suppose there are two mailboxes that are exactly alike—they are the same size, the same colour, made of the same material, equally waterproof, and so on. Now suppose it is suggested that one of these mailboxes is better than the other. This would make no sense, because objects cannot differ only in their goodness—if X is better than Y, there must also be some other difference between them. A mailbox is good *because* it has a certain size, shape, sturdiness, and so on; thus, any other mailbox with these same qualities must be equally good. This may be expressed by saying that a thing's goodness supervenes on its other properties. In this sense, a property like 'yellow' is not supervenient. Two objects can differ only in that one is yellow while the other is not.

Any view about the nature of moral properties must account for their supervenience, and the approach we are now considering can do so easily enough. If being good is the same as being pleasurable, or some other such ordinary property, then it is obvious that two things could not differ only in their goodness—they could not, that is to say, be exactly alike in every other way, including their pleasurableness, and yet one be good while the other is not.

This does not mean, however, that this view is free of difficulties. Even though it avoids the metaphysical and epistemological problems, the motivation problem remains worrisome. If something's being good, or right, is identical with some ordinary fact, why can't we be as indifferent to this fact as to any other? It is not obvious how, within this view, we are to account for the connection between moral belief and conduct.

3. Finally, there is the view that moral properties are similar to what John Locke called 'secondary qualities'. The distinction between primary and secondary qualities is a tricky, contentious business, but for our purposes it may suffice to say, paraphrasing Locke, that secondary qualities are *powers that objects have to produce effects in the consciousness of observers*. Colour is the classic (if disputed) example of a secondary quality. A physical object, like a box, has a shape and mass that exist entirely independently of observers. (Shape and mass are primary qualities.) The box's shape and mass would be the same even if there were no conscious beings in the universe. But what of its colour? Colour is not a thing spread upon the box like a coat of paint. The box's surface reflects light-waves in a certain way. Then, this light strikes the eyes of observers, and as a result the observers have visual experiences of a certain character. If the light-waves falling on the box were different, or if the visual apparatus of the observer were different, then the box would appear to have a different colour, and this would no more be the box's 'real' colour than any other. The box's 'redness', then, just consists in its power, under certain conditions, to cause a certain kind of observer to have a certain kind of visual experience.

We may extend this analysis to include other powers of things to induce other sorts of experience in us. What does it mean for something to be sour? A lemon is sour because, when we put it to our tongues, we experience a certain kind of taste. What is sour for humans might not be sour for animals with different kinds of sense-organs; and if we were made differently, lemons might not be sour for us. Moreover, what is sour for one human being may not be sour for another—although we do have a notion of what is 'normal' for our species in this regard. But, despite all this, to say that lemons are sour is not a 'subjective' remark. It is a perfectly objective fact that lemons have the power to produce the sensation in us. Whether they are sour is not merely a matter of opinion.

Moral properties could be properties of this kind—they could be powers to cause us to have certain sorts of attitude or emotion. Being evil might consist in having whatever it takes to provoke a thoughtful person to hatred, opposition, and contempt. When we think of the murderer and his victim, the (ordinary) facts of the matter are such that they evoke feelings of horror in us; the 'evil' is simply the power to call forth this reaction. Similarly, being good would consist in being so constituted as to evoke our support and approval.

This is a promising form of moral realism. But it is not a robustly realistic view. It is, in an obvious way, a compromise between objective and subjective views of ethics. It is objective in that it identifies good and evil with something that is really 'there' in the world outside us, but at the same time, *what* is there is just the power to produce feelings inside us—the same feelings that Hume described when he wrote that 'When you pronounce any action or character to be vicious, you mean nothing, but that from the constitution of your nature you have a feeling or sentiment of blame from the contemplation of it.' It would not be hard to interpret Hume as a secondary-quality theorist.

This view appears promising because it seems to satisfy the various conditions of adequacy we have discussed. Those conditions are, once again:

An adequate theory must solve the ontological problem: it must account for ethics without assuming the existence of anything that does not actually exist. The secondary-quality view requires only ordinary objects, events, and the like, and human beings who interact with them. It assumes no 'queer' entities and no entities beyond the bounds of our ordinary scientific understanding of what the world is like.

An adequate theory must solve the motivation problem: it must account for the internal connection between moral belief and motivation (or, if there is no such connection, it must offer an alternative account of how morality guides action). On the secondary-quality view, there is a clear, if somewhat complicated, connection between recognizing something as right and being motivated to act. If an act is right (if we ought to do it), then there is something about it that would evoke an attitude of approval in us, if only we would think clearly and non-evasively about it. Attitudes motivate. Therefore, if we ought to do something, then to the extent that we think clearly and non-evasively about it, we will be motivated to act accordingly.

An adequate theory must solve the epistemological problem: if we have knowledge of right and wrong, it must explain how we acquire such knowledge. We learn that a lemon is sour by tasting it; the proof of the sourness is the taste in our mouths. Similarly, we learn that something is wrong by contemplating it and as a result experiencing feelings of disapproval.

Complications arise, however, because such feelings can have other sources—a feeling might be the product of prejudice or cultural conditioning rather than proceeding from what Hume called 'a proper discernment of its object'. Therefore, the process of deliberation must be conducted in such a way as to eliminate these other possible sources—one must try to set aside prejudice and other influences and take an objective look at the matter under consideration. As Hume knew, doing this might require a considerable expenditure of cognitive energy: 'But in order to pave the way for such a sentiment, and give a proper discernment of its object, it is often necessary, we find, that much reasoning should precede, that nice distinctions be made, just conclusions drawn, distant comparisons formed, complicated relations examined, and general facts fixed and ascertained.'[14] A sentiment indicates the presence of moral qualities only to the extent that it results from this kind of thinking. Otherwise, we cannot infer that the object itself has what it takes to cause the feeling.

An adequate theory must account for the place of reason in ethics. Moral judgements require reasons in their support; but what sort of consideration is a good reason? On the secondary-quality view, there is an obvious method for identifying the most basic moral reasons: we ask 'What is it about X, if anything, that causes reflective people to approve or disapprove it?' The answer reveals the reasons, if any, why X is good or bad. What is it about murder, for example, that causes reflective people to recoil from it? There is the fact that a person, who did not want to die, has had her life taken from her; that she will never be able to do all the things she wanted to do; that she will never experience the enjoyments she could have experienced; that her entire future has been cancelled. These are some of the reasons murder is wrong; and they are reasons because they have the power to move us.

An adequate theory must explain the nature of ethical disagreement. There is, of course, a vast amount of agreement in ethics, and the secondary-quality view can account for this easily enough. We agree about good and evil for the same reason we agree about what is sour. Lemons affect most of us in the same way because we have similar sense-organs; and murder affects us in the same way because we are similar in what Hume called 'the constitution of our natures'. The similarity is not hard to understand: we have evolved, by natural selection, as certain sorts of creature, with common desires and needs. We all want and enjoy friends. We take pleasure in our children. We respond to music. We are curious. We all have

---

[14] David Hume, *An Enquiry Concerning the Principles of Morals* (1752) ed. L. A. Selby-Bigge (Oxford: Oxford University Press, 1902), I. 137, p. 173.

reason to want a peaceful, secure society, because only in the context of such a society can our desires be satisfied. Such facts support large-scale agreements about respect for life and property, truthfulness, promise-keeping, friendship, and much more.

All this is compatible, however, with a degree of disagreement. As we have already observed, what is sour for one human being may not be sour for another—although we do have a notion of what is 'normal' for our species in this regard. As a practical matter, however, we need not assume that moral disagreements are expressions of intractable differences between people. More mundanely, and more frequently, disagreement will be the result of people's being influenced by ignorance; prejudice; self-deceit; a wilful refusal to face facts that contradict what one wants to believe; a lack of seriousness; or by just plain logical errors in reasoning. Our working hypothesis should be that we are enough alike that we could be brought to agree about most things, if only these sources of error could be eliminated.

An adequate theory must be consistent with the supervenient character of evaluative concepts. Secondary qualities are supervenient on primary qualities: if a lemon is sour, and there is another lemon that is identical to the first, molecule for molecule, then it must be sour too. Similarly, if X has the power to evoke a certain emotional response from us, and Y is exactly like X, then Y must also have what it takes to evoke that response.

And finally, an adequate theory about ethics must account for the phenomenology of moral experience. The strength of realist accounts of ethics is that they seem more faithful to the nature of moral experience than subjectivist accounts. If I say that something is wicked, and you reply: 'That's only the way you feel about it', I will think you are dismissing my claim, and not merely describing it, because I mean to be saying something more than that I have a certain feeling. A theory of ethics should explain this 'something more'. The secondary-quality view has this in common with other realist theories: it explains the 'something more' as the object's really having the property of being wicked—even though, when we learn what the property consists in, it may be a bit of a let-down.

But there is a difference between (*a*) what we consider ourselves to be doing when we make a moral judgement, and (*b*) the character of the experience we have when we 'perceive' something as good or bad. What, exactly, is moral experience like? What are the phenomena to which moral theories must be faithful? There is no simple answer. Moral experience includes a large variety of items: the inner sense that certain things must, or must not, be done; and feelings of guilt, embarrassment, admiration, outrage, and indignation. Some would add that feelings like love and devotion are 'moral'. But as far as *experiencing wickedness itself* is concerned, there is no use pretending that we experience such things in the way that we experience ordinary properties: we can't see it or touch it. Hume seems to have been right. If we attend closely to our experience, when we confront a murder for example, all we find, in addition to ordinary sensory perceptions, are our thoughts and emotions. We should not expect any theory, realist or otherwise, to imply that there is more.

I

SCIENCE AND ETHICS

BERTRAND RUSSELL

Those who maintain the insufficiency of science . . . appeal to the fact that science has nothing to say about 'values'. This I admit; but when it is inferred that ethics contains truths which cannot be proved or disproved by science, I disagree. The matter is one on which it is not altogether easy to think clearly, and my own views on it are quite different from what they were thirty years ago. But it is necessary to be clear about it if we are to appraise such arguments as those in support of Cosmic Purpose. As there is no consensus of opinion about ethics, it must be understood that what follows is my personal belief, not the dictum of science.

The study of ethics, traditionally, consists of two parts, one concerned with moral rules, the other with what is good on its own account. Rules of conduct, many of which have a ritual origin, play a great part in the lives of savages and primitive peoples. It is forbidden to eat out of the chief's dish, or to seethe the kid in its mother's milk; it is commanded to offer sacrifices to the gods, which, at a certain stage of development, are thought most acceptable if they are human beings. Other moral rules, such as the prohibition of murder and theft, have a more obvious social utility, and survive the decay of the primitive theological systems with which they were originally associated. But as men grow more reflective there is a tendency to lay less stress on rules and more on states of mind. This comes from two sources—philosophy and mystical religion. We are all familiar with passages in the prophets and the Gospels, in which purity of heart is set above meticulous observance of the Law; and St Paul's famous praise of charity, or love, teaches the same principle. The same thing will be found in all great mystics, Christian and non-Christian: what they value is a state of mind, out of which, as they hold, right conduct must ensue; rules seem to them external, and insufficiently adaptable to circumstances.

From Bertrand Russell, *Religion and Science* (New York: Oxford University Press, 1935), 234–55. Reprinted by permission of Oxford University Press.

One of the ways in which the need of appealing to external rules of conduct has been avoided has been the belief in 'conscience', which has been especially important in Protestant ethics. It has been supposed that God reveals to each human heart what is right and what is wrong, so that, in order to avoid sin, we have only to listen to the inner voice. There are, however, two difficulties in this theory: first, that conscience says different things to different people; secondly, that the study of the unconscious has given us an understanding of the mundane causes of conscientious feelings.

As to the different deliverances of conscience: George III's conscience told him that he must not grant Catholic Emancipation, as, if he did, he would have committed perjury in taking the Coronation Oath, but later monarchs have had no such scruples. Conscience leads some to condemn the spoliation of the rich by the poor, as advocated by communists; and others to condemn exploitation of the poor by the rich, as practised by capitalists. It tells one man that he ought to defend his country in case of invasion, while it tells another that all participation in warfare is wicked. During the war, the authorities, few of whom had studied ethics, found conscience very puzzling, and were led to some curious decisions, such as that a man might have conscientious scruples against fighting himself, but not against working on the fields so as to make possible the conscription of another man. They held also that, while conscience might disapprove of all war, it could not, failing that extreme position, disapprove of the war then in progress. Those who, for whatever reason, thought it wrong to fight, were compelled to state their position in terms of this somewhat primitive and unscientific conception of 'conscience'.

The diversity in the deliverances of conscience is what is to be expected when its origin is understood. In early youth, certain classes of acts meet with approval, and others with disapproval; and by the normal process of association, pleasure and discomfort gradually attach themselves to the acts, and not merely to the approval and disapproval respectively produced by them. As time goes on, we may forget all about our early moral training, but we shall still feel uncomfortable about certain kinds of actions, while others will give us a glow of virtue. To introspection, these feelings are mysterious, since we no longer remember the circumstances which originally caused them; and therefore it is natural to attribute them to the voice of God in the heart. But in fact conscience is a product of education, and can be trained to approve or disapprove, in the great majority of mankind, as educators may see fit. While, therefore, it is right to wish to liberate ethics from external moral rules, this can hardly be satisfactorily achieved by means of the notion of 'conscience'.

Philosophers, by a different road, have arrived at a different position in which, also, moral rules of conduct have a subordinate place. They have framed the concept of the Good, by which they mean (roughly speaking) that which, in itself and apart from its consequences, we should wish to see existing—or, if they are theists, that which is pleasing to God. Most people would agree that happiness is preferable to unhappiness, friendliness to unfriendliness, and so on. Moral rules, according to this view, are justified if they promote the existence of what is good on its own account, but not otherwise. The prohibition of murder, in the vast majority of cases, can be justified by its effects, but the practice of burning widows on their husbands' funeral pyres cannot. The former rule, therefore, should be retained, but not the latter. Even the best moral rules, however, will have *some* exceptions, since no class of actions *always* has bad results. We have thus three different senses in which an act may be ethically commendable: (1) it may be in accordance with the received moral code; (2) it may be sincerely intended to have good effects; (3) it may in fact have good effects. The third sense, however, is generally considered inadmissible in morals. According to orthodox theology, Judas Iscariot's act of betrayal had good consequences, since it was necessary for the Atonement; but it was not on this account laudable.

Different philosophers have formed different conceptions of the Good. Some hold that it consists in the knowledge and love of God; others in universal love; others in the enjoyment of beauty; and yet others in pleasure. The Good once defined, the rest of ethics follows: we ought to act in the way we believe most likely to create as much good as possible, and as little as possible of its correlative evil. The framing of moral rules, so long as the ultimate Good is supposed known, is matter for science. For example: Should capital punishment be inflicted for theft, or only for murder, or not at all? Jeremy Bentham, who considered pleasure to be the Good, devoted himself to working out what criminal code would most promote pleasure, and concluded that it ought to be much less severe than that prevailing in his day. All this, except the proposition that pleasure is the Good, comes within the sphere of science.

But when we try to be definite as to what we mean when we say that this or that is 'the Good', we find ourselves involved in very great difficulties. Bentham's creed that pleasure is the Good roused furious opposition, and was said to be a pig's philosophy. Neither he nor his opponents could advance any argument. In a scientific question, evidence can be adduced on both sides, and in the end one side is seen to have the better case—or, if this does not happen, the question is left undecided. But in a question as to whether this or that is the ultimate Good, there is no evidence either way; each disputant can only appeal to his own emotions, and employ such rhetorical devices as shall rouse similar emotions in others.

Take, for example, a question which has come to be important in practical politics. Bentham held that one man's pleasure has the same ethical importance as another man's, provided the quantities are equal; and on this ground he was led to advocate democracy. Nietzsche, on the contrary, held that only the great man can be regarded as important on his own account, and that the bulk of mankind are only means to his well-being. He viewed ordinary men as many people view animals: he thought it justifiable to make use of them, not for their own good, but for that of the superman, and this view has since been adopted to justify the abandonment of democracy. We have here a sharp disagreement of great practical importance, but we have absolutely no means, of a scientific or intellectual kind, by which to persuade either party that the other is in the right. There are, it is true, ways of altering men's opinions on such subjects, but they are all emotional, not intellectual.

Questions as to 'values'—that is to say, as to what is good or bad on its own account, independently of its effects—lie outside the domain of science, as the defenders of religion emphatically assert. I think that in this they are right, but I draw the further conclusion, which they do not draw, that questions as to 'values' lie wholly outside the domain of knowledge. That is to say, when we assert that this or that has 'value', we are giving expression to our own emotions, not to a fact which would still be true if our personal feelings were different. To make this clear, we must try to analyse the conception of the Good.

It is obvious, to begin with, that the whole idea of good and bad has some connection with *desire*. Prima facie, anything that we all desire is 'good', and anything that we all dread is 'bad'. If we all agreed in our desires, the matter could be left there, but unfortunately our desires conflict. If I say, 'What I want is good', my neighbour will say, 'No, what *I* want'. Ethics is an attempt—though not, I think, a successful one—to escape from this subjectivity. I shall naturally try to show, in my dispute with my neighbour, that my desires have some quality which makes them more worthy of respect than his. If I want to preserve a right of way, I shall appeal to the landless inhabitants of the district; but he, on his side, will appeal to the landowners. I shall say: 'What use is the beauty of the countryside if no one sees it?' He will retort: 'What beauty will be left if trippers are allowed to spread devastation?' Each tries to enlist allies by showing that his own desires harmonize with those of other people. When this is obviously impossible, as in the case of a burglar, the man is condemned by public opinion, and his ethical status is that of a sinner.

Ethics is thus closely related to politics: it is an attempt to bring the collective desires of a group to bear upon individuals; or, conversely, it is an attempt by an individual to cause his desires to become those of his group. This latter is, of course, possible only if his desires are not too obviously opposed to the general interest: the burglar will hardly attempt to persuade people that he is doing them good, though plutocrats make similar attempts, and often succeed. When our desires are for things which all can enjoy in common, it seems not unreasonable to hope that others may concur; thus the philosopher who values Truth, Goodness, and Beauty seems, to himself, to be not merely expressing his own desires, but pointing the way to the welfare of all mankind. Unlike the burglar, he is able to believe that his desires are for something that has value in an impersonal sense.

Ethics is an attempt to give universal, and not merely personal, importance to certain of our desires. I say 'certain' of our desires, because in regard to some of them this is obviously impossible, as we saw in the case of the burglar. The man who makes money on the Stock Exchange by means of some secret knowledge does not wish others to be equally well informed: Truth (in so far as he values it) is for him a private possession, not the general human good that it is for the philosopher. The philosopher may, it is true, sink to the level of the stockjobber, as when he claims priority for a discovery. But this is a lapse: in his purely philosophic capacity, he wants only to enjoy the contemplation of Truth, in doing which he in no way interferes with others who wish to do likewise.

To seem to give universal importance to our desires—which is the business of ethics—may be attempted from two points of view, that of the legislator, and that of the preacher. Let us take the legislator first.

I will assume, for the sake of argument, that the legislator is personally disinterested. That is to say, when he recognizes one of his desires as being concerned only with his own welfare, he does not let it influence him in framing the laws; for example, his code is not designed to increase his personal fortune. But he has other desires which seem to him impersonal. He may believe in an ordered hierarchy from king to peasant, or from mine-owner to black indentured labourer. He may believe that women should be submissive to men. He may hold that the spread of knowledge in the lower classes is dangerous. And so on and so on. He will then, if he can, so construct his code that conduct promoting the ends which he values shall, as far as possible, be in accordance with individual self-interest; and he will establish a system of moral instruction which will, where it succeeds, make men feel wicked if they pursue other purposes than his.[1] Thus 'virtue' will come to be in fact, though not in subjective estimation subservience to the desires of the legislator, in so far as he himself considers these desires worthy to be universalized.

The standpoint and method of the preacher are necessarily somewhat different, because he does not control the machinery of the State, and therefore cannot produce an artificial harmony between his desires and those of others. His only method is to try to rouse in others the same desires that he feels himself, and for this purpose his appeal must be to the emotions. Thus Ruskin caused people to like Gothic architecture, not by argument, but by the moving effect of rhythmical prose. *Uncle Tom's Cabin* helped to make people think slavery an evil by causing them to imagine themselves as slaves. Every attempt to persuade people that something is good (or bad) in itself, and not merely in its effects, depends upon the art of rousing feelings, not upon an appeal to evidence. In every case the preacher's skill consists in creating in others emotions similar to his own—or dissimilar, if he is a hypocrite. I am not saying this as a criticism of the preacher, but as an analysis of the essential character of his activity.

When a man says, 'This is good in itself', he *seems* to be making a statement, just as much as if he said, 'This is square' or, 'This is sweet'. I believe this to be a mistake. I think that what the man really means is: 'I wish everybody to desire this', or rather, 'Would that everybody desired this'. If what he says is interpreted as a statement, it is merely an affirmation of his own personal wish; if, on the other hand, it is interpreted in a general way, it states nothing, but merely desires something. The wish, as an occurrence, is personal, but what it desires is universal. It is, I think, this curious interlocking of the particular and the universal which has caused so much confusion in ethics.

The matter may perhaps become clearer by contrasting an ethical sentence with one which makes a statement. If I say, 'All Chinese are Buddhists', I can be refuted by the production of a Chinese Christian or Mohammedan. If I say, 'I believe that all Chinese are Buddhists', I cannot be refuted by any evidence from China, but only by evidence that I do not believe what I say; for what I am asserting is only something about my own

---

[1] Compare the following advice by a contemporary of Aristotle (Chinese, not Greek): 'A ruler should not listen to those who believe in people having opinions of their own and in the importance of the individual. Such teachings cause men to withdraw to quiet places and hide away in caves or on mountains, there to rail at the prevailing government, sneer at those in authority, belittle the importance of rank and emoluments, and despise all who hold official posts' (Arthur Waley, *The Way and its Power* (London: Allen & Unwin, 1934), 37). [The quotation is from Lao-tzu.]

state of mind. If, now, a philosopher says, 'Beauty is good', I may interpret him as meaning either, 'Would that everybody loved the beautiful' (which corresponds to 'All Chinese are Buddhists') or, 'I wish that everybody loved the beautiful' (which corresponds to 'I believe that all Chinese are Buddhists'). The first of these makes no assertion, but expresses a wish; since it affirms nothing, it is logically impossible that there should be evidence for or against it, or for it to possess either truth or falsehood. The second sentence, instead of being merely optative, does make a statement, but it is one about the philosopher's state of mind, and it could be refuted only by evidence that he does not have the wish that he says he has. This second sentence does not belong to ethics, but to psychology or biography. The first sentence, which does belong to ethics, expresses a desire for something, but asserts nothing.

Ethics, if the above analysis is correct, contains no statements, whether true or false, but consists of desires of a certain general kind, namely, such as are concerned with the desires of mankind in general—and of gods, angels, and devils, if they exist. Science can discuss the causes of desires, and the means for realizing them, but it cannot contain any genuinely ethical sentences, because it is concerned with what is true or false.

The theory which I have been advocating is a form of the doctrine which is called the 'subjectivity' of values. This doctrine consists in maintaining that, if two men differ about values, there is not a disagreement as to any kind of truth, but a difference of taste. If one man says, 'Oysters are good', and another says '*I* think they are bad', we recognize that there is nothing to argue about. The theory in question holds that all differences as to values are of this sort, although we do not naturally think them so when we are dealing with matters that seem to us more exalted than oysters. The chief ground for adopting this view is the complete impossibility of finding any arguments to prove that this or that has intrinsic value. If we all agreed, we might hold that we know values by intuition. We cannot *prove*, to a colour-blind man, that grass is green and not red. But there are various ways of proving to him that he lacks a power of discrimination which most men posses, whereas in the case of values there are no such ways, and disagreements are much more frequent than in the case of colours. Since no way can be even imagined for deciding a difference as to values, the conclusion is forced upon us that the difference is one of tastes, not one as to any objective truth.

The consequences of this doctrine are considerable. In the first place, there can be no such thing as 'sin' in any absolute sense; what one man calls 'sin' another may call 'virtue', and though they may dislike each other on account of this difference, neither can convict the other of intellectual error. Punishment cannot be justified on the ground that the criminal is 'wicked', but only on the ground that he has behaved in a way which others wish to discourage. Hell, as a place of punishment for sinners, becomes quite irrational.

In the second place, it is impossible to uphold the way of speaking about values which is common among those who believe in Cosmic Purpose. Their argument is that certain things which have been evolved are 'good', and therefore the world must have had a purpose which was ethically admirable. In the language of subjective values, this argument becomes: 'Some things in the world are to our liking, and therefore they must have been created by a Being with our tastes, Whom, therefore, we also like, and Who, consequently, is good'. Now it seems fairly evident that, if creatures having likes and dislikes were to exist at all, they were pretty sure to like *some* things in their environment, since otherwise they would find life intolerable. Our values have been evolved along with the rest of our constitution, and nothing as to any original purpose can be inferred from the fact that they are what they are.

Those who believe in 'objective' values often contend that the view which I have been advocating has immoral consequences. This seems to me to be due to faulty reasoning. There are, as has already been said, certain ethical consequences of the doctrine of subjective values, of which the most important is the rejection of vindictive punishment and the notion of 'sin'. But the more general consequences which are feared, such as the decay of all sense of moral obligation, are not to be logically deduced. Moral obligation, if it is to influence conduct, must consist not merely of a belief, but of a desire. The desire, I may be told, is the desire to be 'good' in a sense which I no longer allow. But when we analyse the desire to be 'good' it generally resolves itself into a desire to be approved, or, alternatively, to act so as to bring about certain general consequences which we desire. We have wishes which are not purely personal, and, if we had not, no amount of ethical teaching would influence our conduct except through fear of disapproval. The sort of life that most of us admire is one which is guided by large impersonal desires; now such desires can, no doubt, be encouraged by example, education, and knowledge, but they can hardly be created by the mere abstract belief that they are good, nor discouraged by an analysis of what is meant by the word 'good'.

When we contemplate the human race, we may desire that it should be happy, or healthy, or intelligent, or warlike, and so on. Any one of these desires, if it is strong, will produce its own morality; but if we have no such general desires, our conduct, whatever our ethic may be, will serve social purposes only in so far as self-interest and the interests of society are in harmony. It is the business of wise institutions to create such harmony as far as possible, and for the rest, whatever may be our theoretical definition of value, we must depend upon the existence of impersonal desires. When you meet a man with whom you have a fundamental ethical disagreement—for example, if you think that all men count equally, while he selects a class as alone important—you will find yourself no better able to cope with him if you believe in objective values than if you do not. In either case, you can influence his conduct only through influencing his desires: if you succeed in that, his ethic will change, and if not, not.

Some people feel that if a general desire, say, for the happiness of mankind, has not the sanction of absolute good, it is in some way irrational. This is due to a lingering belief in objective values. A desire cannot, in itself, be either rational or irrational. It may conflict with other desires, and therefore lead to unhappiness; it may rouse opposition in others, and therefore be incapable of gratification. But it cannot be considered 'irrational' merely because no reason can be given for feeling it. We may desire *A* because it is a means to *B*, but in the end, when we have done with mere means, we must come to something which we desire for no reason, but not on that account 'irrationally'. All systems of ethics embody the desires of those who advocate them, but this fact is concealed in a mist of words. Our desires are, in fact, more general and less purely selfish than many moralists imagine; if it were not so, no theory of ethics would make moral improvement possible. It is, in fact, not by ethical theory, but by the cultivation of large and generous desires through intelligence, happiness, and freedom from fear, that men can be brought to act more than they do at present in a manner that is consistent with the general happiness of mankind. Whatever our definition of the 'Good', and whether we believe it to be subjective or objective, those who do not desire the happiness of mankind will not endeavour to further it, while those who do desire it will do what they can to bring it about.

I conclude that, while it is true that science cannot decide questions of value, that is because they cannot be intellectually decided at all, and lie outside the realm of truth and falsehood. Whatever knowledge is attainable, must be attained by scientific methods; and what science cannot discover, mankind cannot know.

II

THE CONCEPTION OF INTRINSIC VALUE

G. E. MOORE

My main object in this paper is to try to define more precisely the most important question, which, so far as I can see, is really at issue when it is disputed with regard to any predicate of value, whether it is or is not a 'subjective' predicate. There are three chief cases in which this controversy is apt to arise. It arises, first, with regard to the conceptions of 'right' and 'wrong', and the closely allied conception of 'duty' or 'what *ought* to be done'. It arises, secondly, with regard to 'good' and 'evil', in some sense of those words in which the conceptions for which they stand are certainly quite distinct from the conceptions of 'right' and 'wrong', but in which nevertheless it is undeniable that ethics has to deal with them. And it arises, lastly, with regard to certain aesthetic conceptions, such as 'beautiful' and 'ugly'; or 'good' and 'bad', in the sense in which these words are applied to works of art, and in which, therefore, the question what is good and bad is a question not for ethics but for aesthetics.

In all three cases there are people who maintain that the predicates in question are purely 'subjective', in a sense which can, I think, be fairly easily defined. I am not here going to attempt a perfectly accurate definition of the sense in question; but, as the term 'subjective' is so desperately ambiguous, I had better try to indicate roughly the sense I am thinking of. Take the word 'beautiful' for example. There is a sense of the term 'subjective', such that to say that 'beautiful' stands for a subjective predicate, means, roughly, that any statement of the form 'This is beautiful' merely expresses a psychological assertion to the effect that some particular individual or class of individuals either actually has, or would, under certain circumstances, have, a certain kind of mental attitude towards the thing in question. And what I mean by 'having a mental attitude' towards a thing, can be best explained by saying that to desire a thing is to have one kind of mental attitude towards it, to be pleased with it is to have another, to will

From G. E. Moore, *Philosophical Studies* (London: Routledge & Kegan Paul, 1922), 253–75. Reprinted by permission of Routledge Publishers.

it is to have another; and in short that to have any kind of feeling or emotion *towards* it is to have a certain mental attitude towards it—a different one in each case. Thus anyone who holds that when we say that a thing is beautiful, what we *mean* is merely that we ourselves or some particular class of people actually do, or would under certain circumstances, have, or permanently have, a certain feeling towards the thing in question, is taking a 'subjective' view of beauty.

But in all three cases there are also a good many people who hold that the predicates in question are not, in this sense 'subjective'; and I think that those who hold this are apt to speak as if the view which they wish to maintain in opposition to it consisted simply and solely in holding its contradictory—in holding, that is, that the predicates in question are 'objective', where 'objective' simply means the same as 'not subjective'. But in fact I think this is hardly ever really the case. In the case of goodness and beauty, what such people are really anxious to maintain is by no means merely that these conceptions are 'objective', but that, besides being 'objective', they are also, in a sense which I shall try to explain, 'intrinsic' kinds of value. It is this conviction—the conviction that goodness and beauty are *intrinsic* kinds of value, which is, I think, the strongest ground of their objection to any subjective view. And indeed, when they speak of the 'objectivity' of these conceptions, what they have in mind is, I believe, always a conception which has no proper right to be called 'objectivity', since it includes as an essential part this other characteristic which I propose to call that of being an 'intrinsic' kind of value.

The truth is, I believe, that though, from the proposition that a particular kind of value is 'intrinsic' it does follow that it must be 'objective', the converse implication by no means holds, but on the contrary it is perfectly easy to conceive theories of e.g. 'goodness', according to which goodness would, in the strictest sense, be 'objective', and yet would not be 'intrinsic'. There is, therefore, a very important difference between the conception of 'objectivity', and that which I will call 'internality'; but yet, if I am not mistaken, when people talk about the 'objectivity' of any kind of value, they almost always confuse the two, owing to the fact that most of those who deny the 'internality' of a given kind of value, also assert its 'subjectivity'. How great the difference is, and that it is a fact that those who maintain the 'objectivity' of goodness do, as a rule, mean by this not mere 'objectivity', but 'internality', as well, can, I think, be best brought out by considering an instance of a theory, according to which goodness would be objective but would not be intrinsic.

Let us suppose it to be held, for instance, that what is meant by saying that one type of human being A is 'better' than another type B, is merely that the course of evolution tends to increase the numbers of type *A* and to decrease those of type *B*. Such a view has, in fact, been often suggested, even if it has not been held in this exact form; it amounts merely to the familiar suggestion that 'better' means 'better fitted to survive'. Obviously 'better', on this interpretation of its meaning, is in no sense a 'subjective' conception: the conception of belonging to a type which tends to be favoured by the struggle for existence more than another is as 'objective' as any conception can be. But yet, if I am not mistaken, all those who object to a subjective view of 'goodness', and insist upon its 'objectivity', would object just as strongly to this interpretation of its meaning as to any 'subjective' interpretation. Obviously, therefore, what they are really anxious to contend for is not merely that goodness is 'objective', since they are here objecting to a theory which is 'objective'; but something else. And this something else is, I think, certainly just that it is 'intrinsic'—a character which is just as incompatible with this objective evolutionary interpretation as with any and every subjective interpretation. For if you say that to call type *A* 'better' than type *B* means merely that it is more favoured in the struggle for existence, it follows that the being 'better' is a predicate which does *not depend merely on the intrinsic nature of A and B respectively*. On the contrary, although here and now *A* may be more favoured than *B*, it is obvious that under other circumstances or with different natural laws the very same type *B* might be more favoured than *A*, so that the very same type which, under one set of circumstances, is better than *B*, would, under another set, be worse. Here, then, we have a case where an interpretation of 'goodness', which does make it 'objective', is incompatible with its being 'intrinsic'. And it is just this same fact—the fact that, on any 'subjective' interpretation, the very same kind of thing which, under some circumstances, is better than another, would, under others, be worse—which constitutes, so far as I can see, the fundamental objection to all 'subjective' interpretations. Obviously, therefore, to express this objection by saying that goodness is 'objective' is very incorrect; since goodness might quite well be 'objective' and yet *not* possess the very characteristic which it is mainly wished to assert that it has.

In the case, therefore, of ethical and aesthetic 'goodness', I think that what those who contend for the 'objectivity' of these conceptions really wish to contend for is not mere 'objectivity' at all, but principally and essentially that they are *intrinsic* kinds of value. But in the case of 'right' and 'wrong' and 'duty', the same cannot be said, because many of those who object to the view that these conceptions are 'subjective', nevertheless do not hold that they are 'intrinsic'. We cannot, therefore, say that what those who contend for the 'objectivity' of right and wrong really mean is always chiefly that those conceptions are intrinsic, but we can, I think, say that what they do mean is certainly *not* 'objectivity' in this case any more than the other; since here, just as there, it would be possible to find certain views, which are in every sense 'objective', to which they would object just as strongly as to any subjective view. And though what is meant by 'objectivity' in this case, is not that 'right' and 'wrong' are *themselves* 'intrinsic', what is, I think, meant here too is that they have a fixed relation to a kind of value which *is* 'intrinsic'. It is this fixed relation to an intrinsic kind of value, so far as I can see, which gives to right and wrong that kind and degree of fixity and impartiality which they actually are felt to possess, and which is what people are thinking of when they talk of their 'objectivity'. Here, too, therefore, to talk of the characteristic meant as 'objectivity' is just as great a misnomer as in the other cases; since though it is a characteristic which is incompatible with any kind of 'subjectivity', it is also incompatible, for the same reason, with many kinds of 'objectivity'.

For these reasons I think that what those who contend for the 'objectivity' of certain kinds of value, or for the 'objectivity' of judgements of value, commonly have in mind is not really 'objectivity' at all, but either that the kinds of value in question are themselves 'intrinsic', or else that they have a fixed relation to some kind that is so. The conception upon which they really wish to lay stress is not that of 'objective value', but that of 'intrinsic value', though they confuse the two. And I think this is the case to a considerable extent not only with the defenders of so-called 'objectivity', but also with its opponents. Many of those who hold strongly (as many do) that *all* kinds of value are 'subjective' certainly object to the so-called 'objective' view, not so much because it is *objective*, as because it is not *naturalistic* or *positivistic*—a characteristic which does naturally follow from the contention that value is 'intrinsic', but does not follow from the mere contention that it is 'objective'. To a view which is at the same time both 'naturalistic' or 'positivistic' and also 'objective', such as the evolutionary view which I sketched just now, they do not feel at all the same kind or degree of objection as to any so-called 'objective' view. With regard to so-called 'objective' views they are apt to feel not only that they are false, but that they involve a particularly poisonous kind of falsehood—the erecting into a 'metaphysical' entity of what is really susceptible of a simple naturalistic explanation. They feel that to hold such a view is not merely to make a mistake, but to make a superstitious mistake. They feel the same kind of contempt for those who hold it, which we are apt to feel towards those whom we regard as grossly superstitious, and which is felt by certain persons for what they call 'metaphysics'. Obviously, therefore, what they really object to is not simply the view that these predicates are 'objective', but something else—something which does not at all follow from the contention that they are 'objective', but which does follow from the contention that they are 'intrinsic'.

In disputes, therefore, as to whether particular kinds of value are or are not 'subjective', I think that the issue which is really felt to be important, almost always by one side, and often by both, is not really the issue between 'subjective' and 'non-subjective', but between 'intrinsic' and 'non-intrinsic'. And not only is this felt to be the more important issue; I think it really is so. For the difference that must be made to our view of the universe, according as we hold that some kinds of value are 'intrinsic' or that none are, is much greater than any which follows from a mere difference of opinion as to whether some are 'non-subjective', or all without exception 'subjective'. To hold that any kinds of value are 'intrinsic' entails the recognition of a kind of predicate extremely different from any we should otherwise have to recognize and perhaps unique; whereas it is in any case certain that there are 'objective' predicates as well as 'subjective'.

But now what is this 'internality' of which I have been speaking? What is meant by saying with regard to a kind of value that it is 'intrinsic'? To express roughly what is meant is, I think, simple enough; and everybody will recognize it at once, as a notion which is constantly in people's heads; but I want to dwell upon it at some length, because I know of no place where it is expressly explained and defined, and because, though it seems very simple and fundamental, the task of defining it precisely is by no means easy and involves some difficulties which I must confess that I do not know how to solve.

I have already given incidentally the main idea in speaking of that evolutionary interpretation of 'goodness', according to which, as I said, goodness would be 'objective' but would not be 'intrinsic'. I there used as equivalent to the assertion that 'better', on that definition, would not be 'intrinsic', the assertion that the question whether one type of being A was better than another B would *not* depend *solely on the intrinsic natures of A and B*, but on circumstances and the laws of nature. And I think that this phrase will in fact suggest to everybody just what I do mean by 'intrinsic' value. We can, in fact, set up the following definition. *To say that a kind of value is 'intrinsic' means merely that the question whether a thing possesses it, and in what degree it possesses it, depends solely on the intrinsic nature of the thing in question.*

But though this definition does, I think, convey exactly what I mean, I want to dwell upon its meaning, partly because the conception of 'differing in intrinsic nature' which I believe to be of fundamental importance, is

liable to be confused with other conceptions, and partly because the definition involves notions, which I do not know how to define exactly.

When I say, with regard to any particular kind of value, that the question
whether and in what degree anything possesses it *depends solely on the
intrinsic nature of the thing in question*, I mean to say two different things
at the same time. I mean to say (1) that it is *impossible* for what is strictly
one and the same thing to possess that kind of value at one time, or in one
set of circumstances, and *not* to possess it at another; and equally *impossible* for it to possess it in one degree at one time, or in one set of
circumstances, and to possess it in a different degree at another, or in a
different set. This, I think, is obviously part of what is naturally conveyed
by saying that the question whether and in what degree a thing possesses
the kind of value in question always depends *solely* on the intrinsic nature
of the thing. For if x and y have different intrinsic natures, it follows that x
cannot be quite strictly one and the same thing as y; and hence if x and y
can have a different intrinsic value, only where their intrinsic natures are
different, it follows that one and the same thing must always have the same
intrinsic value. This, then, is part of what is meant; and about this part I
think I need say no more, except to call attention to the fact that it involves
a conception, which as we shall see is also involved in the other part, and
which involves the same difficulty in both cases—I mean, the conception
which is expressed by the word 'impossible'. (2) The second part of what is
meant is that if a given thing possesses any kind of intrinsic value in a
certain degree, then not only must that same thing possess it, under all
circumstances, in the same degree, but also anything *exactly like* it, must,
under all circumstances, possess it in exactly the same degree. Or to put it
in the corresponding negative form: It is *impossible* that of two exactly
similar things one should possess it and the other not, or that one should
possess it in one degree, and the other in a different one.

I think this second proposition also is naturally conveyed by saying that
the kind of value in question depends solely on the intrinsic nature of what
possesses it. For we should naturally say of two things which were *exactly
alike* intrinsically, in spite of their being *two*, that they possessed the *same*
intrinsic nature. But it is important to call attention expressly to the fact
that what I mean by the expression 'having a different intrinsic nature' is
equivalent to 'not exactly alike' because here there is real risk of confusion
between this conception and a different one. This comes about as follows.
It is natural to suppose that the phrase 'having a different intrinsic nature'
is equivalent to the phrase 'intrinsically different' or 'having different
intrinsic properties'. But, if we do make this identification, there is a risk of
confusion. For it is obvious that there is a sense in which, when things are

exactly like, they must be 'intrinsically different' and have different intrinsic properties, merely because they are two. For instance, two patches of colour may be exactly alike, in spite of the fact that each possesses a constituent which the other does not possess, provided only that their two constituents are exactly alike. And yet, in a certain sense, it is obvious that the fact that each has a constituent, which the other has not got, does constitute an intrinsic difference between them, and implies that each has an intrinsic property which the other has not got. And even where the two things are simple the mere fact that they are *numerically* different does in a sense constitute an intrinsic difference between them, and each will have at least one intrinsic property which the other has not got—namely that of being identical with itself. It is obvious therefore that the phrases 'intrinsically different' and 'having different intrinsic properties' are ambiguous. They may be used in such a sense that to say of two things that they are intrinsically different or have different intrinsic properties does *not* imply that they are not exactly alike, but only that they are *numerically* different. Or they may be used in a sense in which two things can be said to be intrinsically different, and to have different intrinsic properties *only* when they are not exactly alike. It is, therefore, extremely important to insist that when I say: Two things can differ in intrinsic value, only when they have different intrinsic natures, I am using the expression 'having different intrinsic natures' in the latter sense and not the former—in a sense in which the mere fact that two things are two, or differ numerically, does *not* imply that they have different intrinsic natures, but in which they can be said to have different intrinsic natures, *only* where, besides different numerically, they are also *not* exactly alike.

But as soon as this is explained, another risk of confusion arises owing to the fact that when people contrast mere numerical difference with a kind of intrinsic difference, which is *not* merely numerical, they are apt to identify the latter with *qualitative* difference. It might, therefore, easily be thought that by 'difference in intrinsic nature' I mean 'difference in quality'. But this identification of difference in quality with difference in intrinsic nature would also be a mistake. It is true that what is commonly meant by difference of quality, in the strict sense, always is a difference of intrinsic nature: two things cannot differ in quality without differing in intrinsic nature; and that fact is one of the most important facts about qualitative difference. But the converse is by no means also true: although two things cannot differ in quality without differing in intrinsic nature, they can differ in intrinsic nature without differing in quality; or, in other words, difference in quality is only *one* species of difference in intrinsic nature. That this is so follows from the fact that, as I explained, I am using the phrase 'different in intrinsic nature' as equivalent to 'not exactly like': for it is quite plain that two things may not be exactly alike, in spite of the fact that they don't differ in quality, e.g. if the only difference between them were in respect of the *degree* in which they possess some quality they do possess. Nobody would say that a very loud sound was exactly like a very soft one, even if they were exactly like in quality; and yet it is plain there is a sense in which their intrinsic nature is different. For this reason alone qualitative difference cannot be identified with difference in intrinsic nature. And there are still other reasons. Difference in size, for instance may be a difference in intrinsic nature, in the sense I mean, but it can hardly be called a difference in quality. Or take such a difference as the difference between two patterns consisting in the fact that the one is a yellow circle with a red spot in the middle, and the other a yellow circle with a blue spot in the middle. This difference would perhaps be loosely called a difference of quality; but obviously it would be more accurate to call it a difference which consists in the fact that the one pattern has a *constituent* which is qualitatively different from any which the other has; and the difference between being qualitatively different and having qualitatively different constituents is important both because the latter can only be defined in terms of the former, and because it is possible for simple things to differ from one another in the former way, whereas it is only possible for complex things to differ in the latter.

I hope this is sufficient to make clear exactly what the conception is which I am expressing by the phrase 'different in intrinsic nature'. The important points are (1) that it is a kind of difference which does *not* hold between two things, when they are *merely* numerically different, but only when, besides being numerically different, they are also *not* exactly alike and (2) that it is *not* identical with qualitative difference; although qualitative difference is one particular species of it. The conception seems to me to be an extremely important and fundamental one, although, so far as I can see, it has no quite simple and unambiguous name: and this is the reason why I have dwelt on it at such length. 'Not exactly like' is the least ambiguous way of expressing it; but this has the disadvantage that it looks as if the idea of exact likeness were the fundamental one from which this was derived, whereas I believe the contrary to be the case. For this reason it is perhaps better to stick to the cumbrous phrase 'different in intrinsic nature'.

So much for the question what is meant by saying of two things that they 'differ in intrinsic nature'. We have now to turn to the more difficult question as to what is meant by the words 'impossible' and 'necessary' in the statement: A kind of value is intrinsic if and only if, it is *impossible* that *x* and *y* should have different values of the kind, unless they differ in intrinsic nature; and in the equivalent statement: A kind of value is intrinsic if and only if, when anything possesses it, that same thing or anything exactly like it would *necessarily* or *must* always, under all circumstances, possess it in exactly the same degree.

As regards the meaning of this necessity and impossibility, we may begin by making two points clear.

(1) It is sometimes contended, and with some plausibility, that what we mean by saying that it is *possible* for a thing which possesses one predicate *F* to possess another *G*, is, sometimes at least, merely that some things which possess *F* do in fact also possess *G*. And if we give this meaning to 'possible', the corresponding meaning of the statement it is *impossible* for a thing which possesses *F* to possess *G* will be merely: Things which possess *F* never do in fact possess *G*. If, then, we understood 'impossible' in this sense, the condition for the 'internality' of a kind of value, which I have stated by saying that if a kind of value is to be 'intrinsic' it must be *impossible* for two things to possess it in different degrees, if they are exactly like one another, will amount merely to saying that no two things which are exactly like one another ever do, in fact, possess it in different degrees. It follows, that, if this were all that were meant, this condition would be satisfied, if only it were true (as for all I know it may be) that, in the case of all things which possess any particular kind of intrinsic value, there happens to be nothing else in the universe exactly like any one of them; for if this were so, it would, of course, follow that no two things which are exactly alike did in fact possess the kind of value in question in different degrees, for the simple reason that everything which possessed it at all would be unique in the sense that there was nothing else exactly like it. If this were all that were meant, therefore, we could prove any particular kind of value to satisfy this condition, by merely proving that there never has in fact and never will be anything exactly like any one of the things which possess it: and our assertion that it satisfied this condition would merely be an empirical generalization. Moreover if this were all that was meant it would obviously be by no means certain that purely subjective predicates could not satisfy the condition in question; since it would be satisfied by any subjective predicate of which it happened to be true that everything which possessed it was, in fact, unique—that there was nothing exactly like it; and for all I know there may be many subjective predicates of which this is true. It is, therefore, scarcely necessary to say that I am not using 'impossible' in this sense. When I say that a kind of value, to be intrinsic, must satisfy the condition that it must be *impossible* for two

things exactly alike to possess it in different degrees, I do not mean by this condition anything which a kind of value could be proved to satisfy, by the mere empirical fact that there was nothing else exactly like any of the things which possessed it. It is, of course, an essential part of my meaning that we must be able to say not merely that no two exactly similar things do *in fact* possess it in different degrees, but that, *if* there had been or were going to be anything exactly similar to a thing which does possess it, even though, in fact, there has not and won't be any such thing, that thing would have possessed or would possess the kind of value in question in exactly the same degree. It is essential to this meaning of 'impossibility' that it should entitle us to assert what *would* have been the case, under conditions which never have been and never will be realized; and it seems obvious that no mere empirical generalization can entitle us to do this.

But (2) to say that I am not using 'necessity' in this first sense, is by no means sufficient to explain what I do mean. For it certainly seems as if causal laws (though this is disputed) do entitle us to make assertions of the very kind that mere empirical generalizations do not entitle us to make. In virtue of a causal law we do seem to be entitled to assert such things as that, if a given thing had had a property or were to have a property F which it didn't have or won't have, it *would* have had or *would* have some other property G. And it might, therefore, be thought that the kind of 'necessity' and 'impossibility' I am talking of is this kind of causal 'necessity' and 'impossibility'. It is, therefore, important to insist that I do *not* mean this kind either. If this were all I meant, it would again be by no means obvious, that purely subjective predicates might not satisfy our second condition. It may, for instance, for all I know, be true that there are causal laws which ensure that in the case of everything that is 'beautiful', anything exactly like any of these things would, in this universe, excite a particular kind of feeling in everybody to whom it were presented in a particular way: and if that were so, we should have a subjective predicate which satisfied the condition that, when a given thing possesses that predicate, it is impossible (in the causal sense) that any exactly similar thing should not also possess it. The kind of necessity I am talking of is not, therefore, mere causal necessity either. When I say that if a given thing possesses a certain degree of intrinsic value, anything precisely similar to it *would* necessarily *have* possessed that value in exactly the same degree, I mean that it *would* have done so, even if it had existed in a universe in which the causal laws were quite different from what they are in this one. I mean, in short, that it is *impossible* for any precisely similar thing to possess a different value, in precisely such a sense as that, in which it is, I think, generally admitted that it is *not* impossible that causal laws should have been different from what they are—a sense of impossibility, therefore, which certainly does not depend merely on causal laws.

That there is such a sense of necessity—a sense which entitles us to say that what has *F would* have *G*, even if causal laws were quite different from what they are—is, I think, quite clear from such instances as the following. Suppose you take a particular patch of colour, which is yellow. We can, I think, say with certainty that any patch exactly like that one, *would* be yellow, even if it existed in a universe in which causal laws were quite different from what they are in this one. We can say that any such patch *must* be yellow, quite unconditionally, whatever the circumstances, and whatever the causal laws. And it is in a sense similar to this, in respect of the fact that it is neither empirical nor causal, that I mean the 'must' to be understood, when I say that if a kind of value is to be 'intrinsic', then, supposing a given thing possesses it in a certain degree, anything exactly like that thing *must* possess it in exactly the same degree. To say, of 'beauty' or 'goodness' that they are 'intrinsic' is only, therefore, to say that this thing which is obviously true of 'yellowness' and 'blueness' and 'redness' is true of them. And if we give this sense to 'must' in our definition, then I think it is obvious that to say of a given kind of value that it is intrinsic *is* inconsistent with its being 'subjective'. For there is, I think, pretty clearly no subjective predicate of which we can say thus unconditionally, that, *if* a given thing possesses it, then anything exactly like that thing, *would*, under any circumstances, and under any causal laws, also possess it. For instance, whatever kind of feeling you take, it is plainly not true that supposing I have that feeling towards a given thing *A*, then *I* should necessarily under any circumstances have that feeling towards anything precisely similar to *A*: for the simple reason that a thing precisely similar to *A might* exist in a universe in which I did not exist at all. And similarly it is not true of any feeling whatever, that if *somebody* has that feeling towards a given thing *A*, then, in any universe, in which a thing precisely similar to *A* existed, *somebody* would have that feeling towards it. Nor finally is it even true, that if it is true of a given thing *A*, that, under actual causal laws, any one to whom *A* were presented in a certain way *would* have a certain feeling towards it, then the same hypothetical predicate would, in any universe, belong to anything precisely similar to *A*: in every case it seems to be possible that there *might* be a universe, in which the causal laws were such that the proposition would not be true.

It is, then, because in my definition of 'intrinsic' value the 'must' is to be understood in this unconditional sense, that I think that the proposition that a kind of value is 'intrinsic' is inconsistent with its being subjective.

But it should be observed that in holding that there is this inconsistency, I am contradicting a doctrine which seems to be held by many philosophers. There are, as you probably know, some philosophers who insist strongly on a doctrine which they express by saying that no relations are purely external. And so far as I can make out one thing which they mean by this is just that, whenever x has any relation whatever which y has not got, x and y *cannot* be exactly alike: That any difference in relation necessarily entails a difference in intrinsic nature. There is, I think, no doubt that when these philosophers say this, they mean by their 'cannot' and 'necessarily' an unconditional 'cannot' and 'must'. And hence it follows they are holding that, if, for instance, a thing A pleases me now, then any other thing, B, precisely similar to A, must, under any circumstances, and in any universe, please me also: since, if B did not please me, it would *not* possess a relation which A does possess, and therefore, by their principle, *could* not be precisely similar to A—*must* differ from it in intrinsic nature. But it seems to me to be obvious that this principle is false. If it were true, it would follow that I can know a priori such things as that no patch of colour which is seen by you and is not seen by me is ever exactly like any patch which is seen by me and is not seen by you; or that no patch of colour which is surrounded by a red ring is ever exactly like one which is not so surrounded. But it is surely obvious, that, whether these things are true or not they are things which I cannot know a priori. It is simply *not* evident a priori that no patch of colour which is seen by A and not by B is ever exactly like one which is seen by B and not by A, and that no patch of colour which is surrounded by a red ring is ever exactly like one which is not. And this illustration serves to bring out very well both what is meant by saying of such a predicate as 'beautiful' that it is 'intrinsic', and why, if it is, it cannot be subjective. What is meant is just that if A is beautiful and B is not, you could know a priori that A and B are *not* exactly alike; whereas, with any such subjective predicate, as that of exciting a particular feeling in me, or that of being a thing which would excite such a feeling in any spectator, you cannot tell a priori that a thing A which did possess such a predicate and a thing B which did not, could not be exactly alike.

It seems to me, therefore, quite certain, in spite of the dogma that no relations are purely external, that there are many predicates, such for instance as most (if not all) subjective predicates or the objective one of being surrounded by a red ring, which do *not* depend solely on the intrinsic nature of what possesses them: or, in other words, of which it is *not* true that if x possesses them and y does not, x and y *must* differ in intrinsic nature. But what precisely is meant by this unconditional 'must', I must confess I don't know. The obvious thing to suggest is that it is the logical 'must', which certainly is unconditional in just this sense: the kind of necessity, which we assert to hold, for instance, when we say that whatever is a right-angled triangle *must* be a triangle, or that whatever is yellow *must* be either yellow or blue. But I must say I cannot see that all unconditional necessity is of this nature. I do not see how it can be deduced from any logical law that, if a given patch of colour be yellow, then any patch which were exactly like the first would be yellow too. And similarly in our case of 'intrinsic' value, though I think it is true that beauty, for instance, is 'intrinsic', I do not see how it can be deduced from any logical law, that if *A* is beautiful, anything that were exactly like *A* would be beautiful too, in exactly the same degree.

Moreover, though I do believe that both 'yellow' (in the sense in which it applies to sense-data) and 'beautiful' are predicates which, in this unconditional sense, depend only on the intrinsic nature of what possesses them, there seems to me to be an extremely important difference between them which constitutes a further difficulty in the way of getting quite clear as to what this unconditional sense of 'must' is. The difference I mean is one which I am inclined to express by saying that though both yellowness and beauty are predicates which *depend* only on the intrinsic nature of what possesses them, yet while yellowness is itself an *intrinsic* predicate, *beauty* is not. Indeed it seems to me to be one of the most important truths about predicates of value, that though many of them *are* intrinsic kinds of value, in the sense I have defined, yet *none* of them are intrinsic properties, in the sense in which such properties as 'yellow' or the property of 'being a state of pleasure' or 'being a state of things which contains a balance of pleasure' are intrinsic properties. It is obvious, for instance, that, if we are to reject *all* naturalistic theories of value, we must not only reject those theories, according to which no kind of value would be intrinsic, but must also reject such theories as those which assert, for instance, that to say that a state of mind is good is to say that it is a state of being pleased; or that to say that a state of things is good is to say that it contains a balance of pleasure over pain. There are, in short, two entirely different types of naturalistic theory, the difference between which may be illustrated by the difference between the assertion, '*A* is good' *means* '*A* is pleasant' and the assertion '*A* is good' *means* '*A* is a state of pleasure'. Theories of the former type imply that goodness is *not* an intrinsic kind of value, whereas theories of the latter type imply equally emphatically that it is: since obviously such predicates as that 'of being a state of pleasure', or 'containing a balance of pleasure', *are* predicates like 'yellow' in respect of the fact that if a given thing possesses them, anything exactly like the thing in question must possess them. It seems to me equally obvious that *both* types of theory are false:

but I do not know how to exclude them both except by saying that two different propositions are both true of *goodness*, namely: (1) that it does depend *only* on the intrinsic nature of what possesses it—which excludes theories of the first type and (2) that, *though* this is so, it is yet not itself an intrinsic property—which excludes those of the second. It was for this reason that I said above that, if there are any intrinsic kinds of value, they would constitute a class of predicates which is, perhaps, unique; for I cannot think of any other predicate which resembles them in respect of the fact, that though *not* itself intrinsic, it yet shares with intrinsic properties the characteristics of depending solely on the intrinsic nature of what possesses it. So far as I know, certain predicates of value are the only non-intrinsic properties which share with intrinsic properties this characteristic of depending only on the intrinsic nature of what possesses them.

If, however, we are thus to say that predicates of value, though *dependent* solely on intrinsic properties, are not themselves intrinsic properties, there must be some characteristic belonging to intrinsic properties which predicates of value never possess. And it seems to me quite obvious that there is; only I can't see *what* it is. It seems to me quite obvious that if you assert of a given state of things that it contains a balance of pleasure over pain, you are asserting of it not only a *different* predicate, from what you would be asserting of it if you said it was 'good'—but a predicate which is of quite a different *kind*; and in the same way that when you assert of a patch of colour that it is 'yellow', the predicate you assert is not only *different* from 'beautiful', but of quite a different *kind*, in the same way as before. And of course the mere fact that many people have thought that goodness and beauty were subjective is evidence that there is *some* great difference of kind between them and such predicates as being yellow or containing a balance of pleasure. But *what* the difference is, if we suppose, as I suppose, that goodness and beauty are *not* subjective, and that they do share with 'yellowness' and 'containing pleasure', the property of depending *solely* on the intrinsic nature of what possesses them, I confess I cannot say. I can only vaguely express the kind of difference I feel there to be by saying that intrinsic properties seem to *describe* the intrinsic nature of what possesses them in a sense in which predicates of value never do. If you could enumerate *all* the intrinsic properties a given thing possessed, you would have given a *complete* description of it, and would not need to mention any predicates of value it possessed; whereas no description of a given thing could be *complete* which omitted any intrinsic property. But, in any case, owing to the fact that predicates of intrinsic value are not themselves intrinsic properties, you cannot define 'intrinsic property', in the way which at first sight seems obviously the right one. You cannot say that an intrinsic property is a property such that, if one thing possesses it and another does not, the intrinsic nature of the two things *must* be different. For this is the very thing which we are maintaining to be true of predicates of intrinsic value, while at that same time we say that they are *not* intrinsic properties. Such a definition of 'intrinsic property' would therefore only be possible if, we could say that the necessity there is that, if x and y possess different intrinsic properties, their nature must be different, is a necessity of a *different kind* from the necessity there is that, if x and y are of different intrinsic values, their nature must be different, although both necessities are unconditional. And it seems to me possible that this is the true explanation. But, if so, it obviously adds to the difficulty of explaining the meaning of the unconditional 'must', since, in this case, there would be two different meanings of 'must', both unconditional, and yet neither, apparently, identical with the logical 'must'.

III

THE NATURE OF
ETHICAL DISAGREEMENT

CHARLES L. STEVENSON

1

When people disagree about the value of something—one saying that it is good or right and another that it is bad or wrong—by what methods of argument or inquiry can their disagreement be resolved? Can it be resolved by the methods of science, or does it require methods of some other kind, or is it open to no rational solution at all?

The question must be clarified before it can be answered. And the word that is particularly in need of clarification, as we shall see, is the word 'disagreement'.

Let us begin by noting that 'disagreement' has two broad senses: In the first sense it refers to what I shall call 'disagreement in belief'. This occurs when Mr A believes p, when Mr B believes $not\text{-}p$, or something incompatible with p, and when neither is content to let the belief of the other remain unchallenged. Thus doctors may disagree in belief about the causes of an illness; and friends may disagree in belief about the exact date on which they last met.

In the second sense the word refers to what I shall call 'disagreement in attitude'. This occurs when Mr A has a favourable attitude to something, when Mr B has an unfavourable or less favourable attitude to it, and when neither is content to let the other's attitude remain unchanged. The term 'attitude' is here used in much the same sense that R. B. Perry uses 'interest'; it designates any psychological disposition of being *for* or *against* something. Hence love and hate are relatively specific kinds of attitudes, as are approval and disapproval, and so on.

This second sense can be illustrated in this way: Two men are planning to have dinner together. One wants to eat at a restaurant that the other

From Charles L. Stevenson, *Facts and Values* (New Haven: Yale University Press, 1963), 1–9. Copyright © Yale University Press (1963). Reprinted by permission of Yale University Press.

doesn't like. Temporarily, then, the men cannot 'agree' on where to dine. Their argument may be trivial, and perhaps only half serious; but in any case it represents a disagreement *in attitude*. The men have divergent preferences and each is trying to redirect the preference of the other— though normally, of course, each is willing to revise his own preference in the light of what the other may say.

Further examples are readily found. Mrs Smith wishes to cultivate only the 400; Mr Smith is loyal to his old poker-playing friends. They accordingly disagree, in attitude, about whom to invite to their party. The progressive mayor wants modern school buildings and large parks; the older citizens are against these 'newfangled' ways; so they disagree on civic policy. These cases differ from the one about the restaurant only in that the clash of attitudes is more serious and may lead to more vigorous argument.

The difference between the two senses of 'disagreement' is essentially this: the first involves an opposition of beliefs, both of which cannot be true, and the second involves an opposition of attitudes, both of which cannot be satisfied.

Let us apply this distinction to a case that will sharpen it. Mr A believes that most voters will favour a proposed tax and Mr B disagrees with him. The disagreement concerns attitudes—those of the voters—but note that A and B are *not* disagreeing in attitude. Their disagreement is *in belief about* attitudes. It is simply a special kind of disagreement in belief, differing from disagreement in belief about head colds only with regard to subject-matter. It implies not an opposition of the actual attitudes of the speakers but only of their beliefs about certain attitudes. Disagreement *in* attitude, on the other hand, implies that the very attitudes of the speakers are opposed. A and B may have opposed beliefs about attitudes without having opposed attitudes, just as they may have opposed beliefs about head colds without having opposed head colds. Hence we must not, from the fact that an argument is concerned with attitudes, infer that it necessarily involves disagreement *in* attitude.

2

We may now turn more directly to disagreement about values, with particular reference to normative ethics. When people argue about what is good, do they disagree in belief, or do they disagree in attitude? A long tradition of ethical theorists strongly suggest, whether they always intend to or not, that the disagreement is one *in belief*. Naturalistic theorists, for instance, identify an ethical judgement with some sort of scientific statement, and so make normative ethics a branch of science. Now a scientific argument typically exemplifies disagreement in belief, and if an ethical argument is simply a scientific one, then it too exemplifies disagreement in belief. The usual naturalistic theories of ethics that stress attitudes—such as those of Hume, Westermarck, Perry, Richards, and so many others—stress disagreement in belief no less than the rest. They imply, of course, that disagreement about what is good is disagreement *in belief* about attitudes; but we have seen that that is simply one sort of disagreement in belief, and by no means the same as disagreement *in* attitude. Analyses that stress disagreement *in* attitude are extremely rare.

If ethical arguments, as we encounter them in everyday life, involved disagreement in belief exclusively—whether the beliefs were about attitudes or about something else—then I should have no quarrel with the ordinary sort of naturalistic analysis. Normative judgements could be taken as scientific statements and amenable to the usual scientific proof. But a moment's attention will readily show that disagreement in belief has not the exclusive role that theory has so repeatedly ascribed to it. It must be readily granted that ethical arguments usually involve disagreement in belief; but they *also* involve disagreement in attitude. And the conspicuous role of disagreement in attitude is what we usually take, whether we realize it or not, as the distinguishing feature of ethical arguments. For example:

Suppose that the representative of a union urges that the wage level in a given company ought to be higher—that it is only right that the workers receive more pay. The company representative urges in reply that the workers ought to receive no more than they get. Such an argument clearly represents a disagreement in attitude. The union is *for* higher wages; the company is *against* them, and neither is content to let the other's attitude remain unchanged. *In addition* to this disagreement in attitude, of course, the argument may represent no little disagreement in belief. Perhaps the parties disagree about how much the cost of living has risen and how much the workers are suffering under the present wage scale. Or perhaps they disagree about the company's earnings and the extent to which the company could raise wages and still operate at a profit. Like any typical ethical argument, then, this argument involves both disagreement in attitude and disagreement in belief.

It is easy to see, however, that the disagreement in attitude plays a unifying and predominating role in the argument. This is so in two ways:

In the first place, disagreement in attitude determines what beliefs are *relevant* to the argument. Suppose that the company affirms that the wage scale of fifty years ago was far lower than it is now. The union will immediately urge that this contention, even though true, is irrelevant. And it is irrelevant simply because information about the wage level of fifty years ago, maintained under totally different circumstances, is not likely to affect the present attitudes of either party. To be relevant, any belief that is introduced into the argument must be one that is likely to lead one side or the other to have a different attitude, and so reconcile disagreement in attitude. Attitudes are often functions of beliefs. We often change our attitudes to something when we change our beliefs about it; just as a child ceases to *want* to touch a live coal when he comes to *believe* that it will burn him. Thus in the present argument any beliefs that are at all likely to alter attitudes, such as those about the increasing cost of living or the financial state of the company, will be considered by both sides to be relevant to the argument. Agreement in belief on these matters may lead to agreement in attitude toward the wage scale. But beliefs that are likely to alter the attitudes of neither side will be declared irrelevant. They will have no bearing on the disagreement in attitude, with which both parties are primarily concerned.

In the second place, ethical argument usually terminates when disagreement in attitude terminates, even though a certain amount of disagreement in belief remains. Suppose, for instance, that the company and the union continue to disagree in belief about the increasing cost of living, but that the company, even so, ends by favouring the higher wage scale. The union will then be content to end the argument and will cease to press its point about living costs. It may bring up that point again, in some future argument of the same sort, or in urging the righteousness of its victory to the newspaper columnists; but for the moment the fact that the company has agreed in attitude is sufficient to terminate the argument. On the other hand: suppose that both parties agreed on all beliefs that were introduced into the argument, but even so continued to disagree in attitude. In that case neither party would feel that their dispute had been successfully terminated. They might look for other beliefs that could be introduced into the argument. They might use words to play on each other's emotions. They might agree (in attitude) to submit the case to arbitration, both feeling that a decision, even if strongly adverse to one party or the other, would be preferable to a continued impasse. Or, perhaps, they might abandon hope of settling their dispute by any peaceable means.

In many other cases, of course, men discuss ethical topics without having the strong, uncompromising attitudes that the present example has illustrated. They are often as much concerned with redirecting their own attitudes, in the light of greater knowledge, as with redirecting the attitudes of others. And the attitudes involved are often altruistic rather than selfish. Yet the above example will serve, so long as that is understood, to suggest the nature of ethical disagreement. Both disagreement in attitude and disagreement in belief are involved, but the former predominates in that (1) it determines what sort of disagreement in belief is relevantly disputed in a given ethical argument, and (2) it determines by its continued presence or its resolution whether or not the argument has been settled. We may see further how intimately the two sorts of disagreement are related: since attitudes are often functions of beliefs, an agreement in belief may lead people, as a matter of psychological fact, to agree in attitude.

3

Having discussed disagreement, we may turn to the broad question that was first mentioned, namely: By what methods of argument or inquiry may disagreement about matters of value be resolved?

It will be obvious that to whatever extent an argument involves disagreement in belief, it is open to the usual methods of the sciences. If these methods are the *only* rational methods for supporting beliefs—as I believe to be so, but cannot now take time to discuss—then scientific methods are the only rational methods for resolving the disagreement in *belief* that arguments about values may include.

But if science is granted an undisputed sway in reconciling beliefs, it does not thereby acquire, without qualification, an undisputed sway in reconciling attitudes. We have seen that arguments about values include disagreement in attitude, no less than disagreement in belief, and that in certain ways the disagreement in attitude predominates. By what methods shall the latter sort of disagreement be resolved?

The methods of science are still available for that purpose, but only in an indirect way. Initially, these methods have only to do with establishing agreement in belief. If they serve further to establish agreement in attitude, that will be due simply to the psychological fact that altered beliefs may cause altered attitudes. Hence scientific methods are conclusive in ending arguments about values only to the extent that their success in obtaining agreement in belief will in turn lead to agreement in attitude.

In other words: the extent to which scientific methods can bring about agreement on values depends on the extent to which a commonly accepted body of scientific beliefs would cause us to have a commonly accepted set of attitudes.

How much is the development of science likely to achieve, then, with regard to values? To what extent *would* common beliefs lead to common attitudes? It is, perhaps, a pardonable enthusiasm to *hope* that science will do everything—to hope that in some rosy future, when all men know the consequences of their acts, they will all have common aspirations and live peaceably in complete moral accord. But if we speak not from our enthusiastic hopes but from our present knowledge, the answer must be far less exciting. We usually *do not know*, at the beginning of any argument about values, whether an agreement in belief, scientifically established, will lead to an agreement in attitude or not. It is logically possible, at least, that two men should continue to disagree in attitude even though they had all their beliefs in common, and even though neither had made any logical or inductive error, or omitted any relevant evidence. Differences in temperament, or in early training, or in social status, might make the men retain different attitudes even though both were possessed of the complete scientific truth. Whether this logical possibility is an empirical likelihood I shall not presume to say; but it is unquestionably a possibility that must not be left out of account.

To say that science can always settle arguments about value, we have seen, is to make this assumption: Agreement in attitude will always be consequent upon complete agreement in belief, and science can always bring about the latter. Taken as purely heuristic, this assumption has its usefulness. It leads people to discover the discrepancies in their beliefs and to prolong enlightening argument that *may* lead, as a matter of fact, from commonly accepted beliefs to commonly accepted attitudes. It leads people to reconcile their attitudes in a rational, permanent way, rather than by rhapsody or exhortation. But the assumption is *nothing more*, for present knowledge, than a heuristic maxim. It is wholly without any proper foundation of probability. I conclude, therefore, that scientific methods cannot be guaranteed the definite role in the so-called normative sciences that they may have in the natural sciences. Apart from a heuristic assumption to the contrary, it is possible that the growth of scientific knowledge may leave many disputes about values permanently unsolved. Should these disputes persist, there are non-rational methods for dealing with them, of course, such as impassioned, moving oratory. But the purely intellectual methods of science, and, indeed, *all* methods of reasoning, may be insufficient to settle disputes about values even though they may greatly help to do so.

For the same reasons I conclude that normative ethics is not a branch of any science. It deliberately deals with a type of disagreement that science deliberately avoids. Ethics is not psychology, for instance; for although psychologists may, of course, agree or disagree in belief about attitudes, they need not, as psychologists, be concerned with whether they agree or disagree with one another *in* attitude. In so far as normative ethics draws from the sciences, in order to change attitudes via changing people's beliefs, it *draws* from *all* the sciences; but a moralist's peculiar aim—that of *redirecting* attitudes—is a type of activity, rather than knowledge, and falls within no science. Science may study that activity and may help indirectly to forward it; but is not *identical* with that activity.

4

I can take only a brief space to explain why the ethical terms, such as 'good', 'wrong', 'ought', and so on, are so habitually used to deal with disagreement in attitude. On account of their repeated occurrence in emotional situations they have acquired a strong emotive meaning. This emotive meaning makes them serviceable in initiating changes in a hearer's attitudes. Sheer emotive impact is not likely, under many circumstances, to change attitudes in any permanent way; but it *begins* a process that can then be supported by other means.

There is no occasion for saying that the meaning of ethical terms is *purely* emotive, like that of 'alas' or 'hurrah'. We have seen that ethical *arguments* include many expressions of *belief*, and the rough rules of ordinary language permit us to say that some of these beliefs are expressed by an ethical judgement itself. But the beliefs so expressed are by no means always the same. Ethical terms are notable for their ambiguity, and opponents in an argument may use them in different senses. Sometimes this leads to artificial issues, but it usually does not. So long as one person says 'this is good' with emotive praise, and another says 'no, it is bad', with emotive condemnation, a disagreement in attitude is manifest. Whether or not the beliefs that these statements express are logically incompatible may not be discovered until later in the argument; but even if they are actually compatible, disagreement in attitude will be preserved by emotive meaning; and this disagreement, so certral to ethics, may lead to an argument that is certainly not artificial in its issues so long as it is taken for what it is.

The many theorists who have refused to identify ethical statements with scientific ones have much to be said in their favour. They have seen that ethical judgements mould or alter attitudes, rather than describe them, and they have seen that ethical judgements can be guaranteed no definitive scientific support. But one need not on that account provide ethics with any extramundane, *sui generis subject-matter*. The distinguishing features of an ethical judgement can be preserved by a recognition of emotive meaning and disagreement in attitude, rather than by some non-natural quality—and with far greater intelligibility. If a unique subject-matter is *postulated*, as it usually is, to preserve the important distinction between normative ethics and science, it serves no purpose that is not served by the very simple analysis I have here suggested. Unless non-natural qualities can be defended by positive arguments, rather than as an 'only resort' from the acknowledged weakness of ordinary forms of naturalism, they would seem nothing more than the invisible shadows cast by emotive meaning.

IV

A MORAL ARGUMENT

R. M. HARE

Ethical theory, which determines the meanings and functions of the moral words, and thus the 'rules' of the moral 'game', provides only a clarification of the conceptual framework within which moral reasoning takes place; it is therefore, in the required sense, neutral as between different moral opinions. But it is highly relevant to moral reasoning because, as with the rules of a game, there could be no such thing as moral reasoning without this framework, and the framework dictates the form of the reasoning. It follows that naturalism is not the only way of providing for the possibility of moral reasoning; and this may, perhaps, induce those who have espoused naturalism as a way of making moral thought a rational activity to consider other possibilities.

The rules of moral reasoning are, basically, two, corresponding to the two features of moral judgements which I argued for in the first half of this book, prescriptivity and universalizability. When we are trying, in a concrete case, to decide what we ought to do, what we are looking for (as I have already said) is an action to which we can commit ourselves (prescriptivity) but which we are at the same time prepared to accept as exemplifying a principle of action to be prescribed for others in like circumstances (universalizability). If, when we consider some proposed action, we find that, when universalized, it yields prescriptions which we cannot accept, we reject this action as a solution to our moral problem—if we cannot universalize the prescription, it cannot become an 'ought'.

It is to be noticed that, troublesome as was the problem of moral weakness when we were dealing theoretically with the logical character of the moral concepts, it cannot trouble us here. For if a person is going to reason seriously at all about a moral question, he has to presuppose that the moral concepts are going, in his reasoning, to be used prescriptively. One cannot start a moral argument about a certain proposal on the basis that, whatever the conclusion of it, it makes no difference to what anybody is to do. When one has arrived at a conclusion, one may then be too weak to put it into practice. But *in arguing* one has to discount this possibility; for, as we shall see, to abandon the prescriptivity of one's moral judgements is to unscrew an essential part of the logical mechanism on which such arguments rely. This is why, if a person were to say 'Let's have an argument about this grave moral question which faces us, but let's not think of any conclusion we may come to as requiring anybody to *do* one thing rather than another', we should be likely to accuse him of flippancy, or worse.

6.3. I will now try to exhibit the bare bones of the theory of moral reasoning that I wish to advocate by considering a very simple (indeed over-simplified) example. As we shall see, even this very simple case generates the most baffling complexities; and so we may be pardoned for not attempting anything more difficult to start with.

The example is adapted from a well-known parable.[1] *A* owes money to *B*, and *B* owes money to *C*, and it is the law that creditors may exact their debts by putting their debtors into prison. *B* asks himself, 'Can I say that I ought to take this measure against *A* in order to make him pay?' He is no doubt *inclined* to do this, or *wants* to do it. Therefore, if there were no question of universalizing his prescriptions, he would assent readily to the *singular* prescription 'Let me put *A* into prison'. But when he seeks to turn this prescription into a moral judgement, and say, 'I *ought* to put *A* into prison because he will not pay me what he owes', he reflects that this would involve accepting the principle 'Anyone who is in my position ought to put his debtor into prison if he does not pay'. But then he reflects that *C* is in the same position of unpaid creditor with regard to himself (*B*), and that the cases are otherwise identical; and that if anyone in this position ought to put his debtors into prison, then so ought *C* to put him (*B*) into prison. And to accept the moral prescription '*C* ought to put me into prison' would commit him (since, as we have seen, he must be using the word 'ought' prescriptively) to accepting the singular prescription 'Let *C* put me into prison'; and this he is not ready to accept. But if he is not, then neither can be accept the original judgement that he (*B*) ought to put *A* into prison for debt. Notice that the whole of this argument would break down if 'ought' were not being used both universalizably *and prescriptively*; for if it were not being used prescriptively, the step from '*C* ought to put me into prison' to 'Let *C* put me into prison' would not be valid.

The structure and ingredients of this argument must now be examined. We must first notice an analogy between it and the Popperian theory of scientific method. What has happened is that a provisional or suggested

[1] Matt. 18: 23.

moral principle has been rejected because one of its particlar consequences proved unacceptable. But an important difference between the two kinds of reasoning must also be noted; it is what we should expect, given that the data of scientific observation are recorded in descriptive statements, whereas we are here dealing with prescriptions. What knocks out a suggested hypothesis, on Popper's theory, is a singular statement of fact: the hypothesis has the consequence that p; but not-p. Here the logic is just the same, except that in place of the observation-statements 'p' and 'not-p' we have the singular *prescriptions* 'Let C put B into prison for debt' and its contradictory. Nevertheless, given that B is disposed to reject the first of these prescriptions, the argument against him is just as cogent as in the scientific case.

We may carry the parallel further. Just as science, seriously pursued, is the search for hypotheses and the testing of them by the attempt to falsify their particular consequences, so morals, as a serious endeavour, consists in the search for principles and the testing of them against particular cases. Any rational activity has its discipline, and this is the discipline of moral thought: to test the moral principles that suggest themselves to us by following out their consequences and seeing whether we can accept *them*.

No argument, however, starts from nothing. We must therefore ask what we have to have before moral arguments of the sort of which I have given a simple example can proceed. The first requisite is that the facts of the case should be given; for all moral discussion is about some particular set of facts, whether actual or supposed. Secondly we have the logical framework provided by the meaning of the word 'ought' (i.e. prescriptivity and universalizability, both of which we say to be necessary). Because moral judgements have to be universalizable, B cannot say that he ought to put A into prison for debt without committing himself to the view that C, who is *ex hypothesi* in the same position *vis-à-vis* himself, ought to put *him* into prison; and because moral judgements are prescriptive, this would be, in effect, prescribing to C to put him into prison; and this he is unwilling to do, since he has a strong inclination not to go to prison. This inclination gives us the third necessary ingredient in the argument: if B were a completely apathetic person, who literally did not mind what happened to himself or to anybody else, the argument would not touch him. The three necessary ingredients which we have noticed, then, are (1) facts; (2) logic; (3) inclinations. These ingredients enable us, not indeed to arrive at an evaluative conclusion, but to *reject* an evaluative proposition. We shall see later that these are not, in all cases, the only necessary ingredients.

6.4. In the example which we have been using, the position was deliberately made simpler by supposing that B actually stood to some other person in exactly the same relation as *A* does to him. Such cases are unlikely to arise in practice. But it is not necessary for the force of the argument that *B* should *in fact* stand in this relation to anyone; it is sufficient that he should consider hypothetically such a case, and see what would be the consequences in it of those moral principles between whose acceptance and rejection he has to decide. Here we have an important point of difference from the parallel scientific argument, in that the crucial case which leads to rejection of the principle can itself be a supposed, not an observed, one. That hypothetical cases will do as well as actual ones is important, since it enables us to guard against a possible misinterpretation of the argument which I have outlined. It might be thought that what moves *B* is the *fear* that *C* will actually do to him as he does to *A*—as happens in the Gospel parable. But this fear is not only irrelevant to the moral argument; it does not even provide a particularly strong non-moral motive unless the circumstances are somewhat exceptional. *C* may, after all, not find out what *B* has done to *A*; or *C*'s moral principles may be different from *B*'s, and independent of them, so that what moral principle *B* accepts makes no difference to the moral principles on which *C* acts.

Even, therefore, if *C* did not exist, it would be no answer to the argument for *B* to say 'But in my case there is no fear that anybody will ever be in a position to do to me what I am proposing to do to *A*'. For the argument does not rest on any such fear. All that is essential to it is that *B* should disregard the fact that he plays the particular role in the situation which he does, without disregarding the inclinations which people have in situations of this sort. In other words, he must be prepared to give weight to *A*'s inclinations and interests as if they were his own. This is what turns selfish prudential reasoning into moral reasoning. It is much easier, psychologically, for *B* to do this if he is actually placed in a situation like *A*'s *vis-à-vis* somebody else; but this is not necessary, provided that he has sufficient imagination to envisage what it is like to be *A*. For our first example, a case was deliberately chosen in which little imagination was necessary; but in most normal cases a certain power of imagination and readiness to use it is a fourth necessary ingredient in moral arguments, alongside those already mentioned, viz. logic (in the shape of universalizability and prescriptivity), the facts, and the inclinations or interests of the people concerned.

It must be pointed out that the absence of even one of these ingredients may render the rest ineffective. For example, impartiality by itself is not enough. If, in becoming impartial, *B* became also completely dispassionate and apathetic, and moved as little by other people's interests as by his own, then, as we have seen, there would be nothing to make him accept or reject one moral principle rather than another. That is why those who, like Adam

Smith and Professor Kneale, advocate what have been called 'Ideal Observer Theories' of ethics, sometimes postulate as their imaginary ideal observer not merely an impartial spectator, but an impartially *sympathetic* spectator.[2] To take another example, if the person who faces the moral decision has no imagination, then even the fact that someone can do the very same thing to him may pass him by. If, again, he lacks the readiness to universalize, then the vivid imagination of the sufferings which he is inflicting on others may only spur him on to intensify them, to increase his own vindictive enjoyment. And if he is ignorant of the material facts (for example about what is likely to happen to a person if one takes out a writ against him), then there is nothing to tie the moral argument to particular choices.

6.5. The best way of testing the argument which we have outlined will be to consider various ways in which somebody in *B*'s position might seek to escape from it. There are indeed a number of such ways; and all of them may be successful, at a price. It is important to understand what the price is in each case. We may classify these manœuvres which are open to *B* into two kinds. There are first of all the moves which depend on his using the moral words in a different way from that on which the argument relied. We saw that for the success of the argument it was necessary that 'ought' should be used universalizably and prescriptively. If *B* uses it in a way that is either not prescriptive or not universalizable, then he can escape the force of the argument, at the cost of resigning from the kind of discussion that we thought we were having with him. We shall discuss these two possibilities separately. Secondly, there are moves which can still be made by *B*, even though he is using the moral words in the same way as we are. We shall examine three different subclasses of these.

Before dealing with what I shall call the *verbal* manœuvres in detail, it may be helpful to make a general remark. Suppose that we are having a simple mathematical argument with somebody, and he admits, for example, that there are five eggs in this basket, and six in the other, but maintains that there are a dozen eggs in the two baskets taken together;

---

[2] It will be plain that there are affinities, though there are also differences, between this type of theory and my own. For such theories see W. C. Kneale, 'Objectivity in Morals', *Philosophy*, 25 (1950), 162; R. Firth and R. B. Brandt, 'Ethical Absolutism and the Ideal Observer', *Philosophy and Phenomenological Research*, 12 (1951–2), 317, and 15 (1954–5), 407, 414, 422; and J. Harrison, 'When is a Principle a Moral Principle?', *Proceedings of the Aristotelian Society*, supp. vol. 28 (1954), 132. Firth, unlike Kneale, says that the observer must be 'dispassionate', but see Brandt, 'Ethical Absolutism and the Ideal Observer', 411 n. For a shorter discussion, see R. B. Brandt, *Ethical Theory* (Englewood Cliffs, NJ: Prentice-Hall, 1959), 173. Since for many Christians God occupies the role of 'ideal observer', the moral judgements which they make may be expected to coincide with those arrived at by the method of reasoning which I am advocating.

and suppose that this is because he is using the expression 'a dozen' to mean 'eleven'. It is obvious that we cannot compel him logically to admit that there are not a dozen eggs, in *his* sense of 'dozen'. But it is equally obvious that this should not disturb us. For such a man only appears to be dissenting from us. His dissent is only apparent, because the proposition which his words express is actually consistent with the conclusion which we wish to draw; he *says* 'There are a dozen eggs'; but he *means* what we should express by saying 'There are eleven eggs'; and this we are not disputing. It is important to remember that in the moral case also the dissent may be only apparent, if the words are being used in different ways, and that it is no defect in a method of argument if it does not make it possible to prove a conclusion to a person when he is using words in such a way that the conclusion does not follow.

It must be pointed out, further (since this is a common source of confusion), that in this argument nothing whatever hangs upon our *actual* use of words in common speech, any more than it does in the arithmetical case. That we use the sound 'dozen' to express the meaning that we customarily do use it to express is of no consequence for the argument about the eggs; and the same may be said of the sound 'ought'. There is, however, something which I, at any rate, customarily express by the sound 'ought', whose character is correctly described by saying that it is a universal or universalizable prescription. I hope that what I customarily express by the sound 'ought' is the same as what most people customarily express by it; but if I am mistaken in this assumption, I shall still have given a correct account, so far as I am able, of that which I express by this sound.[3] Nevertheless, this account will interest other people mainly in so far as my hope that they understand the same thing as I do by 'ought' is fulfilled; and since I am moderately sure that this is indeed the case with many people, I hope that I may be of use to them in elucidating the logical properties of the concept which they thus express.

At this point, however, it is of the utmost importance to stress that the fact that two people express the same thing by 'ought' does not entail that they share the same moral opinions. For the formal, logical properties of the word 'ought' (those which are determined by its *meaning*) are only one of the four factors (listed earlier) whose combination governs a man's moral opinion on a given matter. Thus ethics, the study of the logical properties of the moral words, remains morally neutral (its conclusions neither are substantial moral judgements, nor entail them, even in conjunction with factual premisses); its bearing upon moral questions lies in this,

---

[3] Cf. G. E. Moore, *Principia Ethica* (Cambridge: Cambridge University Press, 1903), 6.

that it makes logically impossible certain combinations of moral and other prescriptions. Two people who are using the word 'ought' in the same way may yet disagree about what ought to be done in a certain situation, either because they differ about the facts, or because one or other of them lacks imagination, or because their different inclinations make one reject some singular prescription which the other can accept. For all that, ethics (i.e. the logic of moral language) is an immensely powerful engine for producing moral agreement; for if two people are willing to use the moral word 'ought', and to use it in the same way (viz. the way that I have been describing), the other possible sources of moral disagreement are all eliminable. People's inclinations about most of the important matters in life tend to be the same (very few people, for example, like being starved or run over by motor cars); and, even when they are not, there is a way of generalizing the argument, to be described in the next chapter, which enables us to make allowance for differences in inclinations. The facts are often, given sufficient patience, ascertainable. Imagination can be cultivated. If these three factors are looked after, as they can be, agreement on the use of 'ought' is the only other necessary condition for producing moral agreement, at any rate in typical cases. And, if I am not mistaken, this agreement in use is already there in the discourse of anybody with whom we are at all likely to find ourselves arguing; all that is needed is to think clearly, and so make it evident.

V

THE SUBJECTIVITY OF VALUES

J. L. MACKIE

1. MORAL SCEPTICISM

There are no objective values. This is a bald statement of the thesis of this chapter, but before arguing for it I shall try to clarify and restrict it in ways that may meet some objections and prevent some misunderstanding.

The statement of this thesis is liable to provoke one of three very different reactions. Some will think it not merely false but pernicious; they will see it as a threat to morality and to everything else that is worth while, and they will find the presenting of such a thesis in what purports to be a book on ethics paradoxical or even outrageous. Others will regard it as a trivial truth, almost too obvious to be worth mentioning, and certainly too plain to be worth much argument. Others again will say that it is meaning-less or empty, that no real issue is raised by the question whether values are or are not part of the fabric of the world. But, precisely because there can be these three different reactions, much more needs to be said.

The claim that values are not objective, are not part of the fabric of the world, is meant to include not only moral goodness, which might be most naturally equated with moral value, but also other things that could be more loosely called moral values or disvalues—rightness and wrongness, duty, obligation, an action's being rotten and contemptible, and so on. It also includes non-moral values, notably aesthetic ones, beauty and various kinds of artistic merit. I shall not discuss these explicitly, but clearly much the same considerations apply to aesthetic and to moral values, and there would be at least some initial implausibility in a view that gave the one a different status from the other.

Since it is with moral values that I am primarily concerned, the view I am adopting may be called moral scepticism. But this name is likely to be misunderstood: 'moral scepticism' might also be used as a name for either of

From J. L. Mackie, *Ethics: Inventing Right and Wrong* (Harmondsworth: Penguin, 1977), 15–49. Copyright © J. L. Mackie (1977). Reproduced by permission of Penguin Books Ltd.

two first-order views, or perhaps for an incoherent mixture of the two. A moral sceptic might be the sort of person who says 'All this talk of morality is tripe', who rejects morality and will take no notice of it. Such a person may be literally rejecting all moral judgements; he is more likely to be making moral judgements of his own, expressing a positive moral condemnation of all that conventionally passes for morality; or he may be confusing these two logically incompatible views, and saying that he rejects all morality, while he is in fact rejecting only a particular morality that is current in the society in which he has grown up. But I am not at present concerned with the merits or faults of such a position. These are first-order moral views, positive or negative: the person who adopts either of them is taking a certain practical, normative, stand. By contrast, what I am discussing is a second-order view, a view about the status of moral values and the nature of moral valuing, about where and how they fit into the world. These first- and second-order views are not merely distinct but completely independent: one could be a second-order moral sceptic without being a first-order one, or again the other way round. A man could hold strong moral views, and indeed ones whose content was thoroughly conventional, while believing that they were simply attitudes and policies with regard to conduct that he and other people held. Conversely, a man could reject all established morality while believing it to be an objective truth that it was evil or corrupt.

With another sort of misunderstanding moral scepticism would seem not so much pernicious as absurd. How could anyone deny that there is a difference between a kind action and a cruel one, or that a coward and a brave man behave differently in the face of danger? Of course, this is undeniable; but it is not to the point. The kinds of behaviour to which moral values and disvalues are ascribed are indeed part of the furniture of the world, and so are the natural, descriptive, differences between them; but not, perhaps, their differences in value. It is a hard fact that cruel actions differ from kind ones, and hence that we can learn, as in fact we all do, to distinguish them fairly well in practice, and to use the words 'cruel' and 'kind' with fairly clear descriptive meanings; but is it an equally hard fact that actions which are cruel in such a descriptive sense are to be condemned? The present issue is with regard to the objectivity specifically of value, not with regard to the objectivity of those natural, factual, differences on the basis of which differing values are assigned.

2. SUBJECTIVISM

Another name often used, as an alternative to 'moral scepticism', for the view I am discussing is 'subjectivism'. But this too has more than one meaning. Moral subjectivism too could be a first-order, normative, view, namely that everyone really ought to do whatever he thinks he should. This plainly is a (systematic) first-order view; on examination it soon ceases to be plausible, but that is beside the point, for it is quite independent of the second-order thesis at present under consideration. What is more confusing is that different second-order views compete for the name 'subjectivism'. Several of these are doctrines about the meaning of moral terms and moral statements. What is often called moral subjectivism is the doctrine that, for example, 'This action is right' *means* 'I approve of this action', or more generally that moral judgements are equivalent to reports of the speaker's own feelings or attitudes. But the view I am now discussing is to be distinguished in two vital respects from any such doctrine as this. First, what I have called moral scepticism is a negative doctrine, not a positive one: it says what there isn't, not what there is. It says that there do not exist entities or relations of a certain kind, objective values or requirements, which many people have believed to exist. Of course, the moral sceptic cannot leave it at that. If his position is to be at all plausible, he must give some account of how other people have fallen into what he regards as an error, and this account will have to include some positive suggestions about how values fail to be objective, about what has been mistaken for, or has led to false beliefs about, objective values. But this will be a development of his theory, not its core: its core is the negation. Secondly, what I have called moral scepticism is an ontological thesis, not a linguistic or conceptual one. It is not, like the other doctrine often called moral subjectivism, a view about the meanings of moral statements. Again, no doubt, if it is to be at all plausible, it will have to give some account of their meanings, and I shall say something about this in Section 7 of this chapter . . . But this too will be a development of the theory, not its core.

It is true that those who have accepted the moral subjectivism which is the doctrine that moral judgements are equivalent to reports of the speaker's own feelings or attitudes have usually presupposed what I am calling moral scepticism. It is because they have assumed that there are no objective values that they have looked elsewhere for an analysis of what moral statements might mean, and have settled upon subjective reports. Indeed, if all our moral statements were such subjective reports, it would follow that, at least so far as we are aware, there are no objective moral values. If we were aware of them, we would say something about them. In this sense this sort of subjectivism entails moral scepticism. But the converse entailment does not hold. The denial that there are objective values does not commit one to any particular view about what moral statements mean, and certainly not to the view that they are equivalent to subjective reports. No doubt if moral values are not objective they are in some very broad sense subjective, and for this reason I would accept 'moral subjectivism' as an alternative name to 'moral scepticism'. But subjectivism in this broad sense must be distinguished from the specific doctrine about meaning referred to above. Neither name is altogether satisfactory: we simply have to guard against the (different) misinterpretations which each may suggest.

3. THE MULTIPLICITY OF SECOND-ORDER QUESTIONS

The distinctions drawn in the last two sections rest not only on the well-known and generally recognized difference between first- and second-order questions, but also on the more controversial claim that there are several kinds of second-order moral question. Those most often mentioned are questions about the meaning and use of ethical terms, or the analysis of ethical concepts. With these go questions about the logic of moral statements: there may be special patterns of moral argument, licensed, perhaps, by aspects of the meanings of moral terms—for example, it may be part of the meaning of moral statements that they are universalizable. But there are also ontological, as contrasted with linguistic or conceptual, questions about the nature and status of goodness or rightness or whatever it is that first-order moral statements are distinctively about. These are questions of factual rather than conceptual analysis: the problem of what goodness is cannot be settled conclusively or exhaustively by finding out what the word 'good' means, or what it is conventionally used to say or to do.

Recent philosophy, biased as it has been towards various kinds of linguistic inquiry, has tended to doubt this, but the distinction between conceptual and factual analysis in ethics can be supported by analogies with other areas. The question of what perception is, what goes on when someone perceives something, is not adequately answered by finding out what words like 'see' and 'hear' mean, or what someone is doing in saying 'I perceive . . .', by analysing, however fully and accurately, any established concept of perception. There is a still closer analogy with colours. Robert Boyle and John Locke called colours 'secondary qualities', meaning that colours as they occur in material things consist simply in patterns of arrangement and movement of minute particles on the surfaces of objects, which make them, as we would now say, reflect light of some frequencies better than others, and so enable these objects to produce colour sensations in us, but that colours as we see them do not literally belong to the surfaces of material things. Whether Boyle and Locke were right about this cannot be settled by finding out how we use colour words and what we mean in using them. Naïve realism about colours might be a correct analysis not only of our pre-scientific colour concepts but also of the conventional meanings of colour words, and even of the meanings with which scientifically sophisticated people use them when they are off their guard, and yet it might not be a correct account of the status of colours.

Error could well result, then, from a failure to distinguish factual from conceptual analysis with regard to colours, from taking an account of the meanings of statements as a full account of what there is. There is a similar and in practice even greater risk of error in moral philosophy. There is another reason, too, why it would be a mistake to concentrate second-order ethical discussions on questions of meaning. The more work philosophers have done on meaning, both in ethics and elsewhere, the more complications have come to light. It is by now pretty plain that no simple account of the meanings of first-order moral statements will be correct, will cover adequately even the standard, conventional, senses of the main moral terms; I think, none the less, that there is a relatively clear-cut issue about the objectivity of moral values which is in danger of being lost among the complications of meaning.

4. IS OBJECTIVITY A REAL ISSUE?

It has, however, been doubted whether there is a real issue here. I must concede that it is a rather old-fashioned one. I do not mean merely that it was raised by Hume, who argued that 'The vice entirely escapes you . . . till you turn your reflexion into your own breast,' and before him by Hobbes, and long before that by some of the Greek Sophists. I mean rather that it was discussed vigorously in the 1930s and 1940s, but since then has received much less attention. This is not because it has been solved or because agreement has been reached: instead it seems to have been politely shelved.

But was there ever a genuine problem? R. M. Hare has said that he does not understand what is meant by 'the objectivity of values', and that he has not met anyone who does. We all know how to recognize the activity called 'saying, thinking it to be so, that some act is wrong', and he thinks that it is to this activity that the subjectivist and the objectivist are both alluding, though one calls it 'an attitude of disapproval' and the other 'a moral intuition': these are only different names for the same thing. It is true that if one person says that a certain act is wrong and another that it is not wrong the objectivist will say that they are contradicting one another; but this yields no significant discrimination between objectivism and subjectivism, because the subjectivist too will concede that the second person is negating what the first has said, and Hare sees no difference between contradicting and negating. Again, the objectivist will say that one of the two must be wrong; but Hare argues that to say that the judgement that a certain act is wrong is itself wrong is merely to negate that judgement, and the subjectivist too must negate one or other of the two judgements, so that still no clear difference between objectivism and subjectivism has emerged. He sums up his case thus:

Think of one world into whose fabric values are objectively built; and think of another in which those values have been annihilated. And remember that in both worlds the people in them go on being concerned about the same things—there is no difference in the 'subjective' concern which people have for things, only in their 'objective' value. Now I ask, 'What is the difference between the states of affairs in these two worlds?' Can any answer be given except 'None whatever'?

Now it is quite true that it is logically possible that the subjective concern, the activity of valuing or of thinking things wrong, should go on in just the same way whether there are objective values or not. But to say this is only to reiterate that there is a logical distinction between first- and second-order ethics: first-order judgements are not necessarily affected by the truth or falsity of a second-order view. But it does not follow, and it is not true, that there is no difference whatever between these two worlds. In the one there is something that backs up and validates some of the subjective concern which people have for things, in the other there is not. Hare's argument is similar to the positivist claim that there is no difference between a phenomenalist or Berkeleian world in which there are only minds and their ideas and the common-sense realist one in which there are also material things, because it is logically possible that people should have the same experiences in both. If we reject the positivism that would make the dispute between realists and phenomenalists a pseudo-question, we can reject Hare's similarly supported dismissal of the issue of the objectivity of values.

In any case, Hare has minimized the difference between his two worlds by considering only the situation where people already have just such subjective concern; further differences come to light if we consider how subjective concern is acquired or changed. If there were something in the fabric of the world that validated certain kinds of concern, then it would be possible to acquire these merely by finding something out, by letting one's thinking be controlled by how things were. But in the world in which objective values have been annihilated the acquiring of some new subjective concern means the development of something new on the emotive side by the person who acquires it, something that eighteenth-century writers would put under the head of passion or sentiment.

The issue of the objectivity of values needs, however, to be distinguished from others with which it might be confused. To say that there are object-ive values would not be to say merely that there are some things which are valued by everyone, nor does it entail this. There could be agreement in valuing even if valuing is just something that people do, even if this activity is not further validated. Subjective agreement would give intersubjective values, but intersubjectivity is not objectivity. Nor is objectivity simply universalizability: someone might well be prepared to universalize his prescriptive judgements or approvals—that is, to prescribe and approve in just the same ways in all relevantly similar cases, even ones in which he was involved differently or not at all—and yet he could recognize that such prescribing and approving were his activities, nothing more. Of course if there were objective values they would presumably belong to *kinds* of things or actions or states of affairs, so that the judgements that reported them would be universalizable; but the converse does not hold.

A more subtle distinction needs to be made between objectivism and descriptivism. Descriptivism is again a doctrine about the meanings of ethical terms and statements, namely that their meanings are purely descriptive rather than even partly prescriptive or emotive or evaluative, or that it is not an essential feature of the conventional meaning of moral statements that they have some special illocutionary force, say of commending rather than asserting. It contrasts with the view that commen-dation is in principle distinguishable from description (however difficult they may be to separate in practice) and that moral statements have it as at least part of their meaning that they are commendatory and hence in some uses intrinsically action-guiding. But descriptive meaning neither entails nor is entailed by objectivity. Berkeley's subjective idealism about material objects would be quite compatible with the admission that mater-ial object statements have purely descriptive meaning. Conversely, the main tradition of European moral philosophy from Plato onwards has combined the view that moral values are objective with the recognition that moral judgements are partly prescriptive or directive or action-guiding. Values themselves have been seen as at once prescriptive and objective. In Plato's theory the Forms, and in particular the Form of the Good, are eternal, extra-mental, realities. They are a very central struc-tural element in the fabric of the world. But it is held also that just knowing them or 'seeing' them will not merely tell men what to do but will ensure that they do it, overruling any contrary inclinations. The philosopher-kings in the *Republic* can, Plato thinks, be trusted with unchecked power because their education will have given them knowledge of the Forms. Being acquainted with the Forms of the Good and Justice and Beauty and the rest they will, by this knowledge alone, without any further motivation, be impelled to pursue and promote these ideals. Similarly, Kant believes that pure reason can by itself be practical, though he does not pretend to be able to explain how it can be so. Again, Sidgwick argues that if there is to be a science of ethics—and he assumes that there can be, indeed he defines ethics as 'the science of conduct'—what ought to be 'must in another sense have objective existence: it must be an object of knowledge and as such the same for all minds'; but he says that the affirmations of this science 'are also precepts', and he speaks of happiness as 'an end *absolutely* prescribed by reason'. Since many philosophers have thus held that values are objectively prescriptive, it is clear that the ontological doctrine of objectivism must be distinguished from descriptivism, a theory about meaning.

But perhaps when Hare says that he does not understand what is meant by 'the objectivity of values' he means that he cannot understand how values could be objective, he cannot frame for himself any clear, detailed, picture of what it would be like for values to be part of the fabric of the world. This would be a much more plausible claim; as we have seen, even Kant hints at a similar difficulty. Indeed, even Plato warns us that it is only through difficult studies spread over many years that one can approach the knowledge of the Forms. The difficulty of seeing how values could be objective is a fairly strong reason for thinking that they are not so; this point will be taken up in Section 9 but it is not a good reason for saying that this is not a real issue.

I believe that as well as being a real issue it is an important one. It clearly matters for general philosophy. It would make a radical difference to our metaphysics if we had to find room for objective values—perhaps something like Plato's Forms—somewhere in our picture of the world. It would similarly make a difference to our epistemology if it had to explain how such objective values are or can be known, and to our philosophical psychology if we had to allow such knowledge, or Kant's pure practical reason, to direct choices and actions. Less obviously, how this issue is settled will affect the possibility of certain kinds of moral argument. For example, Sidgwick considers a discussion between an egoist and a utilitarian, and points out that if the egoist claims that his happiness or pleasure is objectively desirable or good, the utilitarian can argue that the egoist's happiness 'cannot be more objectively desirable or more a good than the similar happiness of any other person: the mere fact . . . that *he is he* can have nothing to do with its objective desirability or goodness'. In other words, if ethics is built on the concept of objective goodness, then egoism as a first-order system or method of ethics can be refuted, whereas if it is assumed that goodness is only subjective it cannot. But Sidgwick correctly stresses what a number of other philosophers have missed, that this argument against egoism would require the objectivity specifically of goodness: the objectivity of what ought to be or of what it is rational to do would not be enough. If the egoist claimed that it was objectively rational, or obligatory upon him, to seek his own happiness, a similar argument about the irrelevance of the fact that he is he would lead only to the conclusion that it was objectively rational or obligatory for each other person to seek *his* own happiness, that is, to a universalized form of egoism, not to the refutation of egoism. And of course insisting on the universalizability of moral judgements, as opposed to the objectivity of goodness, would yield only the same result.

5. STANDARDS OF EVALUATION

One way of stating the thesis that there are no objective values is to say that value statements cannot be either true or false. But this formulation, too, lends itself to misinterpretation. For there are certain kinds of value statements which undoubtedly can be true or false, even if, in the sense I intend, there are no objective values. Evaluations of many sorts are commonly made in relation to agreed and assumed standards. The classing of wool, the grading of apples, the awarding of prizes at sheepdog trials, flower shows, skating and diving championships, and even the marking of examination papers are carried out in relation to standards of quality or merit which are peculiar to each particular subject-matter or type of contest, which may be explicitly laid down but which, even if they are nowhere explicitly stated, are fairly well understood and agreed by those who are recognized as judges or experts in each particular field. Given any sufficiently determinate standards, it will be an objective issue, a matter of truth and falsehood, how well any particular specimen measures up to those standards. Comparative judgements in particular will be capable of truth and falsehood: it will be a factual question whether this sheepdog has performed better than that one.

The subjectivist about values, then, is not denying that there can be objective evaluations relative to standards, and these are as possible in the aesthetic and moral fields as in any of those just mentioned. More than this, there is an objective distinction which applies in many such fields, and yet would itself be regarded as a peculiarly moral one: the distinction between justice and injustice. In one important sense of the word it is a paradigm case of injustice if a court declares someone to be guilty of an offence of which it knows him to be innocent. More generally, a finding is unjust if it is at variance with what the relevant law and the facts together require, and particularly if it is known by the court to be so. More generally still, any award of marks, prizes, or the like is unjust if it is at variance with the agreed standards for the contest in question: if one diver's performance in fact measures up better to the accepted standards for diving than another's, it will be unjust if the latter is awarded higher marks or the prize. In this way the justice or injustice of decisions relative to standards can be a thoroughly objective matter, though there may still be a subjective element in the interpretation or application of standards. But the statement that a certain decision is thus just or unjust will not be objectively prescriptive: in so far as it can be simply true it leaves open the question whether there is any objective requirement to do what is just and to refrain from what is unjust, and equally leaves open the practical decision to act in either way.

Recognizing the objectivity of justice in relation to standards, and of evaluative judgements relative to standards, then, merely shifts the question of the objectivity of values back to the standards themselves. The subjectivist may try to make his point by insisting that there is no objective validity about the choice of standards. Yet he would clearly be wrong if he said that the choice of even the most basic standards in any field was completely arbitrary. The standards used in sheepdog trials clearly bear some relation to the work that sheepdogs are kept to do, the standards for grading apples bear some relation to what people generally want in or like about apples, and so on. On the other hand, standards are not as a rule strictly validated by such purposes. The appropriateness of standards is neither fully determinate nor totally indeterminate in relation to independently specifiable aims or desires. But however determinate it is, the objective appropriateness of standards in relation to aims or desires is no more of a threat to the denial of objective values than is the objectivity of evaluation relative to standards. In fact it is logically no different from the objectivity of goodness relative to desires. Something may be called good simply in so far as it satisfies or is such as to satisfy a certain desire; but the objectivity of such relations of satisfaction does not constitute in our sense an objective value.

6. HYPOTHETICAL AND CATEGORICAL IMPERATIVES

We may make this issue clearer by referring to Kant's distinction between hypothetical and categorical imperatives, though what he called imperatives are more naturally expressed as ought-statements than in the imperative mood. 'If you want X, do Y' (or 'You ought to do Y') will be a hypothetical imperative if it is based on the supposed fact that Y is, in the circumstances, the only (or the best) available means to X, that is, on a causal relation between Y and X. The reason for doing Y lies in its causal connection with the desired end, X; the oughtness is contingent upon the desire. But 'You ought to do Y' will be a categorical imperative if you ought to do Y irrespective of any such desire for any end to which Y would contribute, if the oughtness is not thus contingent upon any desire. But this distinction needs to be handled with some care. An ought-statement is not in this sense hypothetical merely because it incorporates a conditional clause. 'If you promised to do Y, you ought to do Y' is not a hypothetical imperative merely on account of the stated if-clause; what is meant may be either a hypothetical or a categorical imperative, depending upon the implied reason for keeping the supposed promise. If this rests upon some such further unstated conditional as 'If you want to be trusted another time', then it is a hypothetical imperative; if not, it is categorical. Even a desire of the agent's can figure in the antecedent of what, though conditional in grammatical form, is still in Kant's sense of a categorical imperative. 'If you are strongly attracted sexually to young children you ought not to go in for school teaching' is not, in virtue of what it explicitly says, a hypothetical imperative: the avoidance of school teaching is not being offered as a means to the satisfaction of the desires in question. Of course, it could still be a hypothetical imperative, if the implied reason were a prudential one; but it could also be a categorical imperative, a moral requirement where the reason for the recommended action (strictly, avoidance) does not rest upon that action's being a means to the satisfaction of any desire that the agent is supposed to have. Not every conditional ought-statement or command, then, is a hypothetical imperative; equally, not every non-conditional one is a categorical imperative. An appropriate if-clause may be left unstated. Indeed, a simple command in the imperative mood, say a parade-ground order, which might seem most literally to qualify for the title of a categorical imperative, will hardly ever be one in the sense we need here. The implied reason for complying with such an order will almost always be some desire of the person addressed, perhaps simply the desire to keep out of trouble. If so, such an apparently categorical order will be in our sense a hypothetical imperative. Again, an imperative remains hypothetical even if we change the 'if' to 'since': the fact that the desire for X is actually present does not alter the fact that the reason for doing Y is contingent upon the desire for X by way of Y's being a means to X. In Kant's own treatment, while imperatives of skill relate to desires which an agent may or may not have, imperatives of prudence relate to the desire for happiness which, Kant assumes, everyone has. So construed, imperatives of prudence are no less hypothetical than imperatives of skill, no less contingent upon desires that the agent has at the time the imperatives are addressed to him. But if we think rather of a counsel of prudence as being related to the agent's future welfare, to the satisfaction of desires that he does not yet have—not even to a present desire that his future desires should be satisfied—then a counsel of prudence is a categorical imperative, different indeed from a moral one, but analogous to it.

A categorical imperative, then, would express a reason for acting which was unconditional in the sense of not being contingent upon any present desire of the agent to whose satisfaction the recommended action would contribute as a means—or more directly: 'You ought to dance', if the implied reason is just that you want to dance or like dancing, is still a hypothetical imperative. Now Kant himself held that moral judgements are categorical imperatives, or perhaps are all applications of one categorical imperative, and it can plausibly be maintained at least that many moral judgements contain a categorically imperative element. So far as ethics is concerned, my thesis that there are no objective values is specifically the denial that any such categorically imperative element is objectively valid. The objective values which I am denying would be action-directing absolutely, not contingently (in the way indicated) upon the agent's desires and inclinations.

Another way of trying to clarify this issue is to refer to moral reasoning or moral arguments. In practice, of course, such reasoning is seldom fully explicit: but let us suppose that we could make explicit the reasoning that supports some evaluative conclusion, where this conclusion has some action-guiding force that is not contingent upon desires or purposes or chosen ends. Then what I am saying is that somewhere in the input to this argument—perhaps in one or more of the premises, perhaps in some part of the form of the argument—there will be something which cannot be objectively validated—some premiss which is not capable of being simply true, or some form of argument which is not valid as a matter of general logic, whose authority or cogency is not objective, but is constituted by our choosing or deciding to think in a certain way.

7. THE CLAIM TO OBJECTIVITY

If I have succeeded in specifying precisely enough the moral values whose objectivity I am denying, my thesis may now seem to be trivially true. Of

course, some will say, valuing, preferring, choosing, recommending, rejecting, condemning, and so on, are human activities, and there is no need to
look for values that are prior to and logically independent of all such
activities. There may be widespread agreement in valuing, and particular
value-judgements are not in general arbitrary or isolated: they typically
cohere with others, or can be criticized if they do not, reasons can be given
for them, and so on: but if all that the subjectivist is maintaining is that
desires, ends, purposes, and the like figure somewhere in the system of
reasons, and that no ends or purposes are objective as opposed to being
merely intersubjective, then this may be conceded without much fuss.

But I do not think that this should be conceded so easily. As I have said,
the main tradition of European moral philosophy includes the contrary
claim, that there are objective values of just the sort I have denied. I have
referred already to Plato, Kant, and Sidgwick. Kant in particular holds that
the categorical imperative is not only categorical and imperative but
objectively so: though a rational being gives the moral law to himself, the
law that he thus makes is determinate and necessary. Aristotle begins the
Nicomachean Ethics by saying that the good is that at which all things aim,
and that ethics is part of a science which he calls 'politics', whose goal is not
knowledge but practice; yet he does not doubt that there can be *knowledge*
of what is the good for man, nor, once he has identified this as well-being
or happiness, *eudaimonia*, that it can be known, rationally determined, in
what happiness consists; and it is plain that he thinks that this happiness is
intrinsically desirable, not good simply because it is desired. The rationalist
Samuel Clarke holds that

these eternal and necessary differences of things make it *fit and reasonable* for
creatures so to act . . . even separate from the consideration of these rules being the
positive will or *command of God*; and also antecedent to any respect or regard,
expectation or apprehension, of any *particular private and personal advantage or
disadvantage, reward or punishment*, either present or future . . .

Even the sentimentalist Hutcheson defines moral goodness as 'some quality apprehended in actions, which procures approbation', while saying that
the moral sense by which we perceive virtue and vice has been given to us
(by the Author of nature) to direct our actions. Hume indeed was on the
other side, but he is still a witness to the dominance of the objectivist
tradition, since he claims that when we 'see that the distinction of vice and
virtue is not founded merely on the relations of objects, nor is perceiv'd
by reason', this 'wou'd subvert all the vulgar systems of morality'. And
Richard Price insists that right and wrong are 'real characters of actions',
not 'qualities of our minds', and are perceived by the understanding; he
criticizes the notion of moral sense on the ground that it would make virtue

an affair of taste, and moral right and wrong 'nothing in the objects themselves'; he rejects Hutcheson's view because (perhaps mistakenly) he sees it as collapsing into Hume's.

But this objectivism about values is not only a feature of the philosophical tradition. It has also a firm basis in ordinary thought, and even in the meanings of moral terms. No doubt it was an extravagance for Moore to say that 'good' is the name of a non-natural quality, but it would not be so far wrong to say that in moral contexts it is used as if it were the name of a supposed non-natural quality, where the description 'non-natural' leaves room for the peculiar evaluative, prescriptive, intrinsically action-guiding aspects of this supposed quality. This point can be illustrated by reflection on the conflicts and swings of opinion in recent years between non-cognitivist and naturalist views about the central, basic, meanings of ethical terms. If we reject the view that it is the function of such terms to introduce objective values into discourse about conduct and choices of action, there seem to be two main alternative types of account. One (which has importantly different subdivisions) is that they conventionally express either attitudes which the speaker purports to adopt towards whatever it is that he characterizes morally, or prescriptions or recommendations, subject perhaps to the logical constratint of universalizability. Different views of this type share the central thesis that ethical terms have, at least partly and primarily, some sort of non-cognitive, non-descriptive, meaning. Views of the other type hold that they are descriptive in meaning, but descriptive of natural features, partly of such features as everyone, even the non-cognitivist, would recognize as distinguishing kind actions from cruel ones, courage from cowardice, politeness from rudeness, and so on, and partly (though these two overlap) of relations between the actions and some human wants, satisfactions, and the like. I believe that views of both these types capture part of the truth. Each approach can account for the fact that moral judgements are action-guiding or practical. Yet each gains much of its plausibility from the felt inadequacy of the other. It is a very natural reaction to any non-cognitive analysis of ethical terms to protest that there is more to ethics than this, something more external to the maker of moral judgements, more authoritative over both him and those of or to whom he speaks, and this reaction is likely to persist even when full allowance has been made for the logical, formal, constraints of full-blooded prescriptivity and universalizability. Ethics, we are inclined to believe, is more a matter of knowledge and less a matter of decision than any non-cognitive analysis allows. And of course naturalism satisfies this demand. It will not be a matter of choice or decision whether an action is cruel or unjust or imprudent or whether it is likely to produce more distress than pleasure. But in satisfying this demand, it introduces a converse deficiency. On a naturalist analysis, moral judgements can be practical, but their practicality is wholly relative to desires or possible satisfactions of the person or persons whose actions are to be guided; but moral judgements seem to say more than this. This view leaves out the categorical quality of moral requirements. In fact both naturalist and non-cognitive analyses leave out the apparent authority of ethics, the one by excluding the categorically imperative aspect, the other the claim to objective validity or truth. The ordinary user of moral language means to say something about whatever it is that he characterizes morally, for example a possible action, as it is in itself, or would be if it were realized, and not about, or even simply expressive of, his, or anyone else's, attitude or relation to it. But the something he wants to say is not purely descriptive, certainly not inert, but something that involves a call for action or for the refraining from action, and one that is absolute, not contingent upon any desire or preference or policy or choice, his own or anyone else's. Someone in a state of moral perplexity, wondering whether it would be wrong for him to engage, say, in research related to bacteriological warfare, wants to arrive at some judgement about this concrete case, his doing this work at this time in these actual circumstances; his relevant characteristics will be part of the subject of the judgement, but no relation between him and the proposed action will be part of the predicate. The question is not, for example, whether he really wants to do this work, whether it will satisfy or dissatisfy him, whether he will in the long run have a pro-attitude towards it, or even whether this is an action of a sort that he can happily and sincerely recommend in all relevantly similar cases. Nor is he even wondering just whether to recommend such action in all relevantly similar cases. He wants to know whether this course of action would be wrong in itself. Something like this is the everyday objectivist concept of which talk about non-natural qualities is a philosopher's reconstruction.

The prevalence of this tendency to objectify values—and not only moral ones—is confirmed by a pattern of thinking that we find in existentialists and those influenced by them. The denial of objective values can carry with it an extreme emotional reaction, a feeling that nothing matters at all, that life has lost its purpose. Of course this does not follow; the lack of objective values is not a good reason for abandoning subjective concern or for ceasing to want anything. But the abandonment of a belief in objective values can cause, at least temporarily, a decay of subjective concern and sense of purpose. That it does so is evidence that the people in whom this reaction occurs have been tending to objectify their concerns and purposes, have been giving them a fictitious external authority. A claim to objectivity has been so strongly associated with their subjective concerns and purposes that the collapse of the former seems to undermine the latter as well.

This view, that conceptual analysis would reveal a claim to objectivity, is sometimes dramatically confirmed by philosophers who are officially on the other side. Bertrand Russell, for example, says that 'ethical propositions should be expressed in the optative mood, not in the indicative'; he defends himself effectively against the charge of inconsistency in both holding ultimate ethical valuations to be subjective and expressing emphatic opinions on ethical questions. Yet at the end he admits:

Certainly there *seems* to be something more. Suppose, for example, that some one were to advocate the introduction of bullfighting in this country. In opposing the proposal, I should *feel*, not only that I was expressing my desires, but that my desires in the matter are *right*, whatever that may mean. As a matter of argument, I can, I think, show that I am not guilty of any logical inconsistency in holding to the above interpretation of ethics and at the same time expressing strong ethical preferences. But in feeling I am not satisfied.

But he concludes, reasonably enough, with the remark: 'I can only say that, while my own opinions as to ethics do not satisfy me, other people's satisfy me still less.'

I conclude, then, that ordinary moral judgements include a claim to objectivity, an assumption that there are objective values in just the sense in which I am concerned to deny this. And I do not think it is going too far to say that this assumption has been incorporated in the basic, conventional, meanings of moral terms. Any analysis of the meanings of moral terms which omits this claim to objective, intrinsic, prescriptivity is to that extent incomplete; and this is true of any non-cognitive analysis, any naturalist one, and any combination of the two.

If second-order ethics were confined, then, to linguistic and conceptual analysis, it ought to conclude that moral values at least are objective: that they are so is part of what our ordinary moral statements mean: the traditional moral concepts of the ordinary man as well as of the main line of Western philosophers are concepts of objective value. But it is precisely for this reason that linguistic and conceptual analysis is not enough. The claim to objectivity, however ingrained in our language and thought, is not self-validating. It can and should be questioned. But the denial of objective values will have to be put forward not as the result of an analytic approach, but as an 'error theory', a theory that although most people in making moral judgements implicitly claim, among other things, to be pointing to something objectively prescriptive, these claims are all false. It is this that makes the name 'moral scepticism' appropriate.

But since this is an error theory, since it goes against assumptions ingrained in our thought and built into some of the ways in which language is used, since it conflicts with what is sometimes called common sense, it needs very solid support. It is not something we can accept lightly or casually and then quietly pass on. If we are to adopt this view, we must argue explicitly for it. Traditionally it has been supported by arguments of two main kinds, which I shall call the argument from relativity and the argument from queerness, but these can, as I shall show, be supplemented in several ways.

8. THE ARGUMENT FROM RELATIVITY

The argument from relativity has as its premiss the well-known variation in moral codes from one society to another and from one period to another, and also the differences in moral beliefs between different groups and classes within a complex community. Such variation is in itself merely a truth of descriptive morality, a fact of anthropology which entails neither first-order nor second-order ethical views. Yet it may indirectly support second-order subjectivism: radical differences between first-order moral judgements make it difficult to treat those judgements as apprehensions of objective truths. But it is not the mere occurrence of disagreements that tells against the objectivity of values. Disagreement on questions in history or biology or cosmology does not show that there are no objective issues in these fields for investigators to disagree about. But such scientific disagreement results from speculative inferences or explanatory hypotheses based on inadequate evidence, and it is hardly plausible to interpret moral disagreement in the same way. Disagreement about moral codes seems to reflect people's adherence to and participation in different ways of life. The causal connection seems to be mainly that way round: it is that people approve of monogamy because they participate in a monogamous way of life rather than that they participate in a monogamous way of life because they approve of monogamy. Of course, the standards may be an idealization of the way of life from which they arise: the monogamy in which people participate may be less complete, less rigid, than that of which it leads them to approve. This is not to say that moral judgements are purely conventional. Of course there have been and are moral heretics and moral reformers, people who have turned against the established rules and practices of their own communities for moral reasons, and often for moral reasons that we would endorse. But this can usually be understood as the extension, in ways which, though new and unconventional, seemed to them to be required for consistency, of rules to which they already adhered as arising out of an existing way of life. In short, the argument from relativity has some force simply because the actual variations in the moral codes are more readily explained by the hypothesis that they reflect ways of life than by the hypothesis that they express perceptions, most of them seriously inadequate and badly distorted, of objective values.

But there is a well-known counter to this argument from relativity, namely to say that the items for which objective validity is in the first place to be claimed are not specific moral rules or codes but very general basic principles which are recognized at least implicitly to some extent in all society—such principles as provide the foundations of what Sidgwick has called different methods of ethics: the principle of universalizability, perhaps, or the rule that one ought to conform to the specific rules of any way of life in which one takes part, from which one profits, and on which one relies, or some utilitarian principle of doing what tends, or seems likely, to promote the general happiness. It is easy to show that such general principles, married with differing concrete circumstances, different existing social patterns or different preferences, will beget different specific moral rules; and there is some plausibility in the claim that the specific rules thus generated will vary from community to community or from group to group in close agreement with the actual variations in accepted codes.

The argument from relativity can be only partly countered in this way. To take this line the moral objectivist has to say that it is only in these principles that the objective moral character attaches immediately to its descriptively specified ground or subject: other moral judgements are objectively valid or true, but only derivatively and contingently—if things had been otherwise, quite different sorts of actions would have been right. And despite the prominence in recent philosophical ethics of universalization, utilitarian principles, and the like, these are very far from constituting the whole of what is actually affirmed as basic in ordinary moral thought. Much of this is concerned rather with what Hare calls 'ideals' or, less kindly, 'fanaticism'. That is, people judge that some things are good or right, and others are bad or wrong, not because—or at any rate not only because—they exemplify some general principle for which widespread implicit acceptance could be claimed, but because something about those things arouses certain responses immediately in them, though they would arouse radically and irresolvably different responses in others. 'Moral sense' or 'intuition' is an initially more plausible description of what supplies many of our basic moral judgements than 'reason'. With regard to all these starting-points of moral thinking the argument from relativity remains in full force.

9. THE ARGUMENT FROM QUEERNESS

Even more important, however, and certainly more generally applicable, is the argument from queerness. This has two parts, one metaphysical, the other epistemological. If there were objective values, then they would be entities or qualities or relations of a very strange sort, utterly different from anything else in the universe. Correspondingly, if we were aware of them, it would have to be by some special faculty of moral perception or intuition, utterly different from our ordinary ways of knowing everything else. These points were recognized by Moore when he spoke of non-natural qualities, and by the Intuitionists in their talk about a 'faculty of moral intuition'. Intuitionism has long been out of favour, and it is indeed easy to point out its implausibilities. What is not so often stressed, but is more important, is that the central thesis of intuitionism is one to which any objectivist view of values is in the end committed: intuitionism merely makes unpalatably plain what other forms of objectivism wrap up. Of course the suggestion that moral judgements are made or moral problems solved by just sitting down and having an ethical intuition is a travesty of actual moral thinking. But, however complex the real process, it will require (if it is to yield authoritatively prescriptive conclusions) some input of this distinctive sort, either premises or forms of argument or both. When we ask the awkward question, how we can be aware of this authoritative prescriptivity, of the truth of these distinctively ethical premises or of the cogency of this distinctively ethical pattern of reasoning, none of our ordinary accounts of sensory perception or introspection or the framing and confirming of explanatory hypotheses or inference or logical construction or conceptual analysis, or any combination of these, will provide a satisfactory answer; 'a special sort of intuition' is a lame answer, but it is the one to which the clear-headed objectivist is compelled to resort.

Indeed, the best move for the moral objectivist is not to evade this issue, but to look for companions in guilt. For example, Richard Price argues that it is not moral knowledge alone that such an empiricism as those of Locke and Hume is unable to account for, but also our knowledge and even our ideas of essence, number, identity, diversity, solidity, inertia, substance, the necessary existence and infinite extension of time and space, necessity and possibility in general, power, and causation. If the understanding, which Price defines as the faculty within us that discerns truth, is also a source of new simple ideas of so many other sorts, may it not also be a power of immediately perceiving right and wrong, which yet are real characters of actions?

This is an important counter to the argument from queerness. The only adequate reply to it would be to show how, on empiricist foundations, we can construct an account of the ideas and beliefs and knowledge that we have of all these matters. I cannot even begin to do that here, though I have undertaken some parts of the task elsewhere. I can only state my belief that satisfactory accounts of most of these can be given in empirical terms. If some supposed metaphysical necessities or essences resist such treatment, then they too should be included, along with objective values, among the targets of the argument from queerness.

This queerness does not consist simply in the fact that ethical statements are 'unverifiable'. Although logical positivism with its verifiability theory of descriptive meaning gave an impetus to non-cognitive accounts of ethics, it is not only Logical Positivists but also empiricists of a much more liberal sort who should find objective values hard to accommodate. Indeed, I would not only reject the verifiability principle but also deny the conclusion commonly drawn from it, that moral judgements lack descriptive meaning. The assertion that there are objective values or intrinsically prescriptive entities or features of some kind, which ordinary moral judgements presuppose, is, I hold, not meaningless but false.

Plato's Forms give a dramatic picture of what objective values would have to be. The Form of the Good is such that knowledge of it provides the knower with both a direction and an overriding motive; something's being good both tells the person who knows this to pursue it and makes him pursue it. An objective good would be sought by anyone who was acquainted with it, not because of any contingent fact that this person, or every person, is so constituted that he desires this end, but just because the end has to-be-pursuedness somehow built into it. Similarly, if there were objective principles of right and wrong, any wrong (possible) course of action would have not-to-be-doneness somehow built into it. Or we should have something like Clarke's necessary relations of fitness between situations and actions, so that a situation would have a demand for such-and-such an action somehow built into it.

The need for an argument of this sort can be brought out by reflection on Hume's argument that 'reason'—in which at this stage he includes all sorts of knowing as well as reasoning—can never be an 'influencing motive of the will'. Someone might object that Hume has argued unfairly from the lack of influencing power (not contingent upon desires) in ordinary objects of knowledge and ordinary reasoning, and might maintain that values differ from natural objects precisely in their power, when known, automatically to influence the will. To this Hume could, and would need to, reply that this objection involves the postulating of value entities or value features of quite a different order from anything else with which we are acquainted, and of a corresponding faculty with which to detect them. That is, he would have to supplement his explicit argument with what I have called the argument from queerness.

Another way of bringing out this queerness is to ask, about anything that is supposed to have some objective moral quality, how this is linked with its natural features. What is the connection between the natural fact that an action is a piece of deliberate cruelty—say, causing pain just for fun—and the moral fact that it is wrong? It cannot be an entailment, a logical or semantic necessity. Yet it is not merely that the two features occur together. The wrongness must somehow be 'consequential' or 'supervenient'; it is wrong because it is a piece of deliberate cruelty. But just what *in the world* is signified by this 'because'? And how do we know the relation that it signifies, if this is something more than such actions being socially condemned, and condemned by us too, perhaps through our having absorbed attitudes from our social environment? It is not even sufficient to postulate a faculty which 'sees' the wrongness: something must be postulated which can see at once the natural features that constitute the cruelty, and the wrongness, and the mysterious consequential link between the two. Alternatively, the intuition required might be the perception that wrongness is a higher-order property belonging to certain natural properties; but what is this belonging of properties to other properties, and how can we discern it? How much simpler and more comprehensible the situation would be if we could replace the moral quality with some sort of subjective response which could be causally related to the detection of the natural features on which the supposed quality is said to be consequential.

It may be thought that the argument from queerness is given an unfair start if we thus relate it to what are admittedly among the wilder products of philosophical fancy—Platonic Forms, non-natural qualities, self-evident relations of fitness, faculties of intuition, and the like. Is it equally forceful if applied to the terms in which everyday moral judgements are more likely to be expressed—though still, as has been argued in Section 7, with a claim to objectivity—'you must do this', 'you can't do that', 'obligation', 'unjust', 'rotten', 'disgraceful', 'mean', or talk about good reasons for or against possible actions? Admittedly not; but that is because the objective prescriptivity, the element a claim for whose authoritativeness is embedded in ordinary moral thought and language, is not yet isolated in these forms of speech, but is presented along with relations to desires and feelings, reasoning about the means to desired ends, interpersonal demands, the injustice which consists in the violation of what are in the context the accepted standards of merit, the psychological constituents of meanness, and so on. There is nothing queer about any of these, and under cover of them the claim for moral authority may pass unnoticed. But if I am right in arguing that it is ordinarily there, and is therefore very likely to be incorporated almost automatically in philosophical accounts of ethics which systematize our ordinary thought even in such apparently innocent terms as these, it needs to be examined, and for this purpose it needs to be isolated and exposed as it is by the less cautions philosophical reconstructions.

10. PATTERNS OF OBJECTIFICATION

Considerations of these kinds suggest that it is in the end less paradoxical to reject than to retain the common-sense belief in the objectivity of moral values, provided that we can explain how this belief, if it is false, has become established and is so resistant to criticisms. This proviso is not difficult to satisfy.

On a subjectivist view, the supposedly objective values will be based in fact upon attitudes which the person has who takes himself to be recognizing and responding to those values. If we admit what Hume calls the mind's 'propensity to spread itself on external objects', we can understand the supposed objectivity of moral qualities as arising from what we can call the projection or objectification of moral attitudes. This would be analogous to what is called the 'pathetic fallacy', the tendency to read our feelings into their objects. If a fungus, say, fills us with disgust, we may be inclined to ascribe to the fungus itself a non-natural quality of foulness. But in moral contexts there is more than this propensity at work. Moral attitudes themselves are at least partly social in origin: socially established— and socially necessary—patterns of behaviour put pressure on individuals, and each individual tends to internalize these pressures and to join in requiring these patterns of behaviour of himself and of others. The attitudes that are objectified into moral values have indeed an external source, though not the one assigned to them by the belief in their absolute authority. Moreover, there are motives that would support objectification. We need morality to regulate interpersonal relations, to control some of the ways in which people behave towards one another, often in opposition to contrary inclinations. We therefore want our moral judgements to be authoritative for other agents as well as for ourselves: objective validity would give them the authority required. Aesthetic values are logically in the same position as moral ones; much the same metaphysical and epistemological considerations apply to them. But aesthetic values are less strongly objectified than moral ones; their subjective status, and an 'error theory' with regard to such claims to objectivity as are incorporated in aesthetic judgements, will be more readily accepted, just because the motives for their objectification are less compelling.

But it would be misleading to think of the objectification of moral values as primarily the projection of feelings, as in the pathetic fallacy. More important are wants and demands. As Hobbes says, 'whatsoever is the object of any man's Appetite or Desire, that is it, which he for his part calleth *Good*'; and certainly both the adjective 'good' and the noun 'goods' are used in non-moral contexts of things because they are such as to satisfy desires. We get the notion of something's being objectively good, or having intrinsic value, by reversing the direction of dependence here, by making the desire depend upon the goodness, instead of the goodness on the desire. And this is aided by the fact that the desired thing will indeed have features that make it desired, that enable it to arouse a desire, or that make it such as to satisfy some desire that is already there. It is fairly easy to confuse the way in which a thing's desirability is indeed objective with its having in our sense objective value. The fact that the word 'good' serves as one of our main moral terms is a trace of this pattern of objectification.

Similarly related uses of words are covered by the distinction between hypothetical and categorical imperatives. The statement that someone 'ought to' or, more strongly, 'must' do such-and-such may be backed up explicitly or implicitly by reference to what he wants or to what his purposes and objects are. Again, there may be a reference to the purposes of someone else, perhaps the speaker: 'You must do this'—'Why?'—'Because I want such-and-such'. The moral categorical imperative which could be expressed in the same words can be seen as resulting from the suppression of the conditional clause in a hypothetical imperative without its being replaced by any such reference to the speaker's wants. The action in question is still required in something like the way in which it would be if it were appropriately related to a want, but it is no longer admitted that there is any contingent want upon which its being required depends. Again this move can be understood when we remember that at least our central and basic moral judgements represent social demands, where the source of the demand is indeterminate and diffuse. Whose demands or wants are in question, the agent's, or the speaker's, or those of an indefinite multitude of other people? All of these in a way, but there are advantages in not specifying them precisely. The speaker is expressing demands which he makes as a member of a community, which he has developed in and by participation in a joint way of life; also, what is required of this particular agent would be required of any other in a relevantly similar situation; but the agent too is expected to have internalized the relevant demands, to act as if the ends for which the action is required were his own. By suppressing any explicit reference to demands and making the imperatives categorical we facilitate conceptual moves from one such demand relation to another. The moral uses of such words as 'must' and 'ought' and 'should', all of which are used also to express hypothetical imperatives, are traces of this pattern of objectification.

It may be objected that this explanation links normative ethics too closely with descriptive morality, with the mores or socially enforced patterns of behaviour that anthropologists record. But it can hardly be denied that moral thinking starts from the enforcement of social codes. Of course it is not confined to that. But even when moral judgements are detached from the mores of any actual society they are liable to be framed with reference to an ideal community of moral agents, such as Kant's kingdom of ends, which but for the need to give God a special place in it would have been better called a commonwealth of ends.

Another way of explaining the objectification of moral values is to say that ethics is a system of law from which the legislator has been removed. This might have been derived either from the positive law of a state or from a supposed system of divine law. There can be no doubt that some features of modern European moral concepts are traceable to the theological ethics of Christianity. The stress on quasi-imperative notions, on what ought to be done or on what is wrong in a sense that is close to that of 'forbidden', are surely relics of divine commands. Admittedly, the central ethical concepts for Plato and Aristotle also are in a broad sense prescriptive or intrinsically action-guiding, but in concentrating rather on 'good' than on 'ought' they show that their moral thought is an objectification of the desired and the satisfying rather than of the commanded. Elizabeth Anscombe has argued that modern, non-Aristotelian, concepts of *moral* obligation, *moral* duty, of what is *morally* right and wrong, and of the *moral* sense of 'ought' are survivals outside the framework of thought that made them really intelligible, namely the belief in divine law. She infers that 'ought' has 'become a word of mere mesmeric force', with only a 'delusive appearance of content', and that we would do better to discard such terms and concepts altogether, and go back to Aristotelian ones.

There is much to be said for this view. But while we can explain some distinctive features of modern moral philosophy in this way, it would be a mistake to see the whole problem of the claim to objective prescriptivity as merely local and unnecessary, as a post-operative complication of a society from which a dominant system of theistic belief has recently been rather hastily excised. As Cudworth and Clarke and Price, for example, show, even those who still admit divine commands, or the positive law of God, may believe moral values to have an independent objective but still action-guiding authority. Responding to Plato's *Euthyphro* dilemma, they believe that God commands what he commands because it is in itself good or right, not that it is good or right merely because and in that he commands it. Otherwise God himself could not be called good. Price asks, 'What can be more preposterous, than to make the Deity nothing but will; and to exalt this on the ruins of all his attributes?' The apparent objectivity of moral value is a widespread phenomenon which has more than one source: the persistence of a belief in something like divine law when the belief in the divine legislator has faded out is only one factor among others. There are several different patterns of objectification, all of which have left characteristic traces in our actual moral concepts and moral language.

11. THE GENERAL GOAL OF HUMAN LIFE

The argument of the preceding sections is meant to apply quite generally to moral thought, but the terms in which it has been stated are largely those of the Kantian and post-Kantian tradition of English moral philosophy. To those who are more familiar with another tradition, which runs through Aristotle and Aquinas, it may seem wide of the mark. For them, the fundamental notion is that of the good for man, or the general end or goal of human life, or perhaps of a set of basic goods or primary human purposes. Moral reasoning consists partly in achieving a more adequate understanding of this basic goal (or set of goals), partly in working out the best way of pursuing and realizing it. But this approach is open to two radically different interpretations. According to one, to say that something is the good for man or the general goal of human life is just to say that this is what men in fact pursue or will find ultimately satisfying, or perhaps that it is something which, if postulated as an implicit goal, enables us to make sense of actual human strivings and to detect a coherent pattern in what would otherwise seem to be a chaotic jumble of conflicting purposes. According to the other interpretation, to say that something is the good for man or the general goal of human life is to say that this is man's proper end, that this is what he ought to be striving after, whether he in fact is or not. On the first interpretation we have a descriptive statement, on the second a normative or evaluative or prescriptive one. But this approach tends to combine the two interpretations, or to slide from one to the other, and to borrow support for what are in effect claims of the second sort from the plausibility of statements of the first sort.

I have no quarrel with this notion interpreted in the first way. I would only insert a warning that there may well be more diversity even of fundamental purposes, more variation in what different human beings will find ultimately satisfying, than the terminology of '*the* good for man' would suggest. Nor indeed, have I any quarrel with the second, prescriptive, interpretation, provided that it is recognized as subjectively prescriptive, that the speaker is here putting forward his own demands or proposals, or those of some movement that he represents, though no doubt linking these demands or proposals with what he takes to be already in the first, descriptive, sense fundamental human goals. In fact, I shall myself make use of the notion of the good for man, interpreted in both these ways, when I try in chapter 8 [of *Ethics: Inventing Right and Wrong*] to sketch a positive moral system. But if it is claimed that something is objectively the right or proper goal of human life, then this is tantamount to the assertion of something that is objectively categorically imperative, and comes fairly within the scope of our previous argument. Indeed, the running together of what I have here called the two interpretations is yet another pattern of objectification: a claim to objective prescriptivity is constructed by combining the normative element in the second interpretation with the objectivity allowed by the first, by the statement that such-and-such are fundamentally pursued or ultimately satisfying human goals. The argument from relativity still applies: the radical diversity of the goals that men actually pursue and find satisfying makes it implausible to construe such pursuits as resulting from an imperfect grasp of a unitary true good. So too does the argument from queerness; we can still ask what this objectively prescriptive rightness of the true goal can be, and how this is linked on the one hand with the descriptive features of this goal and on the other with the fact that it is *to some extent* an actual goal of human striving.

To meet these difficulties, the objectivist may have recourse to the purpose of God: the true purpose of human life is fixed by what God intended (or, intends) men to do and to be. Actual human strivings and satisfactions have some relation to this true end because God made men for this end and made them such as to pursue it—but only *some* relation, because of the inevitable imperfection of created beings.

I concede that if the requisite theological doctrine could be defended, a kind of objective ethical prescriptivity could be thus introduced. Since I think that theism cannot be defended, I do not regard this as any threat to my argument. But I shall take up the question of relations between morality and religion again in Chapter 10. Those who wish to keep theism as a live option can read the arguments of the interveing chapters hypothetically, as a discussion of what we can make of morality without recourse to God, and hence of what we can say about morality if, in the end, we dispense with religious belief.

12. CONCLUSION

I have maintained that there is a real issue about the status of values, including moral values. Moral scepticism, the denial of objective moral values, is not to be confused with any one of several first-order normative views, or with any linguistic or conceptual analysis. Indeed, ordinary moral judgements involve a claim to objectivity which both non-cognitive and naturalist analyses fail to capture. Moral scepticism must, therefore, take the form of an error theory, admitting that a belief in objective values is built into ordinary moral thought and language, but holding that this ingrained belief is false. As such, it needs arguments to support it against 'common sense'. But solid arguments can be found. The considerations that favour moral scepticism are: first, the relativity or variability of some important starting-points of moral thinking and their apparent dependence on actual ways of life; secondly, the metaphysical peculiarity of the supposed objective values, in that they would have to be intrinsically action-guiding and motivating; thirdly, the problem of how such values could be consequential or supervenient upon natural features; fourthly, the corresponding epistemological difficulty of accounting for our knowledge of value entities or features and of their links with the features on which they would be consequential; fifthly, the possibility of explaining, in terms of several different patterns of objectification, traces of which remain in moral language and moral concepts, how even if there were no such objective values people not only might have come to suppose that there are but also might persist firmly in that belief. These five points sum up the case for moral scepticism; but of almost equal importance are the preliminary removal of misunderstandings that often prevent this thesis from being considered fairly and explicitly, and the isolation of those items about which the moral sceptic is sceptical from many associated qualities and relations whose objective status is not in dispute.

VI

ETHICS AND OBSERVATION

GILBERT HARMAN

1. THE BASIC ISSUE

Can moral principles be tested and confirmed in the way scientific principles can? Consider the principle that, if you are given a choice between five people alive and one dead or five people dead and one alive, you should always choose to have five people alive and one dead rather than the other way round. We can easily imagine examples that appear to confirm this principle. Here is one:

> You are a doctor in a hospital's emergency room when six accident victims are brought in. All six are in danger of dying but one is much worse off than the others. You can just barely save that person if you devote all of your resources to him and let the others die. Alternatively, you can save the other five if you are willing to ignore the most seriously injured person.

It would seem that in this case you, the doctor, would be right to save the five and let the other person die. So this example, taken by itself, confirms the principle under consideration. Next, consider the following case.

> You have five patients in the hospital who are dying, each in need of a separate organ. One needs a kidney, another a lung, a third a heart, and so forth. You can save all five if you take a single healthy person and remove his heart, lungs, kidneys, and so forth, to distribute to these five patients. Just such a healthy person is in room 306. He is in the hospital for routine tests. Having seen his test results, you know that he is perfectly healthy and of the right tissue compatibility. If you do nothing, he will survive without incident; the other patients will die, however. The other five patients can be saved only if the person

in Room 306 is cut up and his organs distributed. In that case, there would be one dead but five saved.

The principle in question tells us that you should cut up the patient in Room 306. But in this case, surely you must not sacrifice this innocent bystander, even to save the five other patients. Here a moral principle has been tested and disconfirmed in what may seem to be a surprising way.

This, of course, was a 'thought experiment'. We did not really compare a hypothesis with the world. We compared an explicit principle with our feelings about certain imagined examples. In the same way, a physicist performs thought experiments in order to compare explicit hypotheses with his 'sense' of what should happen in certain situations, a 'sense' that he has acquired as a result of his long working familiarity with current theory. But scientific hypotheses can also be tested in real experiments, out in the world.

Can moral principles be tested in the same way, out in the world? You can observe someone do something, but can you ever perceive the rightness or wrongness of what he does? If you round a corner and see a group of young hoodlums pour gasoline on a cat and ignite it, you do not need to *conclude* that what they are doing is wrong; you do not need to figure anything out; you can *see* that it is wrong. But is your reaction due to the actual wrongness of what you see or is it simply a reflection of your moral 'sense', a 'sense' that you have acquired perhaps as a result of your moral upbringing?

2. OBSERVATION

The issue is complicated. There are no pure observations. Observations are always 'theory-laden'. What you perceive depends to some extent on the theory you hold, consciously or unconsciously. You see some children pour gasoline on a cat and ignite it. To really see that, you have to possess a great deal of knowledge, know about a considerable number of objects, know about people: that people pass through the life stages infant, baby, child, adolescent, adult. You must know what flesh and blood animals are, and in particular, cats. You must have some idea of life. You must know what gasoline is, what burning is, and much more. In one sense, what you 'see' is a pattern of light on your retina, a shifting array of splotches, although even that is theory, and you could never adequately describe what you see in that sense. In another sense, you see what you do because of the theories you hold. Change those theories and you would see something else, given the same pattern of light.

Similarly, if you hold a moral view, whether it is held consciously or unconsciously, you will be able to perceive rightness or wrongness, goodness or badness, justice or injustice. There is no difference in this respect between moral propositions and other theoretical propositions. If there is a difference, it must be found elsewhere.

Observation depends on theory because perception involves forming a belief as a fairly direct result of observing something; you can form a belief only if you understand the relevant concepts and a concept is what it is by virtue of its role in some theory or system of beliefs. To recognize a child as a child is to employ, consciously or unconsciously, a concept that is defined by its place in a framework of the stages of human life. Similarly, burning is an empty concept apart from its theoretical connections to the concepts of heat, destruction, smoke, and fire.

Moral concepts—Right and Wrong, Good and Bad, Justice and Injustice—also have a place in your theory or system of beliefs and are the concepts they are because of their context. If we say that observation has occurred whenever an opinion is a direct result of perception, we must allow that there is moral observation, because such an opinion can be a moral opinion as easily as any other sort. In this sense, observation may be used to confirm or disconfirm moral theories. The observational opinions that, in this sense, you find yourself with can be in either agreement or conflict with your consciously explicit moral principles. When they are in conflict, you must choose between your explicit theory and observation. In ethics, as in science, you sometimes opt for theory, and say that you made an error in observation or were biased or whatever, or you sometimes opt for observation, and modify your theory.

In other words, in both science and ethics, general principles are invoked to explain particular cases and, therefore, in both science and ethics, the general principles you accept can be tested by appealing to particular judgements that certain things are right or wrong, just or unjust, and so forth; and these judgements are analogous to direct perceptual judgements about facts.

3. OBSERVATIONAL EVIDENCE

Nevertheless, observation plays a role in science that it does not seem to play in ethics. The difference is that you need to make assumptions about certain physical facts to explain the occurrence of the observations that support a scientific theory, but you do not seem to need to make assumptions about any moral facts to explain the occurrence of the so-called moral observations I have been talking about. In the moral case, it would seem that you need only make assumptions about the psychology or moral sensibility of the person making the moral observation. In the scientific case, theory is tested against the world.

The point is subtle but important. Consider a physicist making an observation to test a scientific theory. Seeing a vapour trail in a cloud chamber, he thinks, 'There goes a proton'. Let us suppose that this is an observation in the relevant sense, namely, an immediate judgement made in response to the situation without any conscious reasoning having taken place. Let us also suppose that his observation confirms his theory, a theory that helps give meaning to the very term 'proton' as it occurs in his observational judgement. Such a confirmation rests on inferring an explanation. He can count his making the observation as confirming evidence for his theory only to the extent that it is reasonable to explain his making the observation by assuming that, not only is he in a certain psychological 'set', given the theory he accepts and his beliefs about the experimental apparatus, but furthermore, there really was a proton going through the cloud chamber, causing the vapour trail, which he saw as a proton. (This is evidence for the theory to the extent that the theory can explain the proton's being there better than competing theories can.) But, if his having made that observation could have been equally well explained by his psychological set alone, without the need for any assumption about a proton, then the observation would not have been evidence for the existence of that proton and therefore would not have been evidence for the theory. His making the observation supports the theory only because, in order to explain his making the observation, it is reasonable to assume something about the world over and above the assumptions made about the observer's psychology. In particular, it is reasonable to assume that there was a proton going through the cloud chamber, causing the vapour trail.

Compare this case with one in which you make a moral judgement immediately and without conscious reasoning, say, that the children are wrong to set the cat on fire or that the doctor would be wrong to cut up one healthy patient to save five dying patients. In order to explain your making the first of these judgements, it would be reasonable to assume, perhaps, that the children really are pouring gasoline on a cat and you are seeing them do it. But in neither case is there any obvious reason to assume anything about 'moral facts', such as that it really is wrong to set the cat on fire or to cut up the patient in Room 306. Indeed, an assumption about moral facts would seem to be totally irrelevant to the explanation of your making the judgement you make. It would seem that all we need assume is that you have certain more or less well-articulated moral principles that are reflected in the judgements you make, based on your moral sensibility. It seems to be completely irrelevant to our explanation whether your intuitive immediate judgement is true or false.

The observation of an event can provide observational evidence for or against a scientific theory in the sense that the truth of that observation can be relevant to a reasonable explanation of why that observation was made. A moral observation does not seem, in the same sense, to be observational evidence for or against any moral theory, since the truth or falsity of the moral observation seems to be completely irrelevant to any reasonable explanation of why that observation was made. The fact that an observation of an event was made at the time it was made is evidence not only about the observer but also about the physical facts. The fact that you made a particular moral observation when you did does not seem to be evidence about moral facts, only evidence about you and your moral sensibility. Facts about protons can affect what you observe, since a proton passing through the cloud chamber can cause a vapour trail that reflects light to your eye in a way that, given your scientific training and psychological set, leads you to judge that what you see is a proton. But there does not seem to be any way in which the actual rightness or wrongness of a given situation can have any effect on your perceptual apparatus. In this respect, ethics seems to differ from science.

In considering whether moral principles can help explain observations, it is therefore important to note an ambiguity in the word 'observation'. You see the children set the cat on fire and immediately think, 'That's wrong'. In one sense, your observation is that what the children are doing is wrong. In another sense, your observation is your thinking that thought. Moral principles might explain observations in the first sense but not in the second sense. Certain moral principles might help to explain why it was *wrong* of the children to set the cat on fire, but moral principles seem to be of no help in explaining *your thinking* that that is wrong. It the first sense of 'observation', moral principles can be tested by observation—'That this act is wrong is evidence that causing unnecessary suffering is wrong'. But in the second sense of 'observation', moral principles cannot clearly be tested by observation, since they do not appear to help explain observations in this second sense of 'observation'. Moral principles do not seem to help explain your observing what you observe.

Of course, if you are already given the moral principle that it is wrong to cause unnecessary suffering, you can take your seeing the children setting the cat on fire as observational evidence that they are doing something wrong. Similarly, you can suppose that your seeing the vapour trail is observational evidence that a proton is going through the cloud chamber, if you are given the relevant physical theory. But there is an important apparent difference between the two cases. In the scientific case, your making that observation is itself evidence for the physical theory because the physical theory explains the proton, which explains the trail, which explains your observation. In the moral case, your making your observation does not seem to be evidence for the relevant moral principle because that principle does not seem to help explain your observation. The explanatory chain from principle to observation seems to be broken in morality. The moral principle may 'explain' why it is wrong for the children to set the cat on fire. But the wrongness of that act does not appear to help explain the act, which you observe, itself. The explanatory chain appears to be broken in such a way that neither the moral principle nor the wrongness of the act can help explain why you observe what you observe.

A qualification may seem to be needed here. Perhaps the children perversely set the cat on fire simply 'because it is wrong'. Here it may seem at first that the actual wrongness of the act does help explain why they do it and therefore indirectly helps explain why you observe what you observe just as a physical theory, by explaining why the proton is producing a vapour trail, indirectly helps explain why the observer observes what he observes. But on reflection we must agree that this is probably an illusion. What explains the children's act is not clearly the actual wrongness of the act but, rather their belief that the act is wrong. The actual rightness or wrongness of their act seems to have nothing to do with why they do it.

Observational evidence plays a part in science it does not appear to play in ethics, because scientific principles can be justified ultimately by their role in explaining observations, in the second sense of observation—by their explanatory role. Apparently, moral principles cannot be justified in the same way. It appears to be true that there can be no explanatory chain between moral principles and particular observings in the way that there can be such a chain between scientific principles and particular observings. Conceived as an explanatory theory, morality, unlike science, seems to be cut off from observation.

Not that every legitimate scientific hypothesis is susceptible to direct observational testing. Certain hypothesis about 'black holes' in space cannot be directly tested, for example, because no signal is emitted from within a black hole. The connection with observation in such a case is indirect. And there are many similar examples. Nevertheless, seen in the large, there is the apparent difference between science and ethics we have noted. The scientific realm is accessible to observation in a way the moral realm is not.

4. ETHICS AND MATHEMATICS

Perhaps ethics is to be compared, not with physics, but with mathematics. Perhaps such a moral principle as 'You ought to keep your promises' is confirmed or disconfirmed in the way (whatever it is) in which such a mathematical principle as '5 + 7 = 12' is. Observation does not seem to play the role in mathematics it plays in physics. We do not and cannot perceive numbers, for example, since we cannot be in causal contact with them. We do not even understand what it would be like to be in causal contact with the number 12, say. Relations among numbers cannot have any more of an effect on our perceptual apparatus than moral facts can.

Observation, however, *is* relevant to mathematics. In explaining the observations that support a physical theory, scientists typically appeal to mathematical principles. On the other hand, one never seems to need to appeal in this way to moral principles. Since an observation is evidence for what best explains it, and since mathematics often figures in the explanations of scientific observations, there is indirect observational evidence for mathematics. There does not seem to be observational evidence, even indirectly, for basic moral principles. In explaining why certain observations have been made, we never seem to use purely moral assumptions. In this respect, then, ethics appears to differ not only from physics but also from mathematics.

In what follows, we will be considering a number of possible responses to the apparent fact that ethics is cut off from observational testing in a way that science is not. Some of these responses claim that there is a distinction of this sort between science and ethics and try to say what its implications are. Others deny that there is a distinction of this sort between science and ethics and argue that ethics is not really exempt from observational testing in the way it appears to be.

VII

WHY CONTRACTARIANISM?

DAVID GAUTHIER

I

> As the will to truth thus gains self-consciousness—there can be no
> doubt of that—morality will gradually *perish* now: this is the great
> spectacle in a hundred acts reserved for the next two centuries in
> Europe—the most terrible, most questionable, and perhaps also the
> most hopeful of all spectacles.
>
> (Nietzsche)

Morality faces a foundational crisis. Contractarianism offers the only
plausible resolution of this crisis. These two propositions state my theme.
What follows is elaboration.

Nietzsche may have been the first, but he has not been alone, in recognizing the crisis to which I refer. Consider these recent statements. 'The
hypothesis which I wish to advance is that in the actual world which we
inhabit the language of morality is in . . . [a] state of grave disorder . . . we
have—very largely, if not entirely—lost our comprehension, both theoretical and practical, of morality' (Alasdair MacIntyre).[1] 'The resources of
most modern moral philosophy are not well adjusted to the modern world'
(Bernard Williams).[2] 'There are no objective values. . . . [But] the main
tradition of European moral philosophy includes the contrary claim'

From Peter Vallentyne (ed.), *Contractarianism and Rational Choice* (Cambridge: Cambridge
University Press, 1991), 15–30. Reprinted by permission.

Two paragraphs of Section II and most of Section IV are taken from 'Morality, Rational
Choice, and Semantic Representation—A Reply to my Critics', in E. F. Paul, F. D. Miller, Jr.,
and J. Paul (eds.), *The New Social Contract: Essays on Gauthier* (Oxford: Basil Blackwell, 1988),
173–4, 179–180, 184–5, 188–9 (this volume appears also as *Social Philosophy and Policy* 5 (1988),
same pagination). I am grateful to Annette Baier, Paul Hurley, and Geoffrey Sayre-McCord
for comments on an earlier draft. I am also grateful to discussants at Western Washington
University, the University of Arkansas, the University of California at Santa Cruz, and the
University of East Anglia for comments on a related talk.

[1] *After Virtue* (Notre Dame, Ind.: University of Notre Dame Press, 1981), 2.
[2] *Ethics and the Limits of Philosophy* (Cambridge, Mass.: Harvard University Press, 1985),
197.

(J. L. Mackie).[3] 'Moral hypotheses do not help explain why people observe what they observe. So ethics is problematic and nihilism must be taken seriously. . . . An extreme version of nihilism holds that morality is simply an illusion. . . . In this version, we should abandon morality, just as an atheist abandons religion after he has decided that religious facts cannot help explain observations' (Gilbert Harman).[4]

I choose these statements to point to features of the crisis that morality faces. They suggest that moral language fits a world-view that we have abandoned—a view of the world as purposively ordered. Without this view, we no longer truly understand the moral claims we continue to make. They suggest that there is a lack of fit between what morality presupposes—objective values that help explain our behaviour, and the psychological states—desires and beliefs—that, given our present world-view, actually provide the best explanation. This lack of fit threatens to undermine the very idea of a morality as more than an anthropological curiosity. But how could this be? How could morality *perish*?

II

To proceed, I must offer a minimal characterization of the morality that faces a foundational crisis. And this is the morality of justified constraint. From the standpoint of the agent, moral considerations present themselves as constraining his choices and actions, in ways independent of his desires, aims, and interests. Later, I shall add to this characterization, but for the moment it will suffice. For it reveals clearly what is in question—the ground of constraint. This ground seems absent from our present world-view. And so we ask, what reason can a person have for recognizing and accepting a constraint that is independent of his desires and interests? He may agree that such a constraint would be *morally* justified; he would have a reason for accepting it *if* he had a reason for accepting morality. But what justifies paying attention to morality, rather than dismissing it as an appendage of outworn beliefs? We ask, and seem to find no answer. But before proceeding, we should consider three objections.

The first is to query the idea of constraint. Why should morality be seen as constraining our choices and actions? Why should we not rather say that the moral person chooses most freely, because she chooses in the light of a true conception of herself, rather than in the light of the false conceptions that so often predominate? Why should we not link morality with

---

[3] *Ethics: Inventing Right and Wrong* (Harmondsworth: Penguin, 1977), 15, 30.
[4] *The Nature of Morality* (New York: Oxford University Press, 1977), 11.

self-understanding? Plato and Hume might be enlisted to support this view, but Hume would be at best a partial ally, for his representation of 'virtue in all her genuine and most engaging charms, . . . talk[ing] not of useless austerities and rigours, suffering and self-denial', but rather making 'her votaries . . . during every instant of their existence, if possible, cheerful and happy', is rather overcast by his admission that 'in the case of justice . . . a man, taking things in a certain light, may often seem to be a loser by his integrity'.[5] Plato, to be sure, goes further, insisting that only the just man has a healthy soul, but heroic as Socrates' defence of justice may be, we are all too apt to judge that Glaucon and Adeimantus have been charmed rather than reasoned into agreement, and that the unjust man has not been shown necessarily to be the loser.[6] I do not, in any event, intend to pursue this direction of thought. Morality, as we, heirs to the Christian and Kantian traditions, conceive it, constrains the pursuits to which even our reflective desires would lead us. And this is not simply or entirely a constraint on self-interest; the affections that morality curbs include the social ones of favouritism and partiality, to say nothing of cruelty.

The second objection to the view that moral constraint is insufficiently grounded is to query the claim that it operates independently of, rather than through, our desires, interests, and affections. Morality, some may say, concerns the well-being of all persons, or perhaps of all sentient creatures.[7] And one may then argue, either with Hume, that morality arises in and from our sympathetic identification with our fellows, or that it lies directly in well-being, and that our affections tend to be disposed favourably towards it. But, of course, not all of our affections. And so our sympathetic feelings come into characteristic opposition to other feelings, in relation to which they function as a constraint.

This is a very crude characterization, but it will suffice for the present argument. This view grants that morality, as we understand it, is without purely *rational* foundations, but reminds us that we are not therefore unconcerned about the well-being of our fellows. Morality is founded on the widespread, sympathetic, other-directed concerns that most of us have, and these concerns do curb self-interest, and also the favouritism and partiality with which we often treat others. Nevertheless, if morality depends for its practical relevance and motivational efficacy entirely on our sympathetic feelings, it has no title to the prescriptive grip with which it has been invested in the Christian and Kantian views to which I have referred,

---

[5] David Hume, *An Enquiry Concerning the Principles of Morals* (1751), IX. ii.

[6] See Plato, *Republic*, esp. books 2 and 4.

[7] Some would extend morality to the non-sentient, but sympathetic as I am to the rights of trolley-cars and steam locomotives, I propose to leave this view quite out of consideration.

and which indeed Glaucon and Adeimantus demanded that Socrates defend to them in the case of justice. For to be reminded that some of the time we do care about our fellows and are willing to curb other desires in order to exhibit that care tells us nothing that can guide us in those cases in which, on the face of it, we do not care, or do not care enough—nothing that will defend the demands that morality makes on us in the hard cases. That not all situations in which concern for others combats self-concern are hard cases is true, but morality, as we ordinarily understand it, speaks to the hard cases, whereas its Humean or naturalistic replacement does not.

These remarks apply to the most sustained recent positive attempt to create a moral theory—that of John Rawls. For the attempt to describe our moral capacity, or more particularly, for Rawls, our sense of justice, in terms of principles, plausible in the light of our more general psychological theory, and coherent with 'our considered judgments in reflective equilibrium',[8] will not yield any answer to why, in those cases in which we have no, or insufficient, interest in being just, we should nevertheless follow the principles. John Harsanyi, whose moral theory is in some respects a utilitarian variant of Rawls's contractarian construction, recognizes this explicitly: 'All we can prove by rational arguments is that anybody who wants to serve our common human interests in a rational manner must obey these commands.'[9] But although morality may offer itself in the service of our common human interests, it does not offer itself only to those who want to serve them.

Morality is a constraint that, as Kant recognized, must not be supposed to depend solely on our feelings. And so we may not appeal to feelings to answer the question of its foundation. But the third objection is to dismiss this question directly, rejecting the very idea of a foundational crisis. Nothing justifies morality, for morality needs no justification. We find ourselves, in morality as elsewhere, *in mediis rebus*. We make, accept and reject, justify and criticize moral judgements. The concern of moral theory is to systematize that practice, and so to give us a deeper understanding of what moral justification is. But there are no extramoral foundations for moral justification, any more than there are extra-epistemic foundations for epistemic judgements. In morals as in science, foundationalism is a bankrupt project.

Fortunately, I do not have to defend *normative* foundationalism. One

---

[8] John Rawls, *A Theory of Justice* (Cambridge, Mass.: Harvard University Press, 1971), 51.

[9] John C. Harsanyi, 'Morality and the Theory of Rational Behaviour', in Amartya Sen and Bernard Williams (eds.), *Utilitarianism and Beyond* (Cambridge: Cambridge University Press, 1982), 62.

problem with accepting moral justification as part of our ongoing practice is that, as I have suggested, we no longer accept the world-view on which it depends. But perhaps a more immediately pressing problem is that we have, ready to hand, an alternative mode for justifying our choices and actions. In its more austere and, in my view, more defensible form, this is to show that choices and actions maximize the agent's expected utility, where utility is a measure of considered preference. In its less austere version, this is to show that choices and actions satisfy, not a subjectively defined requirement such as utility, but meet the agent's objective interests. Since I do not believe that we have objective interests, I shall ignore this latter. But it will not matter. For the idea is clear; we have a mode of justification that does not require the introduction of moral considerations.[10]

Let me call this alternative non-moral mode of justification, neutrally, deliberative justification. Now moral and deliberative justification are directed at the same objects—our choices and actions. What if they conflict? And what do we say to the person who offers a deliberative justification of his choices and actions and refuses to offer any other? We can say, of course, that his behaviour lacks *moral* justification, but this seems to lack any hold, unless he chooses to enter the moral framework. And such entry, he may insist, lacks any deliberative justification, at least for him.

If morality perishes, the justificatory enterprise, in relation to choice and action, does not perish with it. Rather, one mode of justification perishes, a mode that, it may seem, now hangs unsupported. But not only unsupported, for it is difficult to deny that deliberative justification is more clearly basic, that it cannot be avoided in so far as we are rational agents, so that if moral justification conflicts with it, morality seems not only unsupported but opposed by what is rationally more fundamental.

Deliberative justification relates to our deep sense of self. What distinguishes human beings from other animals, and provides the basis for rationality, is the capacity for semantic representation. You can, as your dog on the whole cannot, represent a state of affairs to yourself, and consider in particular whether or not it is the case, and whether or not you would want it to be the case. You can represent to yourself the contents of your beliefs, and your desires or preferences. But in representing them, you bring them into relation with one another. You represent to yourself that the Blue Jays will win the World Series, and that a National League

---

[10] To be sure, if we think of morality as expressed in certain of our affections and/or interests, it will incorporate moral considerations to the extent that they actually are present in our preferences. But this would be to embrace the naturalism that I have put to one side as inadequate.

team will win the World Series, and that the Blue Jays are not a National League team. And in recognizing a conflict among those beliefs, you find rationality thrust upon you. Note that the first two beliefs could be replaced by preferences, with the same effect.

Since in representing our preferences we become aware of conflict among them, the step from representation to choice becomes complicated. We must, somehow, bring our conflicting desires and preferences into some sort of coherence. And there is only one plausible candidate for a principle of coherence—a maximizing principle. We order our preferences, in relation to decision and action, so that we may choose in a way that maximizes our expectation of preference fulfilment. And in so doing, we show ourselves to be rational agents, engaged in deliberation and deliberative justification. There is simply nothing else for practical rationality to be.

The foundational crisis of morality thus cannot be avoided by pointing to the existence of a practice of justification within the moral framework, and denying that any extramoral foundation is relevant. For an extramoral mode of justification is already present, existing not side by side with moral justification, but in a manner tied to the way in which we unify our beliefs and preferences and so acquire our deep sense of self. We need not suppose that this deliberative justification is itself to be understood foundationally. All that we need suppose is that moral justification does not plausibly survive conflict with it.

III

In explaining why we may not dismiss the idea of a foundational crisis in morality as resulting from a misplaced appeal to a philosophically discredited or suspect idea of foundationalism, I have begun to expose the character and dimensions of the crisis. I have claimed that morality faces an alternative, conflicting, deeper mode of justification, related to our deep sense of self, that applies to the entire realm of choice and action, and that evaluates each *action* in terms of the reflectively held concerns of its *agent*. The relevance of the agent's concerns to practical justification does not seem to me in doubt. The relevance of anything else, except in so far as it bears on the agent's concerns, does seem to me very much in doubt. If the agent's reflectively endorsed concerns, his preferences, desires, and aims, are, with his considered beliefs, constitutive of his self-conception, then I can see no remotely plausible way of arguing from their relevance to that of anything else that is not similarly related to his sense of self. And, indeed, I can see no way of introducing anything as relevant to practical justification except through the agent's self-conception. My assertion of this practical individualism is not a conclusive argument, but the burden of proof is surely on those who would maintain a contrary position. Let them provide the arguments—if they can.

Deliberative justification does not refute morality. Indeed, it does not offer morality the courtesy of a refutation. It ignores morality, and seemingly replaces it. It pre-empts the arena of justification, apparently leaving morality no room to gain purchase. Let me offer a controversial comparison. Religion faces—indeed, has faced—a comparable foundational crisis. Religion demands the worship of a divine being who purposively orders the universe. But it has confronted an alternative mode of explanation. Although the emergence of a cosmological theory based on efficient, rather than teleological, causation provided warning of what was to come, the supplanting of teleology in biology by the success of evolutionary theory in providing a mode of explanation that accounted in efficient-causal terms for the *appearance* of a purposive order among living beings, may seem to toll the death-knell for religion as an intellectually respectable enterprise. But evolutionary biology and, more generally, modern science do not refute religion. Rather they ignore it, replacing its explanations by ontologically simpler ones. Religion, understood as affirming the justifiable worship of a divine being, may be unable to survive its foundational crisis. Can morality, understood as affirming justifiable constraints on choice independent of the agent's concerns, survive?

There would seem to be three ways for morality to escape religion's apparent fate. One would be to find, for moral facts or moral properties, an explanatory role that would entrench them prior to any consideration of justification.[11] One could then argue that any mode of justification that ignored moral considerations would be ontologically defective. I mention this possibility only to put it to one side. No doubt there are persons who accept moral constraints on their choices and actions, and it would not be possible to explain those choices and actions were we to ignore this. But our explanation of their behaviour need not commit us to their view. Here the comparison with religion should be straightforward and uncontroversial. We could not explain many of the practices of the religious without reference to their beliefs. But to characterize what a religious person is doing as, say, an act of worship, does not commit us to supposing that an object of worship actually exists, though it does commit us to supposing that she believes such an object to exist. Similarly, to characterize what a

---

[11] This would meet the challenge to morality found in my previous quotation from Gilbert Harman.

moral agent is doing as, say, fulfilling a duty does not commit us to supposing that there are any duties, though it does commit us to supposing that he believes that there are duties. The sceptic who accepts neither can treat the apparent role of morality in explanation as similar to that of religion. Of course, I do not consider that the parallel can be ultimately sustained, since I agree with the religious sceptic but not with the moral sceptic. But to establish an explanatory role for morality, one must first demonstrate its justificatory credentials. One may not assume that it has a prior explanatory role.

The second way would be to reinterpret the idea of justification, showing that, more fully understood, deliberative justification is incomplete, and must be supplemented in a way that makes room for morality. There is a long tradition in moral philosophy, deriving primarily from Kant, that is committed to this enterprise. This is not the occasion to embark on a critique of what, in the hope again of achieving a neutral characterization, I shall call universalistic justification. But critique may be out of place. The success of deliberative justification may suffice. For theoretical claims about its incompleteness seem to fail before the simple practical recognition that it works. Of course, on the face of it, deliberative justification does not work to provide a place for morality. But to suppose that it must, if it is to be fully adequate or complete as a mode of justification, would be to assume what is in question, whether moral justification is defensible.

If, independent of one's actual desires, and aims, there were objective values, and if, independent of one's actual purposes, one were part of an objectively purposive order, then we might have reason to insist on the inadequacy of the deliberative framework. An objectively purposive order would introduce considerations relevant to practical justification that did not depend on the agent's self-conception. But the supplanting of teleology in our physical and biological explanations closes this possibility, as it closes the possibility of religious explanation.

I turn then to the third way of resolving morality's foundational crisis. The first step is to embrace deliberative justification, and recognize that morality's place must be found within, and not outside, its framework. Now this will immediately raise two problems. First of all, it will seem that the attempt to establish any constraint on choice and action, within the framework of a deliberation that aims at the maximal fulfilment of the agent's considered preferences, must prove impossible. But even if this be doubted, it will seem that the attempt to establish a constraint *independent of the agent's preferences*, within such a framework, verges on lunacy. Nevertheless, this is precisely the task accepted by my third way. And, unlike its predecessors, I believe that it can be successful; indeed, I believe that my recent book, *Morals by Agreement*, shows how it can succeed.[12]

I shall not rehearse at length an argument that is now familiar to at least some readers, and, in any event, can be found in that book. But let me sketch briefly those features of deliberative rationality that enable it to constrain maximizing choice. The key idea is that in many situations, if each person chooses what, given the choices of the others, would maximize her expected utility, then the outcome will be mutually disadvantageous in comparison with some alternative—everyone could do better.[13] Equilibrium, which obtains when each person's action is a best response to the others' actions, is incompatible with (Pareto-)optimality, which obtains when no one could do better without someone else doing worse. Given the ubiquity of such situations, each person can see the benefit, to herself, of participating with her fellows in practices requiring each to refrain from the direct endeavour to maximize her own utility, when such mutual restraint is mutually advantageous. No one, of course, can have reason to accept any unilateral constraint on her maximizing behaviour; each benefits from, and only from, the constraint accepted by her fellows. But if one benefits more from a constraint on others than one loses by being constrained oneself, one may have reason to accept a practice requiring everyone, including oneself, to exhibit such a constraint. We may represent such a practice as capable of gaining unanimous agreement among rational persons who were choosing the terms on which they would interact with each other. And this agreement is the basis of morality.

Consider a simple example of a moral practice that would command rational agreement. Suppose each of us were to assist her fellows only when either she could expect to benefit herself from giving assistance, or she took a direct interest in their well-being. Then, in many situations, persons would not give assistance to others, even though the benefit to the recipient would greatly exceed the cost to the giver, because there would be no provision for the giver to share in the benefit. Everyone would then expect to do better were each to give assistance to her fellows, regardless of her own benefit or interest, whenever the cost of assisting was low and the benefit of receiving assistance considerable. Each would thereby accept a constraint on the direct pursuit of her own concerns, not unilaterally, but given a like acceptance by others. Reflection leads us to recognize

[12] See David Gauthier, *Morals by Agreement* (Oxford: Oxford University Press, 1986), esp. chs. v and vi.

[13] The now-classic example of this type of situation is the Prisoner's Dilemma; see *Morals by Agreement*, 79–80. More generally, such situations may be said, in economists' parlance, to exhibit market failure. See, for example, 'Market Contractarianism' in Jules Coleman, *Markets, Morals, and the Law* (Cambridge: Cambridge University Press, 1988), ch. 10.

that those who belong to groups whose members adhere to such a practice of mutual assistance enjoy benefits in interaction that are denied to others. We may then represent such a practice as rationally acceptable to everyone.

This rationale for agreed constraint makes no reference to the content of anyone's preferences. The argument depends simply on the *structure* of interaction, on the way in which each person's endeavour to fulfil her own preferences affects the fulfilment of everyone else. Thus, each person's reason to accept a mutually constraining practice is independent of her particular desires, aims, and interests, although not, of course, of the fact that she has such concerns. The idea of a purely rational agent, moved to act by reason alone, is not, I think, an intelligible one. Morality is not to be understood as a constraint arising from reason alone on the fulfilment of non-rational preferences. Rather, a rational agent is one who acts to achieve the maximal fulfilment of her preferences, and morality is a constraint on the manner in which she acts, arising from the effects of interaction with other agents.

Hobbes's Foole now makes his familiar entry onto the scene, to insist that however rational it may be for a person to agree with her fellows to practices that hold out the promise of mutual advantage, yet it is rational to follow such practices only when so doing directly conduces to her maximal preference fulfilment.[14] But then such practices impose no real constraint. The effect of agreeing to or accepting them can only be to change the expected pay-offs of her possible choices, making it rational for her to choose what in the absence of the practice would not be utility maximizing. The practices would offer only true prudence, not true morality.

The Foole is guilty of a twofold error. First, he fails to understand that real acceptance of such moral practices as assisting one's fellows, or keeping one's promises, or telling the truth is possible only among those who are disposed to comply with them. If my disposition to comply extends only so far as my interests or concerns at the time of performance, then you will be the real fool if you interact with me in ways that demand a more rigorous compliance. If, for example, it is rational to keep promises only when so doing is directly utility-maximizing, then among persons whose rationality is common knowledge, only promises that require such limited compliance will be made. And opportunities for mutual advantage will be thereby forgone.

Consider this example of the way in which promises facilitate mutual

---

[14] See Hobbes, *Leviathan* (London, 1651), I. xv.

benefit. Jones and Smith have adjacent farms. Although neighbours, and not hostile, they are also not friends, so that neither gets satisfaction from assisting the other. Nevertheless, they recognize that, if they harvest their crops together, each does better than if each harvests alone. Next week, Jones's crop will be ready for harvesting; a fortnight hence, Smith's crop will be ready. The harvest in, Jones is retiring, selling his farm, and moving to Florida, where he is unlikely to encounter Smith or other members of their community. Jones would like to promise Smith that, if Smith helps him harvest next week, he will help Smith harvest in a fortnight. But Jones and Smith both know that in a fortnight, helping Smith would be a pure cost to Jones. Even if Smith helps him, he has nothing to gain by returning the assistance, since neither care for Smith nor, in the circumstances, concern for his own reputation, moves him. Hence, if Jones and Smith know that Jones acts straightforwardly to maximize the fulfilment of his preferences, they know that he will not help Smith. Smith, therefore, will not help Jones even if Jones pretends to promise assistance in return. Nevertheless, Jones would do better could he make and keep such a promise—and so would Smith.

The Foole's second error, following on his first, should be clear; he fails to recognize that in plausible circumstances, persons who are genuinely disposed to a more rigorous compliance with moral practices than would follow from their interests at the time of performance can expect to do better than those who are not so disposed. For the former, constrained maximizers as I call them, will be welcome partners in mutually advantageous co-operation, in which each relies on the voluntary adherence of the others, from which the latter, straightforward maximizers, will be excluded. Constrained maximizers may thus expect more favourable opportunities than their fellows. Although in assisting their fellows, keeping their promises, and complying with other moral practices, they forgo preference fulfilment that they might obtain, yet they do better overall than those who always maximize expected utility, because of their superior opportunities.

In identifying morality with those constraints that would obtain agreement among rational persons who were choosing their terms of interaction, I am engaged in rational reconstruction. I do not suppose that we have actually agreed to existent moral practices and principles. Nor do I suppose that all existent moral practices would secure our agreement, were the question to be raised. Not all existent moral practices need be justifiable—need be ones with which we ought willingly to comply. Indeed, I do not even suppose that the practices with which we ought willingly to comply need be those that would secure our present agreement. I suppose that justifiable moral practices are those that would secure our agreement *ex ante*, in an appropriate pre-moral situation. They are those to which we should have agreed as constituting the terms of our future interaction, had we been, *per impossibile*, in a position to decide those terms. Hypothetical agreement thus provides a test of the justifiability of our existent moral practices.

IV

Many questions could be raised about this account, but here I want to consider only one. I have claimed that moral practices are rational, even though they constrain each person's attempt to maximize her own utility, in so far as they would be the objects of unanimous *ex ante* agreement. But to refute the Foole, I must defend not only the rationality of agreement, but also that of compliance, and the defence of compliance threatens to pre-empt the case for agreement, so that my title should be 'Why Constraint?' and not 'Why Contractarianism?'" It is rational to dispose oneself to accept certain constraints on direct maximization in choosing and acting, if and only if so disposing oneself maximizes one's expected utility. What then is the relevance of agreement, and especially of hypothetical agreement? Why should it be rational to dispose oneself to accept only those constraints that would be the object of mutual agreement in an appropriate pre-moral situation, rather than those constraints that are found in our existent moral practices? Surely it is acceptance of the latter that makes a person welcome in interaction with his fellows. For compliance with existing morality will be what they expect, and take into account in choosing partners with whom to co-operate.

I began with a challenge to morality—how can it be rational for us to accept its constraints? It may now seem that what I have shown is that it is indeed rational for us to accept constraints, but to accept them whether or not they might be plausibly considered moral. Morality, it may seem, has nothing to do with my argument; what I have shown is that it is rational to be disposed to comply with whatever constraints are generally accepted and expected, regardless of their nature. But this is not my view.

To show the relevance of agreement to the justification of constraints, let us assume an ongoing society in which individuals more or less acknowledge and comply with a given set of practices that constrain their choices in relation to what they would be did they take only their desires, aims, and interests directly into account. Suppose that a disposition to conform to these existing practices is prima facie advantageous, since persons who are not so disposed may expect to be excluded from desirable opportunities by their fellows. However, the practices themselves have, or at least need have, no basis in agreement. And they need satisfy no intuitive standard of fairness or impartiality, characteristics that we may suppose relevant to the identification of the practices with those of a genuine morality. Although we may speak of the practices as constituting the morality of the society in question, we need not consider them morally justified or acceptable. They are simply practices constraining individual behaviour in a way that each finds rational to accept.

Suppose now that our persons, as rational maximizers of individual utility, come to reflect on the practices constituting their morality. They will, of course, assess the practices in relation to their own utility, but with the awareness that their fellows will be doing the same. And one question that must arise is: Why these practices? For they will recognize that the set of actual moral practices is not the only possible set of constraining practices that would yield mutually advantageous, optimal outcomes. They will recognize the possibility of alternative moral orders. At this point it will not be enough to say that, as a matter of fact, each person can expect to benefit from a disposition to comply with existing practices. For persons will also ask themselves: Can I benefit more, not from simply abandoning any morality, and recognizing no constraint, but from a partial rejection of existing constraints in favour of an alternative set? Once this question is asked, the situation is transformed; the existing moral order must be assessed, not only against simple non-compliance, but also against what we may call alternative compliance.

To make this assessment, each will compare her prospects under the existing practices with those she would anticipate from a set that, in the existing circumstances, she would expect to result from bargaining with her fellows. If her prospects would be improved by such negotiation, then she will have a real, although not necessarily sufficient, incentive to demand a change in the established moral order. More generally, if there are persons whose prospects would be improved by renegotiation, then the existing order will be recognizably unstable. No doubt those whose prospects would be worsened by renegotiation will have a clear incentive to resist, to appeal to the status quo. But their appeal will be a weak one, especially among persons who are not taken in by spurious ideological considerations, but focus on individual utility maximization. Thus, although in the real world, we begin with an existing set of moral practices as constraints on our maximizing behaviour, yet we are led by reflection to the idea of an amended set that would obtain the agreement of everyone, and this amended set has, and will be recognized to have, a stability lacking in existing morality.

The reflective capacity of rational agents leads them from the given to the agreed, from existing practices and principles requiring constraint to those that would receive each person's assent. The same reflective capacity, I claim, leads from those practices that would be agreed to, in existing social circumstances, to those that would receive *ex ante* agreement, premoral and pre-social. As the status quo proves unstable when it comes into conflict with what would be agreed to, so what would be agreed to proves unstable when it comes into conflict with what would have been agreed to in an appropriate pre-social context. For as existing practices must seem arbitrary in so far as they do not correspond to what a rational person would agree to, so what such a person would agree to in existing circumstances must seem arbitrary in relation to what she would accept in a pre-social condition.

What a rational person would agree to in existing circumstances depends in large part on her negotiating position *vis-à-vis* her fellows. But her negotiating position is significantly affected by the existing social institutions, and so by the currently accepted moral practices embodied in those institutions. Thus, although agreement may well yield practices differing from those embodied in existing social institutions, yet it will be influenced by those practices, which are not themselves the product of rational agreement. And this must call the rationality of the agreed practices into question. The arbitrariness of existing practices must infect any agreement whose terms are significantly affected by them. Although rational agreement is in itself a source of stability, yet this stability is undermined by the arbitrariness of the circumstances in which it takes place. To escape this arbitrariness, rational persons will revert from actual to hypothetical agreement, considering what practices they would have agreed to from an initial position not structured by existing institutions and the practices they embody.

The content of a hypothetical agreement is determined by an appeal to the equal rationality of persons. Rational persons will voluntarily accept an agreement only in so far as they perceive it to be equally advantageous to each. To be sure, each would be happy to accept an agreement more advantageous to herself than to her fellows, but since no one will accept an agreement perceived to be less advantageous, agents whose rationality is a matter of common knowledge will recognize the futility of aiming at or holding out for more, and minimize their bargaining costs by co-ordinating at the point of equal advantage. Now the extent of advantage is determined in a twofold way. First, there is advantage internal to an agreement.

In this respect, the expectation of equal advantage is assured by procedural fairness. The step from existing moral practices to those resulting from actual agreement takes rational persons to a procedurally fair situation, in which each perceives the agreed practices to be ones that it is equally rational for all to accept, given the circumstances in which agreement is reached. But those circumstances themselves may be called into question in so far as they are perceived to be arbitrary—the result, in part, of compliance with constraining practices that do not themselves ensure the expectation of equal advantage, and so do not reflect the equal rationality of the complying parties. To neutralize this arbitrary element, moral practices to be fully acceptable must be conceived as constituting a possible outcome of a hypothetical agreement under circumstances that are unaffected by social institutions that themselves lack full acceptability. Equal rationality demands consideration of external circumstances as well as internal procedures.

But what is the practical import of this argument? It would be absurd to claim that mere acquaintance with it, or even acceptance of it, will lead to the replacement of existing moral practices by those that would secure presocial agreement. It would be irrational for anyone to give up the benefits of the existing moral order simply because he comes to realize that it affords him more than he could expect from pure rational agreement with his fellows. And it would be irrational for anyone to accept a long-term utility loss by refusing to comply with the existing moral order, simply because she comes to realize that such compliance affords her less than she could expect from pure rational agreement. Nevertheless, these realizations do transform, or perhaps bring to the surface, the character of the relationships between persons that are maintained by the existing constraints, so that some of these relationships come to be recognized as coercive. These realizations constitute the elimination of false consciousness, and they result from a process of rational reflection that brings persons into what, in my theory, is the parallel of Jürgen Habermas's ideal speech situation.[15] Without an argument to defend themselves in open dialogue with their fellows, those who are more than equally advantaged can hope to maintain their privileged position only if they can coerce their fellows into accepting it. And this, of course, may be possible. But coercion is not agreement, and it lacks any inherent stability.

Stability plays a key role in linking compliance to agreement. Aware of the benefits to be gained from constraining practices, rational persons will seek those that invite stable compliance. Now compliance is stable if it

---

[15] See Raymond Geuss, *The Idea of a Critical Theory: Habermas and the Frankfurt School* (Cambridge: Cambridge University Press, 1981), 65 ff.

arises from agreement among persons each of whom considers both that the terms of agreement are sufficiently favourable to herself that it is rational for her to accept them, and that they are not so favourable to others that it would be rational for them to accept terms less favourable to them and more favourable to herself. An agreement affording equally favourable terms to all thus invites, as no other can, stable compliance.

V

In defending the claim that moral practices, to obtain the stable voluntary compliance of rational individuals, must be the objects of an appropriate hypothetical agreement, I have added to the initial minimal characterization of morality. Not only does morality constrain our choices and actions, but it does so in an impartial way, reflecting the equal rationality of the persons subject to constraint. Although it is no part of my argument to show that the requirements of contractarian morality will satisfy the Rawlsian test of cohering with our considered judgements in reflective equilibrium, yet it would be misleading to treat rationally agreed constraints on direct utility maximization as constituting a morality at all, rather than as replacing morality, were there no fit between their content and our pre-theoretical moral views. The fit lies, I suggest, in the impartiality required for hypothetical agreement.

The foundational crisis of morality is thus resolved by exhibiting the rationality of our compliance with mutual, rationally agreed constraints on the pursuit of our desires, aims, and interests. Although bereft of a basis in objective values or an objectively purposive order, and confronted by a more fundamental mode of justification, morality survives by incorporating itself into that mode. Moral considerations have the same status, and the same role in explaining behaviour, as the other reasons acknowledged by a rational deliberator. We are left with a unified account of justification, in which an agent's choices and actions are evaluated in relation to his preferences—to the concerns that are constitutive of his sense of self. But since morality binds the agent independently of the particular content of his preferences, it has the prescriptive grip with which the Christian and Kantian views have invested it.

In incorporating morality into deliberative justification, we recognize a new dimension to the agent's self-conception. For morality requires that a person have the capacity to commit himself, to enter into agreement with his fellows secure in the awareness that he can and will carry out his part of the agreement without regard to many of those considerations that normally and justifiably would enter into his future deliberations. And this is more than the capacity to bring one's desires and interests together with one's beliefs into a single coherent whole. Although this latter unifying capacity must extend its attention to past and future, the unification it achieves may itself be restricted to that extended present within which a person judges and decides. But in committing oneself to future action in accordance with one's agreement, one must fix at least a subset of one's desires and beliefs to hold in that future. The self that agrees and the self that complies must be one. 'Man himself must first of all have become *calculable*, *regular*, *necessary*, even in his own image of himself, if he is to be able to stand security for *his own future*, which is what one who promises does!'[16]

In developing '*the right to make promises*,'[17] we human beings have found a contractarian bulwark against the perishing of morality.

---

[16] Nietzsche, *On the Genealogy of Morals*, tr. Walter Kaufmann and R. J. Hollingdale (New York: Random House, 1967), 2nd essay, sect. 1, p. 58.
[17] Ibid. 57.

VIII

VALUE

THOMAS NAGEL

1

Whether values can be objective depends on whether an interpretation of objectivity can be found that allows us to advance our knowledge of what to do, what to want, and what things provide reasons for and against action. Last week I argued that the physical conception of objectivity was not able to provide an understanding of the mind, but that another conception was available which allowed external understanding of at least some *aspects* of mental phenomena. A still different conception is required to make sense of the objectivity of values, for values are neither physical nor mental. And even if we find a conception, it must be applied with care. Not all values are likely to prove to be objective in any sense.

Let me say in advance that my discussion of values and reasons in this lecture and the next will be quite general. I shall be talking largely about what determines whether something has value, or whether someone has a reason to do or want something. I shall say nothing about how we pass from the identification of values and reasons to a conclusion as to what should be *done*. That is of course what makes reasons important; but I shall just assume that values do often provide the basis for such conclusions, without trying to describe even in outline how the full process of practical reasoning works. I am concerned here only with the general question, whether values have an objective foundation at all.

In general, as I said last time, objectivity is advanced when we step back, detach from our earlier point of view toward something, and arrive at a new view of the whole that is formed by including ourselves and our earlier viewpoint in what is to be understood.

From Thomas Nagel, 'The Limits of Objectivity', from Sterling McMurrin (ed.), *The Tanner Lectures on Human Values*, i (Salt Lake City and Cambridge: University of Utah Press and Cambridge University Press, 1980). Reprinted courtesy of the University of Utah Press and the Trustees of the Tanner Lectures on Human Values, and Cambridge University Press.

In theoretical reasoning this is done by forming a new conception of reality that includes ourselves as components. This involves an alteration, or at least an extension, of our beliefs. Whether the effort to detach will actually result in an increase of understanding depends on the creative capacity to form objective ideas which is called into action when we add ourselves to the world and start over.

In the sphere of values or practical reasoning, the problem is somewhat different. As in the theoretical case, in order to pursue objectivity we must take up a new, comprehensive viewpoint after stepping back and including our former perspective in what is to be understood. But in this case the new viewpoint will be *not* a new set of *beliefs*, but a new, or extended, set of *values*. If objectivity means anything here, it will mean that when we detach from our individual perspective and the values and reasons that seem acceptable from within it, we can sometimes arrive at a new conception which may endorse some of the original reasons but will reject some as subjective appearances and add others. This is what is usually meant by an objective, disinterested view of a practical question.

The basic step of placing ourselves and our attitudes within the world to be considered is familiar, but the form of the result—a new set of values, reasons, and motives—is different. In order to discover whether there are any objective values or reasons we must try to arrive at *normative* judgements, with *motivational content*, from an impersonal standpoint: a standpoint outside of our lives. We cannot use a *non-normative* criterion of objectivity: for *if* any values are objective, they are objective *values*, not objective anything else.

2

There are many opinions about whether what we have reason to do or want can be determined from a detached standpoint toward ourselves and the world. They range all the way from the view that objectivity has *no* place in this domain except what is inherited from the objectivity of those theoretical and factual elements that play a role in practical reasoning, to the view that objectivity applies here, but with a nihilistic result: i.e. that nothing is objectively right or wrong because objectively nothing matters. In between are many positive objectifying views which claim to get some definite results from a detached standpoint. Each of them is criticized by adherents of opposing views either for trying to force too much into a single objective framework or for according too much or too little respect to divergent subjective points of view.

Here as elsewhere there is a direct connection between the goal of objectivity and the belief in *realism*. The most basic idea of practical objectivity is arrived at by a practical analogue of the rejection of solipsism or idealism in the theoretical domain. Just as realism about the facts leads us to seek a detached point of view from which reality can be discerned and appearance corrected, so realism about values leads us to seek a detached point of view from which it will be possible to correct inclination and to discern what we really should do, or want. Practical objectivity means that practical reason can be understood and even engaged in by the objective self.

This assumption, though powerful, is not yet an ethical position. It merely marks the place which an ethical position will occupy if we can make any sense of the subject. It says that the world of reasons, including my reasons, does not exist only from my point of view. I am in a world whose properties are to a certain extent independent of what I think, and if I have reasons to act it is because the person who I am has those reasons, in virtue of his condition and circumstances. One would expect those reasons to be understandable from outside. Here as elsewhere objectivity is a form of understanding not necessarily available for all of reality. But it is reasonable at least to look for such understanding over as wide an area as possible.

3

It is important not to lose sight of the dangers of *false* objectification, which too easily elevate personal tastes and prejudices into cosmic values. But initially, at least, it is natural to look for some objective account of those reasons that appear from one's own point of view.

In fact those reasons usually present themselves with some pretensions of objectivity to begin with, just as perceptual appearances do. When two things look the same size to me, they look at least initially as if they *are* the same size. And when I want to take aspirin because it will cure my headache, I believe at least initially that this *is* a reason for me to take aspirin, that it can be recognized as a reason from outside, and that if I failed to take it into account, that would be a mistake, and others could recognize this.

The ordinary process of deliberation, aimed at finding out what I have reason to do, assumes that the question has an answer. And in difficult cases especially, deliberation is often accompanied by the belief that I may not *arrive* at that answer. I do not assume that the correct answer is just whatever will result or has resulted from consistent application of deliberative methods—even assuming perfect information about the facts. In deliberation we are trying to arrive at conclusions that are correct in virtue of something *independent* of our arriving at them. If we arrive at a conclusion, we believe that it would have been correct even if we *hadn't* arrived at it. And we can also acknowledge that we might be *wrong*, since the process of reasoning doesn't guarantee the correctness of the result. So the pursuit of an objective account of practical reasons has its basis in the realist claims of ordinary practical reasoning. In accordance with pre-theoretical judgement we adopt the working hypothesis that there are reasons which may diverge from actual motivation even under conditions of perfect information—as reality can diverge from appearance—and then consider what form these reasons take. I shall say more about the general issue of realism later on. But first I want to concentrate on the process of thought by which, against a realist background, one might try to arrive at objective conclusions about reasons for action. In other words, if there really are values, how is objective knowledge of them possible?

In this inquiry no particular hypothesis occupies a privileged position, and it is certain that some of our starting-points will be abandoned as we proceed. However, one condition on reasons obviously presents itself for consideration: a condition of generality. This is the condition that if something provides a reason for a particular individual to do something, then there is a general form of that reason which applies to anyone else in comparable circumstances. What count as comparable circumstances depends on the general form of the reason. This condition is not tautological. It is a rather strong condition which may be false, or true only for some kinds of reasons. But the search for generality is a natural beginning.

4

There is more than one type of generality, and no reason to assume that a single form will apply to every kind of reason or value. In fact I think that the choice among types of generality defines some of the central issues of contemporary moral theory.

One respect in which reasons may vary is in their *breadth*. A general principle may apply to everyone but be quite specific in content, and it is an open question to what extent narrower principles of practical reasons (don't lie; develop your talents) can be subsumed under broader ones (don't hurt others; consider your long-term interests), or even at the limit under a single widest principle from which all the rest derive. Reasons may be general, in other words, without forming a unified system that always provides a method for arriving at determinate conclusions about what one should do.

A second respect in which reasons vary is in their *relativity to the agent*, the person for whom they are reasons. The distinction between reasons that are relative to the agent and reasons that are not is an extremely important one. I shall follow Derek Parfit in using the terms 'agent-relative' and 'agent-neutral' to mark this distinction. (Formerly I used the terms 'subjective' and 'objective', but those terms are here reserved for other purposes.)

If a reason can be given a general form which does *not* include an essential reference to the person to whom it applies, it is an *agent-neutral* reason. For example, if it is a reason for *anyone* to do or want something that it would reduce the amount of wretchedness in the world, then that is an agent-neutral reason.

If on the other hand the general form of a reason *does* include an essential reference to the person to whom it applies, it is an *agent-relative* reason. For example, if it is a reason for anyone to do or want something that it would be in *his* interest, then that is an agent-relative reason. In such a case, if something were in Jones's interest but contrary to Smith's, Jones would have reason to want it to happen and Smith would have the *same* reason to want it *not* to happen. (Both agent-relative and agent-neutral reasons are objective, since both can be understood from outside the viewpoint of the individual who has them.)

A third way in which reasons may vary is in their degree of externality, or independence of the interests of sentient beings. Most of the apparent reasons that initially present themselves to us are intimately connected with interests and desires, our own or those of others, and often with experiential satisfaction. But it is conceivable that some of these interests give evidence that their objects have intrinsic value independent of the satisfaction that anyone may derive from them or of the fact that anyone wants them—independent even of the existence of beings who can take an interest in them. I shall call a reason *internal* if it depends on the existence of an interest or desire in someone, and *external* if it does not. External reasons were believed to exist by Plato, and more recently by G. E. Moore, who believed that aesthetic value provided candidates for this kind of externality.

These three types of variation cut across one another. Formally, a reason may be narrow, external, and agent-relative (don't eat pork, keep your promises), or broad, internal, and agent-neutral (promote happiness), or internal and agent-relative (promote your own happiness). There may be other significant dimensions of variation. I want to concentrate on these because they locate the main controversies about what ethics is. Reasons and values that can be described in these terms provide the material for objective judgements. If one looks at human action and its conditions from outside and considers whether some normative principles are plausible, these are the forms they will take.

The actual *acceptance* of a general normative judgement will have motivational implications, for it will commit you under some circumstances to the acceptance of reasons to want and do things *yourself*.

This is most clear when the objective judgement is that something has *agent-neutral* value. That means *anyone* has reason to want it to happen— *and that includes someone considering the world in detachment from the perspective of any particular person within it*. Such a judgement has motivational content even before it is brought back down to the particular perspective of the individual who has accepted it objectively.

Agent-relative reasons are different. An objective judgement that some kind of thing has *agent-relative* value commits us only to believing that someone has reason to want and pursue it if it is related to him in the right way (being in *his* interest, for example). Someone who accepts this judgement is not committed to wanting it to *be the case* that people in general are influenced by such reasons. The judgement commits him to wanting something only when its implications are drawn *for the individual person he happens to be*. With regard to others, the content of the objective judgement concerns only what *they* should do or want.

I believe that judgements of both these kinds, as well as others, are evoked from us when we take up an objective standpoint. And I believe such judgements can be just as true and compelling as objective factual judgements about the real world that contains us.

5

When we take the step to objectivity in practical reasoning by detaching from our own point of view, the question we must ask ourselves is this: What reasons for action can be said to apply to people when we regard them from a standpoint detached from the values of any particular person?

The simplest answer, and one that some people would give, is 'None'. But that is not the only option. The suggested classification of types of generality provides a range of alternative hypotheses. It also provides some flexibility of response, for with regard to any reason that may appear to a particular individual to exist subjectively, the corresponding objective judgement may be that it does not exist at all, or that it corresponds to an agent-neutral, external value, or anything in between.

The choice among these hypotheses, plus others not yet imagined, is difficult, and there is no general method of making it any more than there is a general method of selecting the most plausible objective account of the facts on the basis of the appearances. The only 'method', here or elsewhere, is to try to generate hypotheses and then to consider which of them seems most reasonable, in light of everything else one is fairly confident of.

This is not quite empty, for it means at least that logic alone can settle nothing. We do *not* have to be shown that the denial of some kind of objective values is *self-contradictory* in order to be reasonably led to accept their existence. There is no constraint to pick the weakest or narrowest or most economical principle consistent with the initial data that arise from individual perspectives. Our admission of reasons beyond these is determined *not* by logical entailment, but by what we cannot help believing, or at least finding most plausible among the alternatives.

In this respect it is no different from anything else: theoretical knowledge does not arise by deductive inference from the appearances either. The main difference is that our objective thinking about practical reasons is very primitive, and has difficulty taking even the first step. Philosophical scepticism and idealism about values are much more popular than their metaphysical counterparts. Nevertheless I believe they are no more correct. I shall argue that although no *single* objective principle of practical reason like egoism or utilitarianism covers everything, the acceptance of some objective values is unavoidable—not because the alternative is inconsistent but because it is not *credible*. Someone who, as in Hume's example, prefers the destruction of the whole world to the scratching of his finger, may not be involved in a *contradiction* or in any false *expectations*, but he is unreasonable none the less (to put it mildly), and anyone else not in the grip of an overly narrow conception of what reasoning is would regard his preference as objectively wrong.

6

But even if it is unreasonable to deny that anyone ever objectively has a reason to do anything, it is not easy to find positive objective principles that *are* reasonable. I am going to attempt to defend a few in the rest of this lecture and the next. But I want to acknowledge in advance that it is not easy to follow the objectifying impulse without distoring individual life and personal relations. We want to be able to understand and accept the way we live from outside, but it may not always follow that we should control. our lives from inside by the terms of that external understanding. Often the objective viewpoint will not be suitable as a replacement for the subjective, but will coexist with it, setting a standard with which the subjective is constrained not to clash. In deciding what to do, for example, we should not reach a result different from what we could decide objectively that that *person* should do—but we need not arrive at the result in the same way from the two standpoints.

Sometimes, also, the objective standpoint will allow us to judge how people should *be* or should *live*, without permitting us to translate this into a judgement about what they have *reasons* to do. For in some respects it is better to live and act not for reasons, but because we cannot help it. This is especially true of close personal relations. Here the objective standpoint cannot be brought into the perspective of *action* without destroying precisely what it affirms the value of. Nevertheless the possibility of this objective affirmation is important. We should be *able* to view our lives from outside without extreme dissociation or distaste, and the extent to which we should live without *considering* the objective point of view or even any reasons *at all* is itself *determined* largely from that point of view.

It is also possible that some idiosyncratic individual grounds of action, or the values of strange communities, will prove objectively inaccessible. To take an example in our midst: I don't think that people who want to be able to run twenty-six miles without stopping are irrational, but their reasons can be understood only from the perspective of a value system that is completely alien to me, and will I hope remain so. A correct objective view will have to allow for such pockets of unassimilable subjectivity, which need not clash with objective principles but won't be affirmed by them either. Many aspects of personal taste will come in this category, if, as I think, they cannot all be brought under a general hedonistic principle.

But the most difficult and interesting problems of accommodation appear where objectivity *can* be employed as a standard, but we have to decide *how*. Some of the problems are these: To what extent should an objective view admit *external* values? To what extent should it admit *internal* but *agent-neutral* values? To what extent should the reasons to respect the interests of *others* take an *agent-relative* form? To what extent is it legitimate for each person to give priority to his own interests? These are all questions about the proper form of generality for different kinds of practical reasoning, and the proper relation between objective principles and the deliberations of individual agents. I shall return to some of them later, but there is a great deal that I shall not get to.

I shall not, for example, discuss the question of external values, i.e. values which may be *revealed* to us by the attractiveness of certain things, but whose existence is independent of the existence of any interests or desires. I am not sure whether there are any such values, though the objectifying tendency produces a strong impulse to believe that there are, especially in aesthetics where the object of interest is external and the interest seems perpetually capable of criticism in light of further attention to the object.

What I shall discuss is the proper form of *internal* values or reasons—those which depend on interests or desires. They can be objectified in more than one way, and I believe different forms of objectification are appropriate for different cases.

7

I plan to take up some of these complications in the next lecture. Let me begin, however, with a case for which I think the solution is simple: that of pleasure and pain. I am not an ethical hedonist, but I think pleasure and pain are very important, and they have a kind of neutrality that makes them fit easily into ethical thinking—unlike preferences or desires, for example, which I shall discuss later on.

I mean the kinds of pleasure and pain that do not depend on activities or desires which *themselves* raise questions of justification and value. Many pleasures and pains are just sensory experiences in relation to which we are fairly passive, but toward which we feel involuntary desire or aversion. Almost everyone takes the avoidance of his own pain and the promotion of his own pleasure as subjective reasons for action in a fairly simple way; they are not backed up by any further reasons. On the other hand if someone pursues pain or avoids pleasure, these idiosyncrasies usually *are* backed up by further reasons, like guilt or sexual masochism. The question is, what sort of general value, if any, ought to be assigned to pleasure and pain when we consider these facts from an objective standpoint?

It seems to me that the least plausible hypothesis is the zero position, that pleasure and pain have no value of any kind that can be objectively recognized. That would mean that looking at it from outside, you couldn't even say that someone had a reason not to put his hand on a hot stove. Try looking at it from the outside and see whether you can manage to withhold that judgement.

But I want to leave this position aside, because what really interests me is the choice between two other hypotheses, both of which admit that people have reason to avoid their own pain and pursue their own pleasure. They are the fairly obvious general hypotheses formed by assigning (*a*) agent-relative or (*b*) agent-neutral value to those experiences. If the avoidance of pain has only agent-relative value, then people have reason to avoid their own pain, but not to avoid the pain of others (unless other kinds of reasons come into play). If the avoidance of pain has agent-neutral value as well, then *anyone* has a reason to want *any* pain to stop, whether or not it is his. From an objective standpoint, which of these hypotheses is more plausible? Is the value of sensory pleasure and pain agent-relative or agent-neutral?

I believe it is agent-neutral, at least in part. That is, I believe pleasure is a good thing and pain is a bad thing, and that the most reasonable objective principle which admits that each of us has reason to pursue his own pleasure and avoid his own pain will acknowledge that these are not the only reasons present. This is a normative claim. Unreasonable, as I have said, does not mean inconsistent.

In arguing for this claim, I am somewhat handicapped by the fact that I find it self-evident. It is therefore difficult for me to find something still more certain with which to back it up. But I shall try to say what is wrong with rejecting it, and with the reasons that may lie behind its rejection. What would it be to really *accept* the alternative hypothesis that pleasure and pain are not impersonally good or bad? If I accept this hypothesis, assuming at the same time that each person has reason to seek pleasure and avoid pain for *himself*, then when I regard the matter objectively the result is very peculiar. I will have to believe that I have a reason to take aspirin for a headache, but that there *is no reason* for me to *have* an aspirin. And I will have to believe the same about anyone else. From an objective standpoint I must judge that everyone has reason to pursue a type of result that is *impersonally valueless*, that has value only to *him*.

This needs to be explained. If agent-neutral reasons are not ruled out of consideration from the start (and one would need reasons for that), why do we not have evidence of them here? The avoidance of pain is not an individual project, expressing the agent's personal values. The desire to make pain stop is simply *evoked* in the person who feels it. He may decide for various reasons not to stop it, but in the first instance he doesn't have to *decide* to want it to stop: he just does. He wants it to go away because it's *bad*: it is not *made* bad by his deciding that he wants it to go away. And I believe that when we think about it objectively, concentrating on what pain is *like*, and ask ourselves whether it is (*a*) not bad at all, (*b*) bad only for its possessor, or (*c*) bad *period*, the third answer is the one that needs to be argued *against*, not the one that needs to be argued *for*. The philosophical problem here is to get rid of the obstacles to the admission of the obvious. But first they have to be identified.

Consider how *strange* is the question posed by someone who wants a justification for altruism about such a basic matter as this. Suppose he and some other people have been admitted to a hospital with severe burns after being rescued from a fire. 'I understand, how *my* pain provides *me* with a reason to take an analgesic,' he says, 'and I understand how my groaning neighbour's pain gives *him* a reason to take an analgesic; but how does *his* pain give *me* any reason to want him to be given an analgesic? How can *his* pain give *me* or anyone else looking at it from outside a reason?'

This question is *crazy*. As an expression of puzzlement, it has that characteristic philosophical craziness which indicates that something very fundamental has gone wrong. This shows up in the fact that the *answer* to the question is *obvious*, so obvious that to ask the question is obviously a philosophical act. The answer is that pain is *awful*. The pain of the man groaning in the next bed is just as awful as yours. That's your reason to want him to have an analgesic.

Yet to many philosophers, when they think about the matter theoretically, this answer seems not to be available. The pain of the person in the next bed is thought to need major external help before it can provide me with a reason for wanting or doing anything: otherwise it can't get its hooks into me. Since most of these people are perfectly aware of the force such considerations actually have for them, justifications of some kind are usually found. But they take the form of working *outward* from the desires and interests of the individual for whom reasons are being sought. The burden of proof is thought always to be on the claim that he has reason to care about anything that is not *already* an object of his interest.

These justifications are unnecessary. They plainly falsify the real nature of the case. My reason for wanting my neighbour's pain to cease is just that it's awful, and I know it.

8

What is responsible for this demand for justification with its special flavour of philosophical madness? I believe it is something rather deep, which doesn't surface in the ordinary course of life: an inappropriate sense of the burden of proof. Basically, we are being asked for a demonstration of the *possibility* of real impersonal values, on the assumption that they are *not* possible unless such a general proof can be given.

But I think this is wrong. We can already *conceive* of such a possibility, and once we take the step of thinking about what reality, if any, there is in the domain of practical reason, it becomes a possibility we are bound to consider, that we cannot help considering. If there really are *reasons*, not just motivational pushes and pulls, and if agent-neutral reasons are among the kinds we can conceive of, then it becomes an obvious possibility that physical pain is simply bad: that even from an impersonal standpoint there is reason to want it to stop. When we view the matter objectively, this is one of the general positions that naturally suggests itself.

And once this is seen as a *possibility*, if becomes difficult *not* to accept it. It becomes a hypothesis that has to be *dislodged* by anyone who wishes to claim, for example, that all reasons are agent-relative. The question is, what are the alternatives, once we take up the objective standpoint? We must think *something*. If there is room in the realistic conception of reasons for agent-neutral values, then it is unnatural *not* to ascribe agent-neutral badness to burn pains. That is the natural conclusion from the fact that anyone who has a burn pain and is therefore closest to it wants acutely to be rid of it, and requires no indoctrination or training to want this. This evidence does not *entail* that burn pains are impersonally bad. It is logically conceivable that there is nothing bad about them at all, or that they provide only agent-relative reasons to their possessors to want them to go away. But to take such hypotheses seriously we would need justifications of a kind that seem totally unavailable in this case.

What could possibly show us that acute physical pain, which everyone finds horrible, is in reality not impersonally bad at all, so that except from the point of view of the sufferer it doesn't in itself matter? Only a very remarkable and far-fetched picture of the value of a cosmic order beyond our immediate grasp, in which pain played an essential part which made it good or at least neutral—or else a demonstration that there can *be* no agent-neutral values. But I take it that neither of these is available: the first because the Problem of Evil has not been solved, the second because the absence of a logical demonstration that there *are* agent-neutral values is not a demonstration that there are *not* agent-neutral values.

My position is this. No demonstration is necessary in order to allow us to *consider* the possibility of agent-neutral reasons: the possibility simply *occurs* to us once we take up an objective stance. And there is no mystery about how an individual could have a reason to want something independently of its relation to his particular interests or point of view, because beings like ourselves are not *limited* to the particular point of view that goes with their personal position inside the world. They are also, as I have put it earlier, *objective selves*: they cannot *help* forming an objective conception of the world with themselves in it; they cannot help trying to arrive at judgements of *value* from that standpoint; they cannot help asking whether, from that standpoint, in abstraction from who in the world they are, they have any reason to want anything to be the case or not—any reason to want anything to happen or not.

Agent-neutral reasons do not have to find a miraculous source in our personal lives, because we are not *merely* personal beings: we are also importantly and essentially viewers of the world *from nowhere within it*— and in this capacity we remain open to judgements of value, both general and particular. The possibility of agent-neutral values is evident as soon as we begin to think from this standpoint about the reality of any reasons whatever. If we acknowledge the possibility of realism, then we cannot rule out agent-neutral values in advance.

Realism is therefore the fundamental issue. If there really are values and reasons, then it should be possible to expand our understanding of them by objective investigation, and there is no reason to rule out the natural and compelling objective judgement that pain is impersonally bad and pleasure impersonally good. So let me turn now to the abstract issue of realism about values.

9

Like the presumption that things exist in an external world, the presumption that there are real values and reasons can be defeated in individual cases, if a purely subjective account of the appearances is more plausible. And like the presumption of an external world, its complete falsity is not self-contradictory. The reality of values, agent-neutral or otherwise, is not *entailed* by the totality of appearances any more than the reality of a physical universe is. But if either of them is recognized as a possibility, then its reality in detail can be confirmed by appearances, at least to the extent of being rendered more plausible than the alternatives. So a lot depends on whether the possibility of realism is admitted in the first place.

It is very difficult to argue for such a possibility. Sometimes there will be arguments against it, which one can try to refute. Berkeley's argument against the conceivability of a world independent of experience is an example. But what is the result when such an argument is refuted? Is the possibility in a stronger position? I believe so: in general, there is no way to prove the possibility of realism; one can only refute impossibility arguments, and the more often one does this the more confidence one may have in the realist alternative. So to consider the merits of an admission of realism about value, we have to consider the reasons against it. I shall discuss three. They have been picked for their apparent capacity to convince people.

The first argument depends on the question-begging assumption that if values are real, they must be real objects of some other kind. John Mackie, for example, in his recent book *Ethics*, denies the objectivity of values by saying that they are not part of the fabric of the world, and that if they were, they would have to be 'entities or qualities or relations of a very strange sort, utterly different from anything else in the universe'.[1] Apparently he has a very definite picture of what the universe is like, and assumes that realism about value would require crowding it with extra entities, qualities, or relations—things like Platonic Forms or Moore's non-natural qualities. But this assumption is not correct. The impersonal badness of pain is not some mysterious further property that all pains have, but just the fact that there is reason for anyone capable of viewing the world objectively to want it to *stop*, whether it is his or someone else's. The view that values are real is not the view that they are real occult entities or properties, but that they are real *values*: that our claims about value and about what people have reason to do may be *true* or *false* independently of our beliefs and inclinations. No *other* kinds of truths are involved. Indeed, no other kinds of truths *could* imply the reality of values.[2]

The second argument I want to consider is not, like the first, based on a misinterpretation of moral objectivity. Instead, it tries to represent the unreality of values as an objective *discovery*. The argument is that if claims of value have to be objectively correct or incorrect, and if they are not reducible to any *other* kind of objective claim, then we can just *see* that all positive value claims must be false. Nothing has any objective value, because objectively nothing matters at all. If we push the claims of objective detachment to their logical conclusion, and survey the world from a standpoint completely detached from all interests, we discover that there is

---

[1] J. L. Mackie, *Ethics: Inventing Right and Wrong* (Harmondsworth: Penguin, 1977), 38 (ch. V, p. 76 in this volume).

[2] In discussion, Mackie claimed that I had misrepresented him, and that his disbelief in the reality of values and reasons does not depend on the assumption that to be real they must be strange *entities* or *properties*. As he says in his book, it applies directly to reasons themselves. For whatever they are they are not needed to explain anything that happens, and there is consequently no reason to believe in their existence. But I would reply that this raises the same issue. It begs the question to assume that *explanatory* necessity is the test of reality in this area. The claim that certain reasons exist is a normative claim, not a claim about the best explanation of anything. To assume that only what has to be included in the best explanatory picture of the world is real, is to assume that there are no irreducibly normative truths.

There is much more to be said on both sides of this issue, and I hope I have not misrepresented Mackie in this short footnote.

nothing—no values left of any kind: things can be said to matter at all only to individuals within the world. The result is objective nihilism.

I don't deny that the objective standpoint tempts one in this direction. But I believe this can seem like the required conclusion only if one makes the mistake of assuming that objective judgements of value must emerge from the detached standpoint *alone*. It is true that with nothing to go on but a conception of the world from nowhere, one would have no way of telling whether anything had value. But an objective view has more to go on, for its data include the appearance of value to individuals with particular perspectives, including oneself. In this respect practical reason is no different from anything else. Starting from a pure idea of a possible reality and a very impure set of appearances, we try to fill in the idea of reality so as to make some partial sense of the appearances, using objectivity as a method. To find out what the world is like from outside we have to approach it from within: it is no wonder that the same is true for ethics. And indeed, when we take up the objective standpoint, the problem is not that values seem to disappear but that there seem to be too many of them, coming from every life and drowning out those that arise from our own. It is just as easy to form desires from an objective standpoint as it is to form beliefs. Probably easier. Like beliefs, these desires and evaluations must be criticized and justified partly in *terms* of the appearances. But they are not just further appearances, any more than the beliefs about the world which arise from an impersonal standpoint are just further appearances.

The third type of argument against the objective reality of values is an empirical argument. It is also perhaps the most common. It is intended not to rule out the possibility of real values from the start, but rather to demonstrate that even if their *possibility* is admitted, we have no reason to believe that there are any. The claim is that if we consider the wide cultural variation in normative beliefs, the importance of social pressure and other psychological influences to their formation, and the difficulty of settling moral disagreements, it becomes highly implausible that they are anything but pure appearances.

Anyone offering this argument must admit that not every psychological factor in the explanation of an appearance shows that the appearance corresponds to nothing real. Visual capacities and elaborate training play a part in explaining the physicist's perception of a cloud-chamber track, or a student's coming to believe a proposition of geometry, but the path of the particle and the truth of the proposition also play an essential part in these explanations. So far as I know, no one has produced a general account of the kinds of psychological explanation that discredit an appearance. But some sceptics about ethics feel that because of the way we acquire moral beliefs and other impressions of value, there are grounds for confidence that no real, objective values play a part in the explanation.

I find the popularity of this argument surprising. The fact that morality is socially inculcated and that there is radical disagreement about it across cultures, over time, and even within cultures at a time is a poor reason to conclude that values have no objective reality. Even where there is truth, it is not always easy to discover. Other areas of knowledge are taught by social pressure, many truths as well as falsehoods are believed without rational grounds, and there is wide disagreement about scientific and social facts, especially where strong interests are involved which will be affected by different answers to a disputed question. This last factor is present throughout ethics to a uniquely high degree: it is an area in which one would expect extreme variation of belief and radical disagreement however objectively real the subject actually was. For comparably motivated disagreements about matters of fact, one has to go to the heliocentric theory, the theory of evolution, the Dreyfus case, the Hiss case, and the genetic contribution to racial differences in IQ.

Although the methods of ethical reasoning are rather primitive, the degree to which agreement can be achieved and social prejudices transcended in the face of strong pressures suggests that something real is being investigated, and that part of the explanation of the appearances, both at simple and at complex levels, is that we perceive, often inaccurately, that certain reasons for action exist, and go on to infer, often erroneously, the general form of the principles that best accounts for those reasons.

The controlling conception that supports these efforts at understanding, in ethics as in science, is realism, or the possibility of realism. Without being sure that we will find one, we look for an account of what reasons there really are, an account that can be objectively understood.

I have not discussed all the possible arguments against realism about values, but I have tried to give general reasons for scepticism about such arguments. It seems to me that they tend to be supported by a narrow preconception of what there *is*, and that this is essentially question-begging.

IX

TRUTH, INVENTION, AND THE MEANING OF LIFE

DAVID WIGGINS

Nul n'est besoin d'espérer pour entreprendre, ni de réussir pour persévérer.

(William the Silent)

Eternal survival after death completely fails to accomplish the purpose for which it has always been intended. Or is some riddle solved by my surviving for ever? Is not this eternal life as much of a riddle as our present life?

(Wittgenstein)

1

Even now, in an age not much given to mysticism, there are people who ask 'What is the meaning of life?' Not a few of them make the simple 'unphilosophical' assumption that there is something to be known here. (One might say that they are 'cognitivists' with regard to this sort of question.) And most of these same people make the equally unguarded assumption that the whole issue of life's meaning presupposes a positive answer at least to the question whether it can be plainly and straightforwardly *true* that this or that thing or activity or pursuit is good, has value, or is worth something. And then, what is even harder, they suppose that questions like that of life's meaning must be among the central questions of moral philosophy.

The question of life's having a meaning and the question of truth are not at the centre of moral philosophy as we now have it. The second is

From David Wiggins, *Needs, Values, Truth: Essays in the Philosophy of Value*, 2nd edn. (Oxford: Basil Blackwell, 1991), 87–137. This is a revised version of a lecture delivered on 24 Nov. 1976, which was first published in *Proceedings of the British Academy*, 62 (1976), 331–78 and is reprinted by permission.

The quotations from Richard Taylor are made by kind permission of Macmillan.

normally settled by something bordering on stipulation,[1] and the first is under suspicion of belonging in the same class as 'What is the greatest good of the greatest number?' or 'What is the will?' or 'What holds the world up?' This is the class of questions not in good order, or best not answered just as they stand.

If there is a semantical crux about this sort of occurrence of the word 'meaning', then all logical priority attaches to it; and no reasonable person could pretend that a perfectly straightforward purport attaches to the idea of life's meaning something. But logical priority is not everything; and, most notably, the order of logical priority is not always or necessarily the same as the order of discovery. Someone who was very perplexed or very persistent would be well within his rights to insist that, where a question has been asked as often as this one has, a philosopher must make what he can of it: and that, if the sense really is obscure, then he must find what significance the effort to frame an answer is apt to *force* upon the question.

In what follows, I try to explore the possibility that the question of truth and the question of life's meaning are among the most fundamental questions of moral philosophy. The outcome of the attempt may perhaps indicate that, unless we want to continue to think of moral philosophy as the casuistry of emergencies, these questions and the other questions that they bring to our attention are a better focus for ethics and meta-ethics than the textbook problem 'What (under this or that or the other circumstance) shall I do?' My finding will be that the question of life's meaning does, as the untheoretical suppose, lead into the question of truth—and conversely. Towards the end I shall also claim to uncover the possibility that philosophy has put happiness in the place that should have been occupied in moral philosophy by meaning. This is a purely theoretical claim, but if it is correct, it is not without consequences; and if (as some say) weariness and dissatisfaction have issued from the direct pursuit of happiness as such, then it is not without all explanatory power.

2

I have spoken in favour of the direct approach, but it is impossible to reach out to the perplexity for which the question of meaning is felt to stand without first recording the sense that, during relatively recent times, there has been some shift in the way the question of life's meaning is seen, and

---

[1] Cp. Wiggins, *Needs, Values, Truth*, essay IV. In 1976, at the time of speaking, the remark stood in less need of qualification than it does now.

in the kind of answer it is felt to require. Here is an answer made almost exactly 200 years ago, two years before the death of Voltaire: 'We live in this world to compel ourselves industriously to enlighten one another by means of reasoning and to apply ourselves always to carrying forward the sciences and the arts' (W. A. Mozart to Padre Martini, letter of 4 December 1776).[2] What we envy here is the specificity, and the certainty of purpose. But, even as we feel envy, it is likely that we want to rejoice in our freedom to disbelieve in that which provided the contingent foundation of the specificity and certainty. I make this remark, not because I think that we ought to believe in what Mozart and Padre Martini believed in, but in outright opposition to the hope that some relatively painless accommodation can be made between the freedom and the certainty. The foundation of what we envy was the now (I think) almost unattainable conviction that there exists a God whose purpose ordains certain specific duties for all men, and appoints particular men to particular roles or vocations.

That conviction was not only fallible: there are many who would say that it was positively dangerous—and that the risk it carried was that, if the conviction were false, then one might prove to have thrown one's life away. It is true that in the cases we are considering, 'throwing one's life away' seems utterly the wrong thing to say of the risk carried by the conviction, and seems wrong even for the aspects of these men's lives that were intimately conditioned by the belief in God. But if one doubts that God exists, then it is one form of the problem of meaning to justify not wanting to speak here of throwing a life away. It is a terrible thing to try to live a life without believing in *anything*. But surely that doesn't mean that just any old set of concerns and beliefs will do, provided one *could* live a life by them. Surely if any old set would do, that is the same as life's being meaningless.

If we envy the certainty of the 1776 answer, then most likely this is only one of several differences that we see between our own situation and the situation of those who lived before the point at which Darwin's theory of evolution so confined the scope of the religious imagination. History has not yet carried us to the point where it is impossible for a description of such differences to count as exaggerated. But they are formidable. And, for the sake of the clarity of what is to come, I must pause to express open dissent from two comments that might be made about them.

First, someone more interested in theory than in what it was like to be alive then and what it is like now may try to diminish the differences that

---

[2] Compare the composer's choice of expression on the occasion of his father's birthday anniversary in 1777: 'I wish you as many years as are needed to have nothing left to do in music.'

we sense, by arguing from the accessibility to both eighteenth and twentieth centuries of a core notion of God, a notion that he may say persists
in the concept of God championed by modern theologians. To this use of
their ideas I object that, whatever gap it is which lies between 1776 and
1976, such notions as *God as the ground of our being* cannot bridge it. For
recourse to these exemplifies a tendency towards an a priori conception
of God which, even if the eighteenth century had had it, most of the men
of that age would have hastened to amplify with a more hazardous a
posteriori conception. Faith in God conceived a posteriori was precisely
the cost of the particularity and definiteness of the certainty that we envy.

The other thing someone might say is that, in one crucial respect, our
situation is not different from a late Enlightenment situation, because
there is a conceptually determined need in which the eighteenth century
stood and in which we stand equally. This, it might be said, is the need for
commitment. In the eighteenth-century case, this extra thing was commitment to submission to God's purpose. We shall come in Section 4 to what
these theorists think it is in our case. Faced however with this second
comment, one might well wonder how a man could get to the point of
recognizing or even suspecting that it was God's purpose that he should be
a composer (say) and yet be indifferent to that. Surely no extra anything,
over and above some suspicion that this or that is God's purpose, is
required to create the concern we should expect to find the suspicion itself
would have implanted in him. On the other hand, if this extra thing were
supplied, then it would bring too much. For the commitment to submission
seems to exclude rebellion; and rebellion against what is taken as God's
purpose has never been excluded by the religious attitude as such.

What then are the similarities and the differences between the
eighteenth-century orientation and our own orientation upon the meaning
of life? It seems that the similarities that persist will hold between the
conceptual scheme with which they in that century confronted the world of
everyday experience and the scheme with which we, in spite of our thor-
oughgoing acceptance of natural science, confront it: and the dissimilari-
ties will relate to the specificity and particularity of the focus of the various
concerns in which their world-view involved them and our world-view
involves us. For us there is less specificity and much less focus.

If this is still a dark statement, it is surely not so dark as to obscure the
relationship between this difference between them and us and a cognate
difference that will have signalled its presence and importance so soon as
I prepared to approach the divide between the eighteenth and twentieth
centuries by reference to the purposive or practical certainty of individual
men. Unless we are Marxists, we are much more resistant in the second

half of the twentieth century than eighteenth- or nineteenth-century men knew how to be against attempts to locate the meaning of human life or human history in mystical or metaphysical conceptions—in the emancipation of mankind, or progress, or the onward advance of Absolute Spirit. It is not that we have lost interest in emancipation or progress themselves; but, whether temporarily or permanently, we have more or less abandoned the idea that the importance of emancipation or progress (or a correct conception of spiritual advance) is that these are marks by which our minute speck in the universe can distinguish itself as the spiritual focus of the cosmos. Perhaps that is what makes the question of the meaning we can find in life so difficult and so desolate for us.

With these bare and inadequate historical assertions, however, the time is come to go straight to a modern philosophical account of the matter. There are not very many to choose from.

3

The account I have taken is that given in chapter 18 of Richard Taylor's book *Good and Evil*—an account rightly singled out for praise by the analytical philosopher who reviewed the book for the *Philosophical Review*.[3]

Taylor's approach to the question whether life has any meaning is first to 'bring to our minds a clear image of meaningless existence', and then determine what would need to be inserted into the meaningless existence so depicted in order to make it not meaningless. Taylor writes:

A perfect image of meaninglessness of the kind we are seeking is found in the ancient myth of Sisyphus. Sisyphus, it will be remembered, betrayed divine secrets to mortals, and for this he was condemned by the gods to roll a stone to the top of the hill, the stone then immediately to roll back down, again to be pushed to the top by Sisyphus, to roll down once more, and so on again and again, *forever*.

Two ways are then mentioned in which this meaninglessness could be alleviated or removed. First:

if we supposed that these stones . . . were assembled [by Sisyphus] at the top of the hill . . . in a beautiful and enduring temple, then . . . his labours would have a point, something would come of them all . . .

That is one way. But Taylor is not in the end disposed to place much reliance in this species of meaning, being more impressed by a second mode of enrichment.

---

[3] See Richard Taylor, *Good and Evil* (New York: Macmillan, 1970). The review was by Judith Jarvis Thomson, *Philosophical Review*, 81 (1973), 113.

Suppose that the gods, as an afterthought, waxed perversely merciful by implanting in [Sisyphus] a strange and irrational impulse . . . to roll stones . . . To make this more graphic, suppose they accomplish this by implanting in him some substance that has this effect on his character and drives . . . This little afterthought of the gods . . . was . . . merciful. For they have by this device managed to give Sisyphus precisely what he wants—by making him want precisely what they inflict on him. However it may appear to us, Sisyphus' . . . life is now filled with mission and meaning, and he seems to himself to have been given an entry to heaven . . . The *only* thing that has happened is this: Sisyphus has been reconciled to [his existence] . . . He has been led to embrace it. Not, however, by reason or persuasion, but by nothing more rational than the potency of a new substance in his veins . . .

So much for meaninglessness, and two ways of alleviating it. Meaninglessness, Taylor says,

is essentially endless pointlessness, and meaningfulness is therefore the opposite. Activity, and even long drawn out and repetitive activity, has a meaning if it has some significant culmination, some more or less lasting end that can be considered to have been the direction and purpose of the activity.

That is the temple-building option, of course.

But the descriptions so far also provide something else; namely, the suggestion of how an existence that is objectively meaningless, in this sense, can nevertheless acquire a meaning for him whose existence it is.

This 'something else' is the option of implanting in Sisyphus the impulse to push what he has to push. Here Taylor turns aside to compare, in point of meaninglessness or meaningfulness, the condition of Sisyphus and the lives of various animals, working from the lower to the higher animals—cannibalistic blindworms, the cicada, migratory birds, and so on up to ourselves. His verdict is that the point of any living thing's life is evidently nothing but life itself.

This life of the world thus presents itself to our eyes as a vast machine, feeding on itself, running on and on forever to nothing. And we are part of that life. To be sure, we are not just the same, but the differences are not so great as we like to think; many are merely invented and none really cancels meaninglessness . . . We are conscious of our activity. Our goals, whether in any significant sense we choose them or not, are things of which we are at least partly aware and can . . . appraise . . . Men have a history, as other animals do not. [Still] . . . if we think that, unlike Sisyphus', [our] labours do have a point, that they culminate in something lasting and, independently of our own deep interests in them, very worthwhile, then we simply have not considered the thing closely enough . . . For [Sisyphus' temple] to make any difference it had to be a temple that would at least endure, adding beauty to the world for the remainder of time. Our achievements . . . those that do last, like the sand-swept pyramids, soon become mere curiosities, while around them the rest of mankind continues its perpetual toting of rocks, only to see them roll down . . .

Here is a point that obsesses the author. Paragraph upon paragraph is devoted to describing the lamentable but undoubted impermanence (futility *sub specie aeternitatis*) of the architectural or built monuments of human labour. It is not entirely clear that the same effect could have been contrived if the gradual accumulation of scientific understanding or the multiplication of the sublime utterances of literature or music had been brought into the argument. What is clear is that Taylor is committed to a strong preference for the second method of enriching Sisyphus' life—that is the compulsion caused by the substance put into Sisyphus' veins. For as for the first method, and temple-building for the sake of the temple,

Suppose . . . that after ages of dreadful toil, all directed at this final result [Sisyphus] did at last complete his temple, [so] that now he could say his work was done, and he could rest and forever enjoy the result. Now what? What picture now presents itself to our minds? It is precisely the picture of infinite boredom! Of Sisyphus doing nothing ever again, but contemplating what he has already wrought and can no longer add anything to, and contemplating it for eternity! Now in this picture we have a meaning for Sisyphus' existence, a point for his prodigious labour, because we have put it there; yet, at the same time, that which is really worthwhile seems to have slipped away entirely.

The final reckoning would appear to be this: (*a*) a lasting end or *telos* could constitute a purpose for the work; but (*b*) there is no permanence; and (*c*), even if there were such permanence, its point would be effectively negated by boredom with the outcome of the work. And so we are thrown inexorably into the arms of the other and second sort of meaning.

We can reintroduce what has been resolutely pushed aside in an effort to view our lives and human existence with objectivity; namely, our own wills, our deep interest in what we find ourselves doing . . . Even the glow worms . . . whose cycles of existence over the millions of years seem so pointless when looked at by us, will seem utterly different to us if we can somehow try to view their existence from within. . . . If the philosopher is apt to see in this a pattern similar to the unending cycles of the existence of Sisyphus, and to despair, then it is indeed because the meaning and point he is seeking is not there—but mercifully so. The meaning of life is from within us, it is not bestowed from without, and it far exceeds in its beauty and permanence any heaven of which men have ever dreamed or yearned for.

4

Connoisseurs of twentieth-century ethical theory in its Anglo-Saxon and Continental variants will not be slow to see the affinities of this account. Practitioners of the first of these kinds are sometimes singled out for their failure to say anything about such questions as the meaning of life. But, if the affinities are as strong as I think, then, notwithstanding Taylor's philosophical distance from his contemporaries, what we have just unearthed has a strong claim to be their secret doctrine of the meaning of life.

Consider first the sharp supposedly unproblematic distinction, reinforced by the myth as told and retold here, between what we discover already there in the world—the facts, including the gods' enforcement of their sentence—and what is invented or, by thinking or willing, somehow *put into* or *spread onto* the factual world—namely the values.[4] Nobody who knows the philosophical literature on value will be surprised by Taylor's variant on the myth. . . . Here, however, at the point where the magic stuff is to be injected into the veins of Sisyphus, I must digress for the sake of what is to come, in order to explain the deliberate way in which I shall use the word 'value'.

I propose that we distinguish between *valuations* (typically recorded by such forms as '*x* is good', 'bad', 'beautiful', 'ugly', 'ignoble', 'brave', 'just', 'mischievous', 'malicious', 'worthy', 'honest', 'corrupt', 'disgusting', 'amusing', 'diverting', 'boring', etc.—no restrictions at all on the category of *x*) and *directive* or *deliberative* (or *practical*) *judgements* (e.g. 'I must ψ', 'I ought to ψ', 'it would be best, all things considered, for me to ψ', etc.).[5] It is true that between these there is an important no man's land (comprising, e.g., general judgements of the strongly deprecatory or commendatory kind about vices and virtues, and general or particular statements about actions that it is ignoble or inhuman or unspeakably wicked to do or not to do).[6] But the fact that many other kinds of judgement lie between pure valuations and pure directives is no objection; and it does nothing to obstruct the discrimination I seek to effect between the (spurious) fact–value distinction and the (real) is–ought distinction. The unavailability of any relevant or useful notion of 'factual' by which to secure the fact–value distinction (see below, Sections 6 and 10) serves only to further our understanding of the second distinction (whether we state that as the distinction between *is* and *ought*, or *is* and *must*, or *is* and *had better*). For, if we conceive of the distinction of *is* and *must* as corresponding to the distinction between appreciation and decision and also emancipate ourselves

---

[4] On the differences between discovery and invention, and on some abuses of the distinction, see William Kneale, 'The Idea of Invention', *Proceedings of the British Academy*, 39 (1955), 85–108.

[5] Note that this is not a distinction whose rationale is originally *founded* in a difference in the motivating force of judgements of the two classes, even if such a difference may be forthcoming from the distinction. In both cases, merely thinking that *p* is arguably derivative from *finding* that *p*. (Cp. Wiggins, *Needs, Values, Truth*, essay v, sect. 11.)

[6] For some purposes, judgements that philosophers describe as judgements of prima-facie obligation (better *pro tanto* obligation) might almost, or without excessive distortion be assimilated to valuational judgements.

from a limited and absurd idea of what *is*, then there can be a new verisimilitude in our accounts of appreciation and decision.[7]

This being proposed as the usage of the word 'value' to be adhered to in this paper, let us return now to Sisyphus and the body of doctrine that is illustrated by Taylor's version of his story. At one moment Sisyphus sees his task as utterly futile and degrading: a moment later, supposedly without any initiating change in his cognitive appreciation, we are told that he sees his whole life as infinitely rewarding. What I was about to say before the digression was that there is only one philosophy of value that can even attempt to accommodate this possibility.

Consider next Taylor's account of the escape from meaninglessness—or what he might equally well have followed the Existentialists in calling *absurdity*. Taylor's mode of escape is simply a variation on the habitual philosophical reaction to the perception of the real or supposed meaninglessness of human existence. As a method for escape it is co-ordinate with every other proposal that is known, suicide (always one recognized way), scorn or defiance (Albert Camus), resignation or drift (certain orientally influenced positions), various kinds of commitment (R. M. Hare and J.-P. Sartre), and what may be the most recently enlisted member of this *équipe*, which is irony.[8]

Again, few readers of *Freedom and Reason* will fail to recognize in Sisyphus, after the injection of the gods' substance into his veins, a Mark I, stone-rolling model of R. M. Hare's further elaborated, rationally impregnable 'fanatic'.[9] As for the mysterious substance itself, surely this is some extra oomph, injected afterwards *ad libitum*, that will enable Sisyphus' factual judgements about stone-rolling to take on 'evaluative meaning'.

Finally, nor has nineteenth- or twentieth-century utilitarianism anything to fear from his style of fable-telling. For the *locus* or origin of all value has been firmly confined within the familiar area of psychological states conceived in independence of what they are directed to.[10]

In order to have a name, I shall call Taylor's and all similar accounts non-cognitive accounts of the meaning of life. This choice of name is not inappropriate if it helps to signal the association of these accounts with a

---

[7] At a point roughly corresponding to the no man's land between *is* and *must* or valuation and practical judgement, there is perhaps overall (or *practically focused*) appreciation, lying in between initial (or unweighted) appreciation and practical decision.

[8] See Thomas Nagel, 'The Absurd', *Journal of Philosophy*, 68 (1971), 716–26.

[9] R. M. Hare, *Freedom and Reason* (Oxford: Oxford University Press, 1963). I mean that Sisyphus is the *stuff* of which the fanatic is made.

[10] For efforts in the direction of a better account of some of these states, see below, Sect. 6 and Wiggins, *Needs, Values, Truth*, essay v, *passim*.

long-standing philosophical tendency to strive for descriptions of the human condition by which will and intellect-cum-perception are kept separate and innocent of all insider transactions. The intellect supplies uncontaminated factual perception, deduction, and means–end reasoning. Ends are supplied (in this picture) by feeling or will, which are not conceived either as percipient or as determinants in any interesting way of perception.

What I shall argue next is that, in spite of the well-tried familiarity of these ideas, the non-cognitive account depends for its whole plausibility upon abandoning at the level of theory the inner perspective that it commends as the only possible perspective upon life's meaning. This is a kind of incoherence, and one that casts some doubt upon the distinction of the inside and the outside viewpoints. I also believe that, once we break down the supposed distinction between the inner or participative and the outer, supposedly objective, viewpoints, there will be a route by which we can advance (though not to anything like the particularity of the moral certainty that we began by envying).

5

Where the non-cognitive account essentially depends on the existence and availability of the inner view, it is a question of capital importance whether the non-cognitivist's account of the inner view makes such sense of our condition as it actually has for us from the inside.

The first ground for suspecting distortion is that, if the non-cognitive view is put in the way Taylor puts it, then it seems to make too little difference to the meaningfulness of life how well or badly our strivings are apt to turn out. Stone-rolling for its own sake, and stone-rolling for successful temple-building, and stone-rolling for temple-building that will be frustrated—all seem to come to much the same thing. I object that that is not how it feels to most people. No doubt there are 'committed' individuals like William the Silent or the doctor in Camus's *La Peste* who will constitute exceptions to my claim. But in general, the larger the obstacles that nature or other men put in our way, and the more truly hopeless the prospect, the less point most of us will feel anything has. 'Where there is no hope, there is no endeavour', as Samuel Johnson observed. In the end point is partly dependent on expectation of outcome; and expectation is dependent on past outcomes. So point is not independent of outcome.

The non-cognitivist may make two replies here. The first is that, in so far as the outcome is conceived by the agent as independent of the activity, the activity itself is merely instrumental and must lead back to other activities that are their own outcome. And these he will say are what matter. But in opposition to this,

(a) I shall show in due course how activities that can be regarded as 'their own goals' typically depend on valuations that non-cognitivism makes bad sense of (Section 6 below);

(b) I shall question whether all activities that have a goal independent of the activity itself are perceived by their agents as only derivatively meaningful (Section 13 below).

The non-cognitivists' second reply will be directed against the objection that he makes it matter too little how well or badly our strivings turn out. Is it not a point on *his* side that the emptier and worse worlds where one imagines everything having even less point than it has now are worlds where the will itself will falter? To this I say Yes, I hear the reply. But if the non-cognitive view was to make the sense of our condition that we attribute to it, then something needed to be written into the non-cognitive account about what kinds of object will engage with the will as important. And it is still unclear at this stage how much room can be found within non-cognitivism for the will's own distinctions between good and bad reasons for caring about anything as important. Objectively speaking (once 'we disengage our wills'), any reason is as good or as bad as any other reason, it seems to say. For on the non-cognitive account, life is *objectively* meaningless. So, by the non-cognitivist's lights, it must appear that whatever the will chooses to treat as a good reason to engage itself is, for the will, a good reason. But the will itself, taking the inner view, picks and chooses, deliberates, weighs, and tests its own concerns. It craves objective reasons; and often it could not go forward unless it thought it had them. The extension of the concept *objective* is quite different on the inner view from the extension assigned to it by the outer view. And the rationale for determining the extension is different also.

There is here an incoherence. To avoid it without flying in the face of what we think we know already about the difference between meaning and meaninglessness, the disagreement between the inner and the outer views must be softened somehow. The trouble is that, if we want to preserve any of the distinctive emphases of Taylor's and similar accounts, then we are bound to find that, for purposes of the validation of any given concern, the non-cognitive view always readdresses the problem to the inner perspective *without itself adopting that perspective*. It cannot adopt the inner perspective because, according to the picture that the non-cognitivist paints of these things, the inner view has to be unaware of the outer one, and has to enjoy essentially illusory notions of objectivity, importance, and significance: whereas the outer view has to hold that life is objectively meaningless. The non-cognitivist mitigates the outrageousness of so categorical a denial of meaning as the outer view issues by pointing to the availability of the participant perspective. But the most that he can do is to point to it. Otherwise the theorist is himself engulfed by a view that he must maintain to be false.

So much for the first distortion I claim to find in non-cognitivism and certain inconclusive defences of that approach. There is also a second distortion.

To us there seems to be an important difference between the life of the cannibalistic blindworms that Taylor describes and the life of (say) a basking seal or a dolphin at play, creatures that are conscious, can rest without sleeping, can adjust the end to the means as well as the means to the end, and can take in far more about the world than they have the immediate or instrumental need to take in. There also seems to us to be a difference, a different difference, between the life of seals or dolphins and the life of human beings living in communities with a history. And there is even a third difference, which as participants we insist upon, between the life of a man who contributes something to a society with a continuing history and a life lived on the plan of a southern pig-breeder who (in the economics textbooks, if not in real life) buys more land to grow more corn to feed more hogs to buy more land, to grow more corn to feed more hogs . . . The practical concerns of this man are at once regressive and circular. And we are keenly interested, on the inner view, in the difference between these concerns and non-circular practical reasonings or life plans.

For the inner view, this difference undoubtedly exists. If the outside view is right to commend the inside view, then the outside view must pay some heed to the differences that the inner view perceives—if only to depreciate them. But it can accord them no importance that is commensurate with the weight that the non-cognitive theory of life's meaning thrusts upon the inner view. 'The differences are merely invented,' Taylor has to say, 'and none really cancels the kind of meaninglessness we found in Sisyphus.'

To the participant it may seem that it is far harder to explain what is so good about buying more land to grow more corn to feed more hogs to buy more land, to grow more corn to feed more hogs . . . than it is to explain what is good about digging a ditch with a man whom one likes, or helping the same man to talk or drink the sun down the sky. It might seem to a participant that the explanation of the second sort of thing, so far from having nowhere to go but round and round in circles, fans out into a whole arborescence of concerns; that, unlike any known explanation of what is so good about breeding hogs to buy more land to breed more hogs . . . it can be pursued backwards and outwards to take in all the concerns of a whole life. But on the non-cognitive view of the inner view there is no way to make these differences stick. They count for so little that it is a mystery why the non-cognitivist doesn't simply say: life is meaningless; and that's all there is to it. If only he would make that pronouncement, we should know where we were.

But why do the differences just mentioned count for so little for the non-cognitivist? Because they all arise from subjective or anthropocentric considerations, and what is subjective or anthropocentric is not by the standards of the outer view objective. (Taylor insists that to determine whether something matters, we have to view it 'independently of our own deep interest'.) I shall come back to this when I reconstruct the non-cognitive view; but let me point out immediately the prima-facie implausibility of the idea that the distinction between objectivity and non-objectivity (which appears to have to do with the existence of publicly accepted and rationally criticizable standards of argument, or of ratiocination towards truth) should coincide with the distinction between the anthropocentric and the non-anthropocentric (which concerns orientation towards human interests or a human point of view). The distinctions are not without conceptual links, but the prima-facie appearance is that a matter that is anthropocentric may be either more objective or less objective, or (at the limit) *merely* subjective.[11] This is how things will appear until we have an argument to prove rigorously the mutual coincidence of independently plausible accounts of the anthropocentric–non-anthropocentric distinction, the non-objective–objective distinction, and the subjective–non-subjective distinction.[12]

The third and last distortion of experience I find in Taylor's presentation of non-cognitivism I shall try to convey by an anecdote. Two or three years ago, when I went to see some film at the Academy Cinema, the second feature of the evening was a documentary film about creatures fathoms

[11] For an independent account of the subjective, see Wiggins, *Needs, Values, Truth*, essay v.

[12] A similar observation needs to be entered about all the other distinctions that are in the offing here—the distinctions between the neutral and the committed, the neutral and the biased, the descriptive and the prescriptive, the descriptive and the evaluative, the quantifiable and the unquantifiable, the absolute and the relative, the scientific and the unscientific, the not essentially contestable and the essentially contestable, the verifiable or falsifiable and the neither verifiable nor falsifiable, the factual and the normative. . . . In common parlance, and in sociology and economics—even in political science, which should know better—these distinctions are used almost interchangeably. But they are different, and they are separately interesting. Each of these contrasts seems to have its own rationale.

down on the ocean-bottom. When it was over, I turned to my companion and asked, 'What is it about these films that makes one feel so utterly desolate?' Her reply was: 'apart from the fact that so much of the film was about sea monsters eating one another, the unnerving thing was that nothing down there ever seemed to *rest*'. As for play, disinterested curiosity, or merely contemplating, she could have added, these seemed inconceivable.

At least about the film we had just seen, these were just the points that needed to be made—untrammelled by all pseudo-philosophical inhibitions, which are irrelevant in any case to the 'inner' or participant perspective. And the thought the film leads to is this. If we can project upon a form of life nothing but the pursuit of life itself, if we find there no non-instrumental concerns and no interest in the world considered as lasting longer than the animal in question will need the world to last in order to sustain the animal's own life; then the form of life must be to some considerable extent alien to us.[13] Any adequate description of the point we can attach to our form of life must do more than treat our appetitive states in would-be isolation from their relation to the things they are directed at.

For purposes of his eventual philosophical destination, Taylor has had to forge an intimate and very direct link between contemplation, permanence, and boredom. But, at least on the inner view, the connection between these things is at once extremely complex and relatively indirect.[14] And, once one has seen the final destination towards which it is Taylor's design to move the whole discussion, then one sees in a new light his obsession with monuments. Surely these are his hostages for the objects of psychological states in general; and all such objects are due to be in some sense discredited. (Discredited on the outer view, or accorded a stultifyingly indiscriminate tolerance on the outer account of the inner view.) And one comprehends all too well Taylor's sour grapes insistence on the impermanence of monuments—as if by this he could reduce to nil

---

[13] Here, I think, or in this neighbourhood, lies the explanation of the profound unease that some people feel at the systematic and unrelenting exploitation of nature and animals which is represented by factory farming, by intensive livestock-rearing, or by the mindless spoliation of non-renewable resources. This condemnation of evil will never be understood till it is distinguished by its detractors from its frequent, natural, but only contingent concomitant—the absolute prohibition of all killing not done in self-defence.

[14] On permanence, cf. Wittgenstein, *Tractatus Logico-Philosophicus* (London: Routledge, 1922), 6.4312, quoted *ad init.*; F. P. Ramsey, 'Is there Anything to Discuss?', in *Foundations of Mathematics and other Essays* (London: Routledge, 1931): 'I apply my perspective not merely to space but also to time. In time the world will cool and everything will die; but that is a long time off still and its percent value at compound discount is almost nothing. Nor is the present less valuable because the future will be blank.'

the philosophical (as opposed, he might say, to subjective) importance of all the objects of psychological states, longings, lookings, reverings, contemplatings, or whatever.

6

Leaving many questions still dangling, I shall conclude discussion of the outer account of the inner perspective with a general difficulty, and a suggestion.

There is a tendency, in utilitarian writings and in the writings of economists,[15] to locate all ultimate or intrinsic value in human appetitive states.[16] They are contrasted (as we also see Taylor contrasting them for his purposes) with everything else in the world. According to this sort of view, the value of anything that is not a psychological state derives from the psychological state or states for which it is an actual or potential object. See here what Bentham says in *An Introduction to the Principles of Morals and Legislation*: 'Strictly speaking, nothing can be said to be good or bad, but either in itself; which is the case only with pain or pleasure; or on account of its effects; which is the case only with things that are the causes or preventives of pain and pleasure.' One has only to put the matter like this, however, to be troubled by a curious instability. Since nothing at all can count for the outer view as inherently or intrinsically good, the doctrine must belong to the inner or inside view. But, as experienced, the inner view too will reject this view of value. For, adopting that inner view,[17] and supposing with Bentham that certain conscious states are good in

[15] Cf. Wilfred Beckerman, 'Growth, Virtue, and Equality', *New Statesman*, 21 June 1974, 880: 'The second, and real question is: at what rate should we use up resources in order to maximise the welfare of human beings . . . Throughout existence man has made use of the environment, and the only valid question for those who attach—as I do (in accordance with God's first injunction to Adam)—*complete and absolute priority to human welfare* is what rate of use provides the maximum welfare for humans, including future generations.' I quote this relatively guarded specimen to illustrate the hazards of making too easy a distinction between human welfare on the one side and the environment on the other. But it also illustrates the purely ornamental role which has devolved upon the Hebrew scriptures. They constitute matter for the literary decoration of sentiments formed and apprehended by quite different methods of divination. It is irrelevant for instance that the world-view given voice in the first chapters of Genesis is perceptibly more complicated than Beckerman's is.

[16] Or in the case of vegetarian utilitarian writings, to locate all ultimate value in conscious animal appetitive states.

[17] Perhaps some one individual man's inner view. For here and only here could it be held to be perfectly or fully obvious that the special goodness in themselves of certain of his pleasurable states is something simply above or beyond argument for him. Beyond that point—notwithstanding utilitarian explanations of the superfluity of argument on something so allegedly evident—it is less obvious to him.

themselves, we must take these states as they appear to the inner view. But then one cannot say without radical misconception that these states are all that is intrinsically valuable. For (a) many of these conscious states have intentional objects; (b) many of the conscious states in which intrinsic value supposedly resides are strivings *after* objects that are not states, or are contemplations *of* objects that are not themselves states; and (c) it is of the essence of these conscious states, experienced as strivings or contemplations or whatever, to accord to their intentional objects a non-instrumental value. For from the inside of lived experience, and by the scale of value that that imposes, the shape of an archway or the sound of the lapping of the sea against the shore at some place at some time may appear to be of an altogether different order of importance from the satisfaction that some human being once had from his breakfast.[18]

The participant, with the going concepts of the objective and the worth while, descries certain external properties in things and states of affairs. And the presence there of these properties is what invests them with importance in his eyes. The one thing that properties cannot be, at least for him, is mere projections resulting from a certain kind of efficacy in the causation of satisfaction. For no appetitive or aesthetic or contemplative state can see its own object as having a value that is derivative in the special way that is required by the thesis that all non-instrumental value resides in human states of satisfaction. But, if that is right, then the outer view cannot rely for its credibility upon the meaning that the inner view perceives in something. To see itself and its object in the alien manner of the outer view, the state as experienced would have to be prepared to suppose that it, the state, could just as well have lighted on any other object (even any other kind of object), provided only that the requisite attitudes could have been induced. But in this conception of such states we are entitled to complain that nothing remains that we can recognize, or that the inner perspective will not instantly disown.[19]

[18] This feature of experience is of course lamented by thinkers who seek to make moral philosophy out of ((('formal value theory' + moral earnestness) + some values of the theorist's own, generalized and thereby tested) + applications. But the feature is part of what is given in the phenomenology of some of the very same 'satisfaction' experiences that are the starting-point of the utilitarians themselves. And there is nothing to take fright at in this feature of them, inconsistent though it is with absurd slogans of the literally absolute priority of human welfare.

[19] An example will make these claims clearer perhaps. A man comes at dead of night to a hotel in a place where he has never been before. In the morning he stumbles out from his darkened room and, following the scent of coffee out of doors, he finds a sunlit terrace looking out across a valley on to a range of blue mountains in the half-distance. The sight of them—a veritable vale of Tempe—entrances him. In marvelling at the valley and mountains he thinks only how overwhelmingly beautiful they are. The value of the state depends on the value attributed to the object. But the theory I oppose says all non-instrumental value resides here in the man's own state, and in the like states of others who are actually so affected by the

I promised to conclude the critique of non-cognitivism with a suggestion about values. It is this: no attempt to make sense of the human condition can make sense of it if it treats the objects of psychological states as unequal partners or derivative elements in the conceptual structure of values and states and their objects. This is far worse than Aristotle's opposite error: 'We desire the object because it seems good to us, rather than the object's seeming good to us because we desire it' (*Metaphysics*, 1072ª29; cf. *Nicomachean Ethics*, 1175ª).

Spinoza appears to have taken this sentence as it stood and deliberately negated it (*Ethics*, part III, proposition 9, note). But maybe it is the beginning of real wisdom to see that we may have to side against both Aristotle and Spinoza here and ask: 'Why should the *because* not hold both ways round?' Surely an adequate account of these matters will have to treat psychological states and their objects as equal and reciprocal partners, and is likely to need to see the identifications of the states and of the properties under which the states subsume their objects as interdependent. (If these interdependencies are fatal to the distinction of inner and outer, we are already in a position to be grateful for that.)

Surely it can be true both that we desire *x* because we think *x* good, and that *x* is good because we desire *x*. It does not count against the point I am making that the explanation of the 'because' is different in each direction. Nor does it count against the particular anti-non-cognitivist position that is now emerging in opposition to non-cognitivism that the second 'because' might have to be explained in some such way as this: such desiring by human beings directed in this way is one part of what is required for there to be such a thing as the perspective from which the non-instrumental goodness of *x* is there to be perceived.

There is an analogy for this suggestion. We may see a pillar-box as red because it is red. But also pillar-boxes, painted as they are, *count* as red only because there actually exists a perceptual apparatus (e.g. our own) that discriminates, and learns on the direct basis of experience to group together, all and only the actually red things. Not every sentient animal that sees a red post-box sees it as red. But this in no way impugns the idea that redness is an external, monadic property of a post-box. 'Red post-box' is not short for 'red to human beings post-box'. Red is not a relational

mountains. The more numerous such states are, the greater, presumably, the theory holds, is the 'realized' value of the mountains. The theory says that the whole actual value of the beauty of the valley and mountains is dependent upon arranging for the full exploitation of the capacity of these things to produce such states in human beings. (Exploitation now begun and duly recorded in Paul Jennings's Wordsworthian emendation: 'I wandered lonely as a crowd.') What I am saying about the theory is simply that it is untrue to the actual experience of the object-directed states that are the starting-point of that theory.

property. (It is certainly not relational in the way in which 'father of' is relational, or 'moves' is relational on a Leibniz–Mach view of space.) All the same, it is in one interesting sense a *relative* property. For the category of colour is an anthropocentric category. The category corresponds to an interest that can only take root in creatures with something approaching our own sensory apparatus.

Philosophy has dwelt nearly exclusively on differences between 'good' and 'red' or 'yellow'. I have long marvelled at this.[20] For there resides in the combined objectivity and anthropocentricity of colour a striking analogy to illuminate not only the externality that human beings attribute to the

[20] Without of course wishing to deny the difference that good is 'attributive' to a marked degree, whereas colour words are scarcely attributive at all. I think that, in these familiar discussions, philosophers have misdescribed the undoubted fact that, because there is no standing interest to which yellowness answers, 'yellow' is not such as to be *cut out* (by virtue of standing for what it stands for) to commend a thing or evaluate it favourably. But, surely, if there were such a standing interest, 'yellow' would be at least as well suited to commend as 'sharp' or 'beautiful' or even 'just' are.

Against the suggestion that axiological predicates are a species of predicate not clearly marked off from the factual, there is a trick the non-cognitivist always plays and he ought not to be allowed to play. He picks himself a 'central case' of a descriptive predicate, and a 'central case' of a valuational predicate. Then he remarks how very different the predicates he has picked are. But what on earth can that show? Nobody thinks you could prove a bat was not an animal by contrasting some bat (a paradigm case of a bat) with some elephant (a paradigm case of an animal). Nothing can come clear from such procedures in advance of explanation of the point of the contrast. In the present case the point of the factual–non-factual distinction has not been explained; and it has to be explained without begging the question in favour of the non-cognitivist, who picked the quarrel in the first place. What was the nature or rationale of the difference which was by these means to have been demonstrated? Till it is explained there must remain all of the following possibilities:

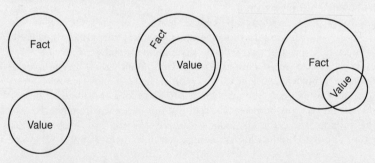

It would be unfair to say there have been no attempts at all to elucidate the point of the fact–value contrast. Wittgenstein tried (quite unsuccessfully, I think) to explain it in his 'Lecture on Ethics', *Philosophical Review*, 74 (1965), 6. And prescriptivists explain it by reference to the link they allege holds between evaluation and action. But, although there is some such link between deliberative judgement and action, the required link does not hold between evaluation and action. That was one part of the point of the contrast I proposed at the beginning of Sect. 4.

properties by whose ascription they evaluate things, people, and actions, but also the way in which the quality *by* which the thing qualifies as good and the desire *for* the thing are equals—are 'made for one another' so to speak. Compare the way in which the quality by which a thing counts as funny and the mental set that is presupposed to being amused by it are made for one another.

7

The time has come to sort out the non-cognitive theory to accommodate these findings and expel contradiction. But it is just possible that I have not convinced you that sorting out is necessary, and that you have found more coherent than I have allowed it to be the non-cognitivist's use of the idea of perspective, and of different and incompatible perspectives.

Perspective is not a form of illusion, distortion, or delusion. All the different perspectives of a single array of objects are perfectly consistent with one another. Given a set of perspectives, we can recover, if only they be reliably collected, a unified true account of the shape, spatial relations, and relative dimensions of the objects in the array. If we forget these platitudes then we may think it is much more harmless than it really is that the so-called outer and inner perspectives should straightforwardly contradict one another. There is nothing whatever in the idea of a perspective to license this scandalous idea—no more than the truism that two perspectives may include or exclude different aspects will create the licence to think that the participant and external views, as the non-cognitivist has described them, may unproblematically conflict over whether a certain activity or pursuit is really (or objectively) worth while or not.[21]

The non-cognitivist theory must be redeployed, then, if it is to continue to be taken seriously. The traditional twentieth-century way of amending the theory into self-consistency would have been *meta-ethics*, conceived as an axiologically neutral branch of 'logic'. Meta-ethics is not as neutral as was supposed, or so I shall claim. But it may be that it is still the best way for us to understand ourselves better.

Let us take the language of practice or morals as an object language. Call it *L*. The theorist's duty is then to discover, and to explain in the

---

[21] Still less does the language of perspective license the supposition that the philosopher who answers the question of the meaning of life could make a virtue out of committing himself to neither, or neither and both perspectives. Where on earth is *he* looking at things from? Or does he think of himself as one who mysteriously somehow looks at everything from no perspective at all? For the closest approximation he could coherently conceive of attaining to this aspiration, see Sect. 10 below.

metalanguage which is his own language, both a *formal theory* and a more discursive *informal theory* of L-utterances, not least L-utterances concerning what is worth while or a good thing to do with one's life.

What does this involve? First, and this is the humble formal task that is presupposed to his more distinctively ethical aspirations, the theorist needs to be able to say, or assume that someone can say, what each of the sentences of the object language means. To achieve this, a procedure is needed for parsing L-sentences into their primitive semantic components, and an axiom is required for each primitive component accounting for its particular contribution to assertion conditions. Then, given any L-sentence s, the axioms can be deployed to derive a pairing of s with an assertion condition p, the pairing being stated in the metalanguage by a theorem in the form:

s is assertible if and only if p.

Moral philosophy as we now know it makes many sophisticated claims about meanings, some of them very hard to assess. Compared with everything that would be involved in making those assessments, what we are assuming here is minimal. It is only that the discursive or informal comments that the moral theorist hopes to make about the status of this, that, or the other judgement in L will presuppose that such a biconditional can be constructed for each sentence of L. There assertion conditions give the meaning of the judgements he wants to comment upon. If no such principled understanding of what they mean may be thought of as obtainable, then (whatever other treasures he possesses) he cannot even count on the first thing.

I speak of *assertion* conditions as that by which meaning is given, and not yet of *truth* conditions, but only because within this meta-ethical framework the non-cognitivist's most distinctive non-formal thesis is likely to be the denial that the assertibility of a value judgement or of a deliberative judgement can amount to anything as objective as we suppose truth to be. The aim must be then to leave undecided *pro tempore*—as Dummett in one way and Davidson and McDowell in another have shown to be possible—the relationship of truth and assertibility.[22] In this way we arrange

---

[22] See M. A. E. Dummett, *Frege: Philosophy of Language* (London: Duckworth, 1973) and John McDowell, 'Bivalence and Verificationism', in Gareth Evans and John McDowell (eds.), *Truth and Meaning: Essays in Semantics* (Oxford: Oxford University Press, 1972). McDowell shows how we can build up an independent account of what a semantical predicate F will have to be like if the sentences of an object language are to be interpreted by means of equivalences which will say what the object language sentences mean. His way of showing that it can be a *discovery*, so to speak, that it is the truth predicate which fulfils the requirements on F is prefigured at p. 210 of Donald Davidson, 'Truth and Meaning', *Synthèse*, 17 (1967).

matters so that it can turn out—as it does for empirical or scientific utterances—that truth is a special case of assertibility; but it is not theoretically excluded that, for certain classes of judgements, assertibility should fall short of truth. The matter is left open, and it is for meta-ethics and the informal theory that is built around the formal theory to close it. I come now to this informal theory.

Adapting Tarski's so-called 'convention T' to the purposes of the formal theory, we may say now that the metalanguage has a materially adequate definition of the predicate 'assertible' just in case it has as consequences all sentences obtained from the schema '*s* is assertible if and only if *p*' by substituting for '*s*' a name of any sentence of *L* and substituting for '*p*' the translation or interpretation of this sentence in the metalanguage.[23] So if the ethical theorist is to erect a theory of objectivity, subjectivity, relativism, or whatever upon these foundations, then the next thing we need to say some more about is how a theory of *L*-assertibility is to be constrained in order to ensure that the sentence used on the right-hand side of any particular equivalence that is entailed by the theory of assertibility should indeed interpret or translate the sentence mentioned on the left. What is *interpretation* or *translation* in this context? If we can supply this constraint then, as a bonus, we shall understand far better the respective roles of participant and theorist and what assertibility would have to amount to.

It seems obvious that the only way to bypass Tarski's explicit use of the word 'translation' is by reference to what Davidson has called radical interpretation.[24] A promising proposal is this. Rewrite convention T to state that the metalanguage possesses an empirically correct definition of 'assertible' just in case the semantical axioms, in terms of which the definition of assertibility is given, all taken together, entail a set Σ of equivalences '*s* is assertible just in case *p*', one equivalence for each sentence of *L*, with the following overall property: a theorist who employs the condition *p* with which each sentence *s* is mated in a Σ-equivalence, and who employs the equivalence to interpret utterances of *s*, is in the best position he can be to make the *best possible overall sense* there is to be

---

[23] See p. 187 of A. Tarski, 'The Concept of Truth in Formalized Languages', in *Logic, Semantics, and Metamathematics* (Oxford: Oxford University Press, 1956). For my present doubts that there is anything to be gained, except an expository point, by the fabrication of a predicate of semantic assessment that is independent of 'true' in the fashion that 'assertible' might seem to promise to be, see Wiggins, *Needs, Values, Truth*, essay IV, sect. 18.

[24] See D. Davidson, 'Radical Interpretation', *Dialectica*, 27 (1973), 313–28. The original problem is of course Quine's. See W. V. O. Quine, *Word and Object* (Cambridge, Mass.: MIT Press, 1960). Davidson's own conception has been progressively refined by many philosophers, notably by Richard Grandy, Donald Davidson, Christopher Peacocke, Gareth Evans, and John McDowell. See also *Needs, Values, Truth*, 141–7.

made of L-speakers. This goal sets a real constraint—witness the fact that the theorist may test his theory, try it out as a way of making sense of his subjects, even as he constructs it. By 'making sense of them' would be meant ascribing to the speakers of L, on the strength of their linguistic and other actions, an intelligible collection of beliefs, needs, and concerns. That is a collection that diminishes to the bare minimum the need for the interpreter to ascribe inexplicable error or inexplicable irrationality to them.[25] By 'interpreting an utterance of s' is intended here: saying what it is that s is used to say.

This general description is intended to pass muster for the interpretation of a totally alien language. But now suppose that we envisage the object language and metalanguage both being English. Then we can turn radical interpretation to advantage in order to envisage ourselves as occupying simultaneously the roles of theorist or interpreter and subject or participant. That will be to envisage ourselves as engaged in an attempt to understand ourselves.

Whether we think of things in this way or not, it is very important to note how essentially similar are the positions of the linguistic theorist and his subjects. The role of the theorist is only to *supplement*, for theoretical purposes, the existing understanding of L-speakers. It is true that, subject to the constraint upon which the whole exercise of interpretation itself rests—namely sufficient agreement in beliefs, concerns, and conceptions of what is rational and what is not—the theorist need not have exactly the same beliefs as his subjects. But the descriptions of the world that are available to him are essentially the same sorts of description as those available to his subjects. He uses the very same sort of sentence to describe the conditions under which s is assertible as the sentence s itself: and the

---

[25] See Richard Grandy, 'Reference, Meaning, and Belief', *Journal of Philosophy*, 70 (1973), 439–52; John McDowell, 'Bivalence and Verificationism'. The requirement that we diminish to the minimum the theoretical need to postulate inexplicable error or irrationality is a precondition of trying to project any interpretation at all upon alien speakers. It was phrased by Davidson in another way, and called by him the requirement of charity. The replacement given here is closer to what has been dubbed by Richard Grandy the requirement of *humanity*. The further alterations reflect the belief that philosophy must desist from the systematic destruction of the sense of the word 'want', and that what Davidson calls 'primary reasons' must be diversified to embrace a wider and more diverse class of affective states than *desire*. (For a little more on these points, see now my *Sameness and Substance* (Oxford: Basil Blackwell, 1980), longer note 6.36.)

Note that, even though we must for purposes of radical interpretation project upon L-speakers our own notions of rationality (and there is no proof they are the sole possible), and even though we take all the advantage we can of the fact that the speakers of the object language are like us in being men, there is no guarantee that there must be a unique best theory of the assertibility conditions of their utterances. It has not been excluded that there might be significant disagreement between interpreters who have made equally good overall sense of the shared life of speakers of L, but at some points rejected one another's interpretations of L.

metalanguage is at no descriptive distance from the object language. If the theorist believes his own semantic theory, then he is committed to be ready to put his mind where his mouth is at least once for each sentence s of the object language, in a statement of assertion conditions for s in which he himself uses either s or a faithful translation of s. It follows that the possibility simply does not exist for the theorist to stand off entirely from the language of his subjects or from the viewpoint that gives this its sense. He has to begin at least by embracing—or by making as if to embrace—the very same commitments and world-view as the ordinary speakers of the object language. (This is not to say that having understood them, he cannot then back off from that world-view. What requires careful statement is how he is to do so.)

8

Even if this is a disappointment to those who have supposed that by means of meta-ethics, the theorist of value could move straight to a position of complete neutrality, it faces us in the right direction for the reconstitution of the non-cognitive theory. In fact the framework I have been proposing precisely enables him to register his own distinctive point. He can do so in at least two distinctive ways. The first accepts and the second actually requires that framework.

First, using the language of his subjects but thinking (as a moralist like a Swift or an Aristophanes should, or as any moral theorist may) a bit harder than the generality of his subjects, he may try to make them look at themselves; and he may prompt them to see their own pursuits and concerns in unaccustomed ways. There is an optical metaphor that is much more useful here than that of perspective. Staying within the participant perspective, what the theorist may do is *lower the level of optical resolution*. Suppressing irrelevancies and trivialities he may perceive, and then persuade others to perceive, the capriciousness of some of the discriminations we unthinkingly engage in; or the obtuseness of some of the assimilations that we are content with. Again, rather differently but placing the non-cognitivist closer within reach of his own hobby-horse, he may direct the attention of his audience to what Aurel Kolnai called 'the incongruities of ordinary practice'.[26] Here Kolnai alluded to the irremovable disproportion between how heroic is the effort that it is biologically instinct in us to put into the pursuit of certain of our concerns, and how 'finite, limited,

---

[26] 'The Utopian Mind', MS, 77.

transient, perishable, tiny, tenuous' we ourselves and our goods and satisfactions all are. To lower the level of resolution, not down to the point where human concerns themselves are invisible—we shall come to that— but to the point where both the disproportion and its terms are manifest, is a pre-condition of human (as opposed to merely animal) resilience, of humour, of sense of proportion, of sanity even. It is the traditional function of the moralist who is a participant and of the satirist (who may want not to be). But this way of seeing is not the seeing of the total meaninglessness that Taylor spoke of. Nor, in the existentialist philosopher's highly techni- cal sense, is it the perception of absurdity. For the participant perspective can contain together both the perception of incongruity and a nice appre- ciation of the limited but not necessarily infinitesimal importance of this or that particular object or concern. (It is not perfectly plain what Kolnai thought about the affinity of existentialist absurdity and incongruity—and his manuscript is unrevised—but, if Kolnai had doubted the compatibility of the perceptions of incongruity and importance, I think I could have convinced him by a very Kolnaistic point. The disproportion between our effort and our transience is a fugitive quantity. It begins to disappear as soon as one is properly impressed by it. For it is only to us or our kind that our own past or future efforts can seem heroic.)

So much then for the non-cognitivist's first way of making his chief point. It will lead to nothing radical enough for him. The second way to make his point is to abstract it from the long sequence of preposterous attempts at traditional philosophical analysis of *good*, *ought*, *right*, etc. in terms of pleasure or feeling or approval ... and to transform it into an informal observation concerning the similarity or difference between the status of assertibility enjoyed by evaluative judgements and practical judgements, on the one hand, and the status of plain, paradigmatic, or canonical truth enjoyed by (for example) historical or geographical judgements on the other hand.[27]

What then is plain truth? Well, for purposes of the comparison, perhaps it will be good enough to characterize it by what may be called the truisms of plain truth. These truisms I take to be (1) the primacy of truth as a dimension of the assessment of judgements: (2) the answerability of truth to evidenced argument that will under favourable conditions converge upon agreement whose proper explanation involves that very truth; and (3) the independence of truth both from our will and from our own limited means of recognizing the presence or absence of the property in a state- ment. (2) and (3) together suggest the truism (4) that every truth is true in

---

[27] See in this connection Wiggins, *Needs, Values, Truth*, essay IV.

virtue of something. We shall expect further (5) that every plain truth is compatible with every other plain truth. Finally, a putative further truism (6*) requires the complete determinacy of truth and of all questions whose answers can aspire to that status.[28]

Does the assertibility of evaluative judgements and/or deliberative judgements come up to this standard? If we press this question within the framework just proposed, the non-cognitivist's distinctive doctrine becomes the contention that the answer is *no*. The question can be pressed from a point that is well within reach. We do not need to pretend to be outside our own conceptual scheme, or at a point that ought to have been both inaccessible and unthinkable.[29] The question is one we can pursue by working with informal elucidations of truth and assertibility that can be fruitfully constrained by the project of radical interpretation.[30] And as regards the apparent incoherence of Taylor's non-cognitivism, we can supersede the separate outer and inner perspectives by a common perspective that is accessible to both theorist and participant. Suppose it is asserted that this, that, or the other thing is worth doing, and that the assertion is made on the best sort of grounds known to participant or theorist. Or suppose that a man dies declaring that his life has been marvellously worth while. The non-cognitive theory is first and foremost a theory not about the meaning but about the *status* of those remarks: that their assertibility is not plain truth and reflects no fact of the matter. What is more, this is precisely the suspicion that sometimes troubles and perplexes the untheoretical participant who is moved to ask the questions from which we began this inquiry. Finally, let it be noticed, and put down to the credit of the framework being commended, that within this it was entirely predictable that the question was there to be asked.

9

The non-cognitivist's answer to the question can now be considered under two separate heads, value judgements (strict valuations) in general (this section) and deliberative judgements in general (Section 11).

[28] These formulations are superseded by the statement of the marks of truth given in Wiggins, *Needs, Values, Truth*, essay IV, sect. 5. (6*) does not survive there, for reasons that emerge in Sect. 10 below.

[29] Compare the manner in which we could ascertain from within the space that we occupy certain of the geometrical properties of that very space: e.g. discover whether all equilateral triangles we encounter, of whatever size, are in fact similar triangles. If not, then the space is non-Euclidean.

[30] Cp. Wiggins, *Needs, Values, Truth*, essay IV, sect. 4.

For the non-cognitive critique of the assertibility predicate as it applies to value judgements I propose to employ a formulation given by Bernard Williams. [31]

Relativism will be true, Williams says, just in case there are or can be systems of beliefs S_1 and S_2 such that:

(1) S_1 and S_2 are distinct and to some extent self-contained;

(2) Adherents of S_1 can understand adherents of S_2;

(3) S_1 and S_2 exclude one another—by (a) being comparable and (b) returning divergent yes–no answers to at least one question identifying some action or object type which is the locus of disagreement under some agreed description;

(4) S_1 and S_2 do not (for us here now, say) stand in real confrontation because, whichever of S_1 and S_2 is ours, the question of whether the other one is right lacks the relation to our concerns 'which alone gives any point or substance to appraisal: the only real questions of appraisal [being] about real options' (p. 255). 'For we recognize that there can be many systems S which have insufficient relation to our concerns for our [own] judgments to have any grip on them.'

If this is right then the non-cognitivist critique of valuations comes to this. Their mere assertibility as such lacks one of the truistic properties of plain truth: for an assertible valuation may fail even under favourable conditions to command agreement (cf. truism (2), Section 8). Again, there is nothing in the assertibility property itself to guarantee that all one by one assertible evaluations are *jointly* assertible (cf. truism (5)). Nor is it clear that where there is disagreement there is always something or other at issue (cf. truism (4)). For truth on the other hand we expect and demand all of this.

The participant will find this disturbing, even discouraging. But is Williams right about the compatibility of his four conditions?[32] He mentions among other things undifferentiated judgements of 'right' and 'wrong', 'ought' and 'ought not'. Here, where the point of agreement of disagreements or opting one way or another lies close to action, and radical

[31] 'The Truth in Relativism', *Proceedings of the Aristotelian Society*, 75 (1974–5), 215–28.

[32] Both for Williams's purposes and for ours—which is the status of the assertibility concept as it applies to value judgements, and then as it applies (Sect. 11) to deliberative or practical judgements—we have to be able to convert a relativism such as this, concerning as it does overall systems S_1 and S_2, into a relativism concerning this or that particular judgement or class of judgements identifiable and reidentifiable across S_1 and S_2. Williams requires this in order that disagreement shall be focused. I require it in order to see whether it is possible to distinguish judgements in S_1 or S_2 whose assertibility conditions coincide with plain truth from other judgements where this is dubious.

interpretation is correspondingly less problematical, I think he is on strong ground. We can make good sense of conditions (2) and (3) being satisfied together. We can easily imagine condition (4) being satisfied. But for valuations in the strict and delimited sense, such as 'brave', 'dishonest', 'ignoble', 'just', 'malicious', 'priggish', there is a real difficulty. The comparability condition (3) requires that radical interpretation be possible. But radical interpretation requires the projection by one man upon an alien man of a collection of beliefs, desires, and concerns that differ from the interpreter's own only in a fashion that the interpreter can describe and, to some extent, explain: and the remoter the link between the word to be interpreted and action, and (which is different) the more special the flavour of the word, the more detailed and delicate the projection that has to be possible to anchor interpretation. Evaluations raise both of these problems at once. (And one of the several factors that make the link between strict valuations and action so remote is something that Williams himself has prominently insisted upon in other connections—the plurality, mutual irreducibility, and incommensurability of goods.) The more feasible interpretation is here, the smaller must be the distance between the concerns of interpreter and subject.[33] But then the harder condition (4) is to satisfy.

In the theoretical framework of radical interpretation we shall suddenly see the point of Wittgenstein's dictum 'If language is to be a means of communication there must be agreement not only in definitions but, queer as this may sound, agreement in judgements also.'[34]

10

The difficulty the non-cognitivist is having in pressing his claim at this point is scarcely a straightforward vindication of cognitivism. If the case for the coincidence of truth and assertibility in evaluative judgements is made in the terms of Section 9, then truth itself is in danger of coming in the process to seem a fairly parochial thing. It is strange to be driven to the conclusion that the more idiosyncratic the customs of a people, the more inscrutable their form of life, and the more special and difficult their language to interpret, the smaller the problem of the truth status of their evaluations.

---

[33] There are valuations which are so specific, and so special in their point, that interpretation requires interpreter and subject to have in some area of concern the very same interests and the same precise focus. But specificity is only one part of the problem.

[34] *Philosophical Investigations*, § 242. Cf. § 241 and the rest of § 242. Cf. also p. 223 (*passim*): 'If a lion could talk, we couldn't understand him.'

It would be natural for someone perplexed by the question of the meaning of life to insist at this point that we shall not have found what it takes for individual lives to have the meaning we attribute to them unless we link meaning with rationality. He will say that the threat of relativism does not depend on Williams's condition (3) in Section 9 being satisfied. The threat is rather that, contrary to the tenor of Section 5, the reasons that impress us as good reasons have no foundation in reason at all. Or as Hume states the point in a famous passage of the First Appendix to the *Enquiry Concerning the Principles of Morals*:

It appears evident that the ultimate ends of human actions can never, in any case, be accounted for by *reason*, but recommend themselves entirely to the sentiments and affections of mankind, without any dependence on the intellectual faculties. Ask a man *why he uses exercise*; he will answer, *because he desires to keep his health*. If you then enquire, *why he desires health*, he will readily reply, *because sickness is painful*. If you push your enquiries farther, and desire a reason *why he hates pain*, it is impossible he can ever give any. This is an ultimate end, and is never referred to any other object.

Perhaps to your second question, *why he desires health*, he may also reply, that *it is necessary for the exercise of his calling*. If you ask, *why he is anxious on that head*, he will answer, *because he desires to get money*. If you demand *Why? It is the instrument of pleasure*, says he. And beyond this it is an absurdity to ask for a reason. It is impossible there can be a progress *in infinitum*; and that one thing can always be a reason why another is desired. Something must be desirable on its own account, and because of its immediate accord or agreement with human sentiment and affection.

Not only is it pointless to hope to discover a *rational* foundation in human sentiment and affection. It is not even as if human sentiment and affection will *effectively* determine the difference between the worth while and the not worth while. Each culture, and each generation in each culture, confronts the world in a different way and reacts to it in a different way.

This scepticism pointedly ignores all the claims I made earlier, in Section 5. Rallying to their support, I ask: What does this scepticism show about our own judgements of significance or importance? After all there is no such thing as a rational creature of no particular neurophysiological formation or a rational man of no particular historical formation. And even if, inconceivably, there were such, why should we care about what this creature would find compelling? It is not in this make-believe context that we are called upon to mount a critique of our own conceptions of the objective, the true, and the worth while.

So much seems to hang on this, but the reply comes so close to simply repeating the words of the relativist whom it is meant to challenge, that there is no alternative but to illustrate what happens when we do try to think of rationality in the absolute impersonal or cosmic fashion that it seems our interlocutor requires.

It is interesting that, so far as rationality in theoretical beliefs is concerned, it is by no means impossible for us to conceive of thinking in the impersonal way. Suppose we take a Peircean view of Science as discovering that which is destined, the world being what it is, to be ultimately agreed by all who investigate.[35] Let 'all' mean 'all actual or possible intelligent beings competent, whatever their conceptual scheme, to look for the fundamental explanatory principles of the world'. Then think of all these theories gradually converging through isomorphism towards identity. Cosmic rationality in belief will then consist in conforming one's beliefs so far as possible to the truths that are destined to survive in this process of convergence.[36]

Perhaps this is all make-believe. (Actually I think it isn't.) But the important thing is that, if we identify properties across all theories that converge upon what are destined to be agreed upon (by us or any other determined natural researchers) as the fundamental principles of nature, then the only non-logical, non-mathematical predicates we shall not discard from the language of rational belief are those which, in one guise or another, will always pull their weight in all explanatorily adequate theories of the world. As a result, and corresponding to predicates fit and not fit so to survive, we shall have a wonderful contrast between the primary qualities of nature and all other qualities. We can then make for ourselves a fact–value distinction that has a real and definite point. We can say that no value predicate stands for any real primary quality, and that the real properties of the world, the properties which inhere in the world *however it is viewed*, are the primary qualities.[37]

[35] Cf. C. S. Peirce: 'How to Make our Ideas Clear', *Popular Science Monthly*, 12 (1878), 286–302. 'Different minds may set out with the most antagonistic views, but the progress of investigations carries them by a force outside themselves to one and the same conclusion. This activity of thought by which we are carried, not where we wish but to a foreordained goal, is like the operation of destiny. No modification of the point of view taken, no selection of other facts for study, no natural bent of mind even, can enable a man to escape the predestinate opinion. This great law is embodied in the conception of truth and reality. The opinion which is fated to be ultimately agreed to by all who investigate is what we mean by the truth, and the object represented in this opinion is the real. That is the way I would explain reality.'

[36] Inasmuch as there is a reality which dictates the way a scientific theory has to be in order that what happens in the world be explained by the theory, the difficulties of radical interpretation, attempted against the background of the truth about the world and the unwaveringly constant desire of speakers of the language to understand the material world, are at their slightest.

[37] One should talk here also of the fundamental physical constants. Cf. B. A. W. Russell, *Human Knowledge* (London: Allen & Unwin, 1948), 41: 'These constants appear in the fundamental equations of physics ... it should be observed that we are much more certain of the importance of these constants than we are of this or that interpretation of them. Planck's

This is a very stark view. It expresses what was an important element of truth in the 'external' perspective. Seeing the world in this way, one sees no meaning in anything.[38] But it is evidently absurd to try to reduce the sharpness of the viewpoint by saying that meaning can be introduced into the world thus seen by the addition of human commitment. Commitment to what? This Peircean conceptual scheme *articulates* nothing that it is humanly possible to care about. It does not even have the expressive resources to pick out the extensions of 'red', 'chair', 'earthquake', 'person', 'famine' . . . For none of these has any claim to be a factual predicate by the scientific criterion. The distinction of fact and value we reach here, at the very limit of our understanding of scientific understanding, cannot be congruent with what the non-cognitivists intended as their distinction. It is as dubious as ever that there is anything for them to have intended. Starting out with the idea that value properties are mental projections, they have discovered that, if value properties are mental projections, then, except for the primary qualities, all properties are mental projections.

We come now to practical rationality for all conceivable rational agents. (Cosmically valid practical rationality.) The idea here would be, I suppose, that to be serious about objective reasons, or why anything matters, one must try to ascend closer to the viewpoint of an impersonal intelligence;[39] and that the properties of such an intelligence should be determinable a priori. A great deal of time and effort has been channelled into this effort. It might have been expected that the outcome would be the transformation of the bareness of our conception of an impersonal intelligence into the conception of an impersonal intelligence of great bareness. What was not so plainly to be expected was that the most elementary part of the subject should immediately collide—as it has—with a simple and (within the discipline thus a priori conceived) unanswerable paradox—the so-called

constant, in its brief history since 1900, has been represented in various ways, but its numerical value has not been affected . . . Electrons may disappear completely from modern physics but e [charge] and m [mass] are pretty certain to survive. In a sense it may be said that the discovery and measurement of these constants is what is most solid in modern physics.

[38] Cf. Tolstoy, *Anna Karenina* (Harmondsworth: Penguin, 1978), 820: '[Levin was] stricken with horror, not so much at death, as at life, without the least conception of its origin, its purpose, its reason, its nature. The organism, its decay, the indestructibility of matter, the law of the conservation of energy, evolution, were the terms that had superseded those of his early faith.' This is a description of what might pass as one stage in the transition we have envisaged as completed.

[39] Or of a human being surviving, Nagel, 'The Absurd', 720, 'with that detached amazement which comes from watching an ant struggle up a heap of sand'. Cf. p. 722, 'the philosophical judgement [of absurdity] contrasts the pretensions of life with a larger context in which *no* standards can be discovered, rather than with a context from which alternative overriding standards may be applied'.

'Prisoner's Dilemma'.[40] What underlies the paradox (or the idea that there *is* here some paradox) is the supposition that it is simply obvious that an a priori theory of rational action ought to be possible—that some cosmic peg must exist on which we can fasten a set of concerns clearly and unproblematically identified *independently* of all ideals of agency and rationality themselves. First you have a set of concerns; then you think of a way that they might be best brought about. That was the picture. But, in a new guise, it was nothing other than the absurd idea that all deliberation is really of means.[41]

11

I conclude that there is no such thing as a pure a priori theory of rationality: and that even if there were such, it would always have been irrelevant to the problem of finding a meaning in life, or seeing anything as worth while. What we need is to define non-cognitivist relativism in a way that is innocent of all dependence on a contrast between our rationality and objective rationality yet restates Taylor.

It now says: Perhaps all strict valuations of the more specific and interesting kind have the interesting property that the interpretation of the value predicate itself presupposes a shared viewpoint, and a set of concerns common between interpreter and subject. Let it be admitted that this does the fact–value distinction no good. If someone insists, then there is

---

[40] Cf. R. C. Jeffrey, *The Logic of Decision* (New York: McGraw-Hill, 1965), 11–12. I take this as a 'paradox' in the following sense: a general principle of decision-theoretic prudence, generalizable to any agent whatever caught in the relevant circumstances, will lead in a wide variety of applications to what must be agreed by everybody to be a situation which is worse than it might have been for each participant if he had not acted on the generalizable principle—or if there had been another generalizable decision-theoretic principle to recommend (which there is not).

To say this is not to 'solve' the paradox. It cannot be solved. But it could only be accounted a real paradox if there were some antecedent grounds to suppose that it *should* have been possible to construct an a priori theory of rationality or prudence such that 'rational (*A*)' is incompatible with 'rational (not-*A*)', and such that that rationality is definable both independently of morality and ideals of agency and in such a way as to have independent leverage in these ancient disputes. (Cf. Plato, *Republic*, 445a.)

For an illuminating account of some of the asymmetries it is rational to expect between an a priori theory of belief and an a priori theory of practical reasonableness, see Ronald de Sousa, 'The Good and the True', *Mind*, 83 (1974), 534–51.

[41] That practically all interesting deliberation relates to ends and their practical specification in the light of actually or potentially available constituents, and that the place of means–ends reasoning is subordinate in practical reason, is argued by A. T. Kolnai, 'Deliberation is of Ends', *Proceedings of the Aristotelian Society*, 36 (1962), 195–218, and in Wiggins, *Needs, Values, Truth*, essay VI, a divergent interpretation of Aristotle's thought on this point, but an account similar to Kolnai's of the problem itself.

nothing to prevent him from exploiting the collapse of that distinction in order to redescribe in terms of a shift or wandering of the 'value focus' all the profound changes in valuation that have occurred in history, when the Greek world became the Christian world, or the Christian world the Renaissance world. He may elect to say with Nicolai Hartmann, as John Findlay reports him, that these changes were all by-products of an intense consciousness of new values, whose swimming into the focus pushed out the old: that such newly apprehended values were not really new, only hitherto ignored.[42]

All this the non-cognitivist may let pass as harmless, however eccentrically expressed; and may in less colourful language himself assert. He may even allow *totidem verbis* that, just as the world cannot be prised by us away from our manner of conceiving it, so our manner of conceiving it cannot be prised apart from our concerns themselves.[43] (It is also open to him to assert the compatibility of anthropocentricity with the only thing that there is for us to mean by objectivity, and to concede that the differences between higher and lower forms of life are not fictitious. They are even objective, he will say, if you use the word 'objective' like that.) But here he will stick. Where he will not back down from Taylor's original position is in the denial that the differences are simply discovered. Rather they are invented. Not only are some of them invented in the strictest and most straightforward sense. All of them depend for their significance upon a framework that is a free construct.

Here at last we approach the distinctive nucleus of non-cognitivism (married, without the consent of either, to Williams's relativism). What the new position will say is that, in so far as anything matters, and in so far as human life has the meaning we think it has, that possibility is rooted in something that is arbitrary, contingent, unreasoned, objectively non-defensible—and not one whit the less arbitrary, contingent, and indefensible by virtue of the fact that the unconstrained inventive processes underlying it have been gradual, unconscious, and communal. Our form of life—or that in our form of life which gives individual lives a meaning—is

---

[42] See J. N. Findlay, *Axiological Ethics* (London: Macmillan, 1970). Cf. William James, *Talks to Teachers on Psychology: and to Students on some of Life's Ideals* (London: Longman, Green, 1899), 299. 'In this solid and tridimensional sense, so to call it, those philosophers are right who contend that the world is a standing thing with no progress, no real history. The changing conditions of history touch only the surface of the show. The altered equilibriums and redistributions only diversify our opportunities and open chances to us for new ideals. But, with each new ideal that comes into life, the chance for a life based on some old ideal will vanish; and he would needs be a presumptuous calculator who should with confidence say that the total sum of significance is positively and absolutely greater at any one epoch than at any other of the world.'

[43] Cf. A. J. Ayer, *The Central Questions of Philosophy* (London: Macmillan, 1974), 235: 'we have seen that the world cannot be prised away from our manner of conceiving it'.

not something that men have ever (as they are apt to say) found or discovered. It is not something that they can criticize or regulate or adjust with an eye to what is true or correct or reasonable. Even within the going enterprise of existing concerns and deliberations, it would be a sad illusion to suppose that the judgement that this or that is worth while, or that life is worth living (or worth leaving), would be simply and plainly true. That sort of terra firma is simply not to be had.

The doctrine thus reconstructed from the assets of bankrupted or naïve non-cognitivism I shall call the doctrine of cognitive underdetermination. Unlike the positions it descends from, this position does not contradict itself. It is consistent with its own rationale. And it can be explained without entering at all into the difficulties and ineffabilities of cultural relativism.

Suppose someone says: 'For me it is neither here nor there that I cannot prise my way of seeing the world apart from my concerns. This does nothing to answer my complaint that there is not *enough* meaning in the world. My life doesn't add up. Nothing matters sufficiently to me. My concerns themselves are too unimportant, too scattered, and too disparate.' Equally devastatingly to the naïve cognitivism that the doctrine of cognitive underdetermination bids us abandon, another man may say he finds that the objects of his concern beckon to him too insistently, too cruelly beguilingly, from too many different directions. 'I have learned that I cannot strive after all of these objects, or minister even to most of the concerns that stand behind them. To follow more than a minute subset is to be doomed to be frustrated in all. The mere validity—if it were valid— of the total set from which I am to choose one subset would provide no guarantee at all that any subset I can actually have will *add up* to anything that means anything to me.'

It is the non-cognitivist's continuing role to comment here that things can never add up for the complainant who finds too frustratingly much, or for the complainant who finds too inanely little, unless each man supplies something extra, some conception of his own, to make sense of things *for himself*.

The problem of living a life, he may say, is to realize or respect a long and incomplete or open-ended list of concerns which are always at the limit conflicting. The claims of all true beliefs (about how the world is) are reconcilable. Everything true must be consistent with everything else that is true (cf. truism (5) of Section 8). But not all the claims of all rational concerns or even of all moral concerns (that the world *be* thus or so) need be actually reconcilable. When we judge that this is what we must do now,[44]

---

[44] I have put '*must*', because *must* and *must not*, unlike *ought* and *ought not*, are genuine contraries.

or that that is what we'd better do, or that our life must now take one direction rather than another direction, we are not fitting truths (or even probabilities) into a pattern where a discrepancy proves that we have mistaken a falsehood for a truth.[45] Often we have to make a practical choice that another rational agent might understand through and through, not fault or even disagree with, but (as Winch has stressed)[46] make differently himself; whereas, if there is disagreement over what is factually true and two rational men have come to different conclusions, then we think it has to be theoretically possible to uncover some discrepancy in their respective views of the evidence. In matters of fact, we suppose that, if two opposing answers to a yes–no question are equally good, then they might as well have been equally bad. But in matters of practice, we are grateful for the existence of alternative answers. The choice between them is then up to us. Here is our freedom. But here too is the bareness of the world we inhabit. If there were practical truth it would have to violate the third and fifth truisms of truth ((3) and (5) of Section 8 above). In living a life there is no truth, and there is nothing *like* regular truth, for us to aim at. Anybody who supposes that the assertibility of 'I must do this' or the assertibility of 'This is the way for me to live, not that' consists in their plain truth is simply deluded.

Aristotle wrote (*Nicomachean Ethics*, 1094[a]23): 'Will not knowledge of the good have a great influence on life? Shall we not, like archers who have a mark to aim at, be more likely to hit upon the right thing?' But in reality there is no such thing as *The Good*, no such thing as knowledge of it, and nothing fixed independently of ourselves to aim at. Or that is what is implied by the thesis of cognitive underdetermination.

12

If there is any common ground to be discovered in modern literature and one broad stream of modern philosophy it is here. What philosophers,

---

[45] See B. A. O. Williams, 'Consistency and Realism', *Proceedings of the Aristotelian Society*, suppl. vol. 40 (1966), 1–22, and cf. Findlay, *Axiological Ethics*, 74–5. 'What is good [Hartmann tells us] necessarily lies in a large number of incompatible directions, and it is intrinsically impossible that all of these should be followed out into realisation. One cannot, for example, achieve pure simplicity and variegated richness in the same thing or occasion, and yet both incontestably make claims upon us . . . in practice we sacrifice one good to another, or we make compromises and accommodations . . . such practical accommodations necessarily override the claims of certain values and everywhere consummate something that in some respect [ideally] ought not to be . . . a man [ideally should] be as wise as a serpent and gentle as a dove, but that does not mean that . . . it is *possible* for him to be both of them.'

[46] Peter Winch, 'The Universalizability of Moral Judgements', *Monist*, 49 (1965), 196–214.

even philosophers of objectivist formation, have constantly stressed is the absence of the unique solutions and unique determinations of the practical that naïve cognitivism would have predicted.[47] They have thus supplied the theoretical basis for what modern writers (not excluding modern writers who have believed in God) have felt rather as a void in our experience of the apprehension of value, and have expressed not so much in terms of the plurality and mutual irreducibility of goods as in terms of the need for an organizing focus or meaning or purpose that we ourselves *bring* to life. The mind is not only a receptor: it is a projector.[48]

At the end of *Anna Karenina* Levin says to himself:

> I shall still lose my temper with Ivan the coachman, I shall still embark on useless discussions and expressing my opinions inopportunely; there will still be the same wall between the sanctuary of my inmost soul and other people, even my wife . . . but my life now, my whole life, independently of anything that can happen to me, every minute of it is no longer meaningless as it was before, but has a positive meaning of goodness with which I have the power to invest it.

However remote such declarations may appear from the language of the non-cognitivist philosopher, this need for autonomous making or investing of which Levin speaks is one part of what, in my presentation of him, the non-cognitive philosopher means by cognitive underdetermination. The familiar idea is that we do not discover a meaning for life or strictly find one: we have to make do with an artefact or construct or projection— something as it were invented.[49] And, whereas discovery is answerable to truth, invention and construction are not. From this he concludes that a

---

[47] The plurality and mutual irreducibility of things good has been stressed by F. Brentano (*Origins of our Knowledge of Right and Wrong*, tr. R. Chisholm and E. Schneewind (New York: Humanities Press, 1961); see esp. para. 32); by N. Hartmann (see Findlay, *Axiological Ethics*); by Isaiah Berlin, see, for instance, *Four Essays on Liberty* (Oxford: Oxford University Press, 1969), introd., p. xlix; by Kolnai ('Deliberation is of Ends') and Williams ('Consistency and Realism'). See also Leszek Kolakowski, 'In Praise of Inconsistency', in *Marxism and Beyond* (London: Pall Mall, 1969); Stuart Hampshire, *Morality and Pessimism* (Cambridge: Cambridge University Press, 1972); and Wiggins, *Needs, Values, Truth*, essay VII.

[48] For the seed of this idea in Plotinus' theory of cognition and for its transplantation and subsequent growth, see M. H. Abrams, *The Mirror and the Lamp* (Oxford: Oxford University Press, 1953), Plotinus, *Ennead*, 4. 6. 2–3: 'The mind affirms something not contained within impression: this is the characteristic of a power—within its allotted sphere to act.' 'The mind gives radiance to the objects of sense out of its own store.'

[49] For a remarkable expression of the non-cognitivist's principal point and some others, see Aldous Huxley, *Do as you Will* (London: Chatto & Windus, 1929), 101. 'The purpose of life, outside the mere continuance of living (already a most noble and beautiful end), is the purpose we put into it. Its meaning is whatever we may choose to call the meaning. Life is not a crossword puzzle, with an answer settled in advance and a prize for the ingenious person who noses it out. The riddle of the universe has as many answers as the universe has living inhabitants. Each answer is a working hypothesis, in terms of which the answerer experiments with reality. The best answers are those which permit the answerer to live most fully, the worst are those which condemn him to partial or complete death . . . Every man has an inalienable right to the major

limited and low-grade objectivity is the very best one could hope for in predications of meaning or significance.

The non-cognitivist takes two steps here and the assessment of the second step concerning objectivity depends markedly on the notion of truth that is employed at the first. What is this notion, we need to know, and to what extent does the cognitivist's position depend upon a naïve and pre-critical understanding of it? Give or take a little—subtract perhaps the more indeterminate among subjunctive conditionals—the pre-critical notion of truth covers empirical judgements fairly well. But it consorts less well with conceptions of truth or assertibility defended in mathematics by mathematical intuitionists or mathematical constructivists. It is well worth remarking that, for someone who wanted to combine objectivity with a doctrine of qualified cognitivism or of underdetermination, there might be no better model than Wittgenstein's normative conception of the objectivity of mathematics; and no better exemplar than Wittgenstein's extended description of how a continuing cumulative process of making or constructing can amount to the creation of a shared form of life that is constitutive of rationality itself, furnishing proofs that are not compulsions but procedures to guide our conceptions, explaining, without explaining away, our sense that sometimes we have no alternative but to infer this from that.[50]

Perhaps this is a million miles from ethics. Or perhaps Wittgenstein's philosophy of mathematics is completely unsuccessful. But if the subject-matter of moral philosophy had any of the features that Wittgenstein attributed to the sort of subject-matter he thought he was treating, then the issue whether the assertibility of practical judgements was truth, and did or did not sufficiently approximate to the truth of statements universally agreed to be factual, might become relatively unimportant.[51] We could measure the distance, assess its importance, and think how to live with it. (Is there an independent case for tampering in certain ways with the received truisms of truth? Or should we leave them to define an ideal that practical judgement must fall far short of? How important really is the shortfall?)

---

premiss of his philosophy of life.' If anything need be added to this, presumably it is only that, concerning what 'living most fully' is for each man, the final authority must be the man himself. There is something right with this; but there is something wrong with it too.

[50] Cf. L. Wittgenstein, *Remarks on the Foundations of Mathematics* (Oxford: Basil Blackwell, 1956), III. 30.

[51] There is a cheap victory to be won even here of course. For it has proved much easier to achieve convergence or reflective equilibrium within our culture about the value of, say, civil liberty than about how exactly printing extra banknotes will act upon conditions of economic recession. But this is not the point I am making.

Of course, if practical judgements were candidates to be accounted simply true, then what made them true, unlike valuations,[52] could not be the world itself, whatever that is.[53] But, saying what they say, the world is not really what they purport to characterize. (Compare what Wittgenstein, whether rightly or wrongly, wanted to say about statements of arithmetic.) In the assertibility (or truth) of mathematical statements we see what perhaps we can never see in the assertibility of empirical (such as geographical or historical) statements: the compossibility of objectivity, discovery, *and* invention.

If we combine Wittgenstein's conception of mathematics with the constructivist or intuitionist views that are its cousins, then we find an illuminating similarity. One cannot get more out of the enterprise of making than one has in one way or another put there. ('What if someone were to reply to a question: "So far there is no such thing as an answer to this question"?'[54] And at any given moment one will have put less than everything into it. So however many determinations have been made, we never have a reason to think we have reached a point where no more decisions or determinations will be needed. No general or unrestricted affirmation is possible of the law of excluded middle. But then anyone who wishes to defend the truth status for practical judgements is released from claiming that every practical question already has an answer. For reasons both independent of the practical and helpful to its pretensions, we may doubt how mandatory it ever was to enter into the system of ideas and preconceptions that issues in such declarations as truism (6*) of Section 8 above.

I shall break off from these large questions with two points of comparison and contrast.

[52] Note that the distinction proposed at Sect. 4 between evaluation and practical judgement is observed both here and throughout this essay.

[53] Everything would be the wrong way round. Cf. Williams, 'Consistency and Realism', 19: 'the line on one side of which consistency plays its peculiarly significant role is the line between the theoretical and the practical, the line between discourse which (to use a now familiar formula) has to fit the world, and discourse which the world must fit. With discourse that is practical in these terms, we can see why . . . consistency . . . should admit of exception and should be connected with coherence notions of a less logical character.' This whole passage suggests something important, not only about statements of what ideally should be, but also about deliberative judgements—namely that the exigencies of having to decide what to believe are markedly dissimilar from the exigencies of having to decide how to act. What the argument does not show is that the only truth there could be in a practical judgement is a peculiar truth which transposes the onus of match on to the world. (Still less that, if one rejects that idea, then the onus of match would be from the sentence or its annexed action to an *ideal* world.) Williams has illuminatingly glossed (1) precisely why truth in a practical judgement would not be like that; (2) the reasons why 'Ought (A)' and 'Ought (not-A)' are actually consistent; and (3) why 'must (A)' (which *is* inconsistent with 'must (not-A)') is only strictly assertible or true if A is the unique thing you must here do.

[54] *Remarks on the Foundations of Mathematics*, IV. 9.

(i) It seems that in the sphere of the practical we may know for certain that there exist absolutely undecidable questions—e.g. cases where the situation is so calamitous or the choices so insupportable that nothing could count as the reasonable practical answer. In mathematics, on the other hand, it appears to be an undecidable question even how much sense attaches to the idea of an absolutely undecidable question. This is a potentially important discrepancy between the two subject-matters. If we insist upon the actuality of some absolute undecidability in the practical sphere, then we shall burst the bounds of ordinary, plain truth. To *negate* the law of excluded middle is to import a contradiction into the intuitionist logic which our comparison makes the natural choice for practical judgements. The *denial* of '((A would be right) or not (A would be right))' contradicts the intuitionist theorem '(not (not (p or not p)))'.

(ii) If a man makes an arithmetical mistake he may collide with a brick wall or miss a train. He may bankrupt himself. For each calculatión there is some risk, and for each risk a clear mark of the worst's having befallen us. There is nothing so definite with practical judgements. But surely it is begging the question to require it. Equally, it is begging the question to shrug this off without another word.

13

Let us review what has been found, before trying to advance further.

Whether practical judgements can attain to truth or not, and whatever is the extent and importance of cognitive underdetermination, we have found no overwhelming reason to deny all objectivity to practical judgements. That practical questions often have more than one answer, and that there is not always an ordering of better or worse answers, is no reason to conclude that good and bad answers cannot be argumentatively distinguished.

It is either false or senseless to deny that what valuational predicates stand for are properties in a world. It is neither here nor there that these value properties are not primary qualities, provided that they be objectively discriminable and can impinge upon practical appreciation and judgement. No extant argument shows that they cannot.

Individual human lives can have more or less point in a manner partially dependent upon the disposition in the world of these value properties. The naïve non-cognitivist has sometimes given the impression that the way we give point to our lives is as if by blindfolding ourselves and attaching to something—anything—some free-floating commitment, a commitment that is itself sustained by the mere fact of our animal life. But that was a mistake. There is no question here of blindfolding. And that is not what is said or implied by the reconstructed doctrine of cognitive underdetermination.

Inasmuch as invention and discovery are distinguishable, and in so far as either or these ideas properly belongs here, life's having a point may depend as much upon something contributed by the person whose life it is as it depends upon something discovered. Or it may depend upon what the owner of the life brings to the world in order to see the world in such a way as to discover meaning. This cannot happen unless world and person are to some great extent reciprocally suited. And unluckily, all claims of human adaptability notwithstanding, those things are often not well suited to one another.

14

To get beyond here, something now needs to be said about the connection of meaning and happiness. In most moral philosophy, the requirement to treat meaning is commuted into the requirement to specify the end; and the end is usually identified with happiness. One thing that has seemed to make this identification plausible is the apparent correctness of the claim that happiness is the state of one's life having a point or meaning. But on any natural account of the relation of point and end, this claim is actually inconsistent with the equation 'Happiness = The End'. (Unless happiness can consist in simply having happiness as one's end.) It is also worth observing that, in the very special cases where it is straightforward to say what the point of someone's life is, we may say what he stands for, or may describe his life's work. (I choose these cases not because I think they are specially central but because they are specially clear.) The remarkable thing is that these specifications are not even categorially of a piece with happiness. That does not prove that happiness is *never* the point. The works of practical moralists are replete, however, with warnings of the difficulty or futility of making happiness the aim. If they are right then, by the same token, it would be futile to make it the point.

The misidentification—if misidentification it is—of happiness and end has had a long history. The first fully systematic equation of the end, the good for man, and happiness is Aristotle's. The lamentable and occasionally comical effects of this are much palliated by the close observation and good sense that Aristotle carried to the *specification* of happiness. And it may be said in Aristotle's defence that the charge of misidentification of

happiness and the good for man is captious, because his detailed specification of *eudaimonia* can perfectly well stand in—if this be what is
required—as a description of the point of human existence: also that
Aristotle meant by *eudaimonia* not exactly happiness but a certain kind of
success. But that is too quick. Unless we want to walk the primrose path to
the trite and solemn conclusion that a meaningful life is just a sum (cf.
Nicomachean Ethics, 1097^b 17) of activities worth while in themselves, or
self-complete (in the sense of *Metaphysics*, 1048^b 17), the question is worth
taking some trouble over. Not only is this proposition trite and solemn.
Read in the way Aristotle intended it is absurd.

Out of good nature a man helps his neighbour dig a drainage ditch. The
soil is hard but not impossibly intractable, and together the two of them
succeed in digging the ditch. The man who offers to help sees what he is
doing in helping dig the ditch as worth while. In so far as meaning is an
issue for him, he may see the episode as all of a piece with a life that has
meaning. He would not see it so, and he would not have taken on the task,
if it were impossible. In the case as we imagine it, the progress of the
project is integral to his pleasure in it. But so equally is the fact that he likes
his neighbour and enjoys working with him (provided it be on projects that
it is within their joint powers to complete).

Shall we say here that the man's helping dig the ditch is instrumental and
has the meaning or importance it has for the helper only derivatively?
Derivatively from what, on the non-cognitivist view? Or shall we say that
the ditch-digging is worth while in itself? But it isn't. It is end-directed. If
we cannot say either of these things, can we cut the Gordian knot by saying
both? In truth, the embracing of the end depends on the man's feeling
for the task of helping someone he likes. But his feeling for the project
of helping equally depends on the existence and attainability of the end of
digging the ditch.

This is not to deny that Aristotle's doctrine can be restored to plausibility if we allow the meaning of the particular life that accommodates the
activity to *confer* intrinsic worth upon the activity. But this is to reverse
Aristotle's procedure (which is the only procedure available to a pure
cognitivist). And I doubt we have to choose (cf. Section 6). At its modest
and most plausible best the doctrine of cognitive underdetermination can
say that we need to be able to think in both directions, down from point to
the human activities that answer to it, and up from activities whose intrinsic worth can be demonstrated by Aristotle's consensual method to forms
of life in which we are capable by nature of finding point.[55]

[55] Maybe neither the consensual method nor the argued discussion of such forms would be
possible in the absence of the shared neurophysiology that makes possible such community of
concepts and such agreement as exists in evaluative and deliberative judgements. Nor would

15

It might be interesting and fruitful to pick over the wreckage of defunct and discredited ethical theories and see what their negligence of the problem of life's having a meaning contributed to their ruin. I have little to report under this head. But it does seem plain that the failure of naturalistic theories, theories reductively identifying the Good or the End with some natural reality, has been bound up with the question of meaning. Surely the failure of all the reductive naturalisms of the nineteenth century—Pleasure and Pain Utilitarianism, Marxism, Evolutionary Ethics—was precisely the failure to discover in brute nature itself (either in the totality of future pleasures or in the supposedly inevitable advance of various social or biological-cum-evolutionary processes), anything that the generality of untheoretical men could find reason to invest with overwhelming *importance*. These theories offered nothing that could engage in the right way with human concerns or give point or focus to anyone's life. (This is the cognitivist version of a point that ought to be attributed to David Hume.)

Naturalistic theories have been replaced in our own time by prescriptivism, emotivism, existentialism, and neutral (satisfaction-based) utilitarianism. It is misleading to speak of them together. The second and third have had important affinities with moral Pyrrhonism. The first and fourth are very careful and, in the promotion of formal or second-order goods such as equality, tolerance, or consistency, rather earnest. But it is also misleading not to see these positions together.

Suppose that, when pleasure and absence of pain give place in an ethical theory to unspecified merely determinable satisfaction (and when the last drop of mentality is squeezed from the revealed preference theory which is the economic parallel of philosophical utilitarianism) a man looks to modern utilitarianism for meaning or happiness. The theory points him towards the greatest satisfaction of human beings' desires. He might embrace that end, if he could understand what that satisfaction consisted in.

there exist such faint prospects as do exist of attaining reflective equilibrium or finding a shared mode of criticism. But nature plays only a causal and enabling role here, not the unconvincing speaking part assigned to it by Ethical Naturalism and by Aristotelian Eudaimonism. Aristotle qualified by the addition 'in a complete life' (1098^a 16) the equation *eudaimonia = activity of soul in accordance with virtue*. And, tempering somewhat the *sum of goods* conception, he could agree with my strictures on the idea that the philosopher describes a meaning for life by building upwards from the special condition of its meaninglessness. But, as J. L. Austin used to complain, 'If *life* comes in at all, it should not come into Aristotle's argument as an afterthought.' And no help is to be had here from Aristotle's idea that, just as an eye has a function f such that the eye's goodness in respect of f = the good *for* the eye, so a man has his function. Eye:body::man:what? Cf. 1194^b 12. What is it for a man to find some function f that he can *embrace as his*, as giving his life meaning? Nature does not declare.

He might if he could see from his own case what satisfaction consisted in. But that is very likely where he started—unless, more wisely, he started closer to the real issue and was asking himself where he should look to find a point for his life. But, so far as either question is concerned, the theory has crossed out the infantile proposal 'pleasure and lack of pain',[56] and distorted and degraded (in description if not in fact) the complexity of the structure within which a man might have improved upon the childish answer for himself. For all questions of ends, all problems about what constitutes the attainment of given human ends, and all perplexities of meaning, have been studiously but fallaciously transposed by this theory into questions of instrumental means. But means to what? The theory is appreciably further than the nineteenth-century theory was from a conceptual appreciation of the structure of values and focused unfrustrated concerns presupposed to a man's finding a point in his life; and of the need to locate correctly happiness, pleasure, and a man's conception of his own unfolding life within that structure.

If we look to existentialism, we find something curiously similar. Going back to the formation of some of these ideas, I found André Maurois's description in *Call no Man Happy* of his teacher Alain (Émile-Auguste Chartier):

> what I cannot convey by words is the enthusiasm inspired in us by this search, boldly pursued with such a guide; the excitement of those classes which are entered with the persistent hope of discovering, that very morning, the secret of life, and from which one departed with the joy of having understood that perhaps there was no such secret but that nevertheless it was possible to be a human being and to be so with dignity and nobility. When I read in *Kim* the story of the Lama who sought so piously for the River of the Arrow, I thought of *our* search.[57]

What happens here—and remember that Alain was the teacher not only of Maurois but also of Sartre—goes wrong even in the question 'What is *the* meaning of life?' We bewitch ourselves to think that we are looking for some one thing like the Garden of the Hesperides, the Holy Grail . . . Then finding nothing like that in the world, no one thing from which all values can be derived and no one focus by which all other concerns can be organized, we console ourselves by looking inwards, but again for some one substitute thing, one thing in us now instead of the world. Of course if the search is conducted in this way it is more or less inevitable that the one consolation will be *dignity* or *nobility* or *commitment*: or more

---

[56] For the thought that this might be literally infantile, I am indebted indirectly to Bradley and directly to Richard Wollheim, 'The Good Self and the Bad Self', *Proceedings of the British Academy*, 61 (1975), 373–98.

[57] Tr. D. Lindley (London: Cape, 1943), 43.

spectatorially *irony, resignation, scorn* ... But, warm though its proper place is for each of these—important though each of them is in its own non-substitutive capacity—it would be better to go back to the 'the' in the original question; and to interest ourselves afresh in what everybody knows about—the set of concerns he actually has, their objects, and the focus he has formed or seeks to bring to bear upon these: also the prospects of purifying, redeploying or extending this set.[58]

Having brought the matter back to this place, how can a theorist go on? I think he must continue from the point where I myself ought to have begun if the products of philosophy itself had not obstructed the line of sight. Working within an intuitionism or moral phenomenology as tolerant of low-grade non-behavioural evidence as is literature (but more obsessively elaborative of the commonplace, and more theoretical, in the interpretive sense, than literature), he has to appreciate and describe the quotidian complexity of what is experientially involved in a man's seeing a point in living. It is no use to take a going moral theory—utilitarianism or whatever it is—and paste on to it such *postscripta* as the Millian insight 'It really is of importance not only what men do, but what manner of men they are that do it': or the insight that to see a point in living a man has to be such that he can like himself: or to try to superimpose upon the theory the structure that we have complained that utilitarianism degrades. If life's having a point is at all central to moral theory then room must be made for these things right from the very beginning. The phenomenological account I advocate would accommodate all these things in conjunction with (1) ordinary anthropocentric objectivity, (2) the elements of value focus and discovery, and (3) the element of invention that it is the non-cognitivist's conspicuous distinction to have imported into the argument.

Let us not underestimate what would have been done if this work were realized. But ought the theorist to be able to do more? Reluctant though I am to draw any limits to the potentiality or enterprise of discursive reason, I see no reason why he should. Having tamed non-cognitivism into a doctrine of cognitive underdetermination, which allows the world to impinge upon but not to determine the point possessed by individual lives, and which sees value properties not as created but as *lit up* by the focus that the man who lives the life brings to the world; and, having described what

---

[58] Cf. Williams, 'Persons, Character and Morality', in Amelie Rorty (ed.), *The Identities of Persons* (Berkeley: University of California Press, 1976): 'The categorical desires which propel one forward do not have to be even very evident to consciousness, let alone grand or large; one good testimony to one's existence having a point is that the question of its point does not arise, and the propelling concerns may be of a relatively everyday kind such as certainly provide the ground of many sorts of happiness' (cf. *Identities*, 209).

finding meaning is, it will not be for the theorist as such to intrude himself further. As Bradley says in *Appearance and Reality*: 'If to show theoretical interest in morality and religion is taken as setting oneself up as a teacher or preacher, I would rather leave these subjects to whoever feels that such a character suits him.'[59]

[59] 2nd edn. rev. (Oxford: Clarendon Press, 1946).

X

ETHICS AND THE FABRIC OF
THE WORLD

BERNARD WILLIAMS

John Mackie held[1] that values, in particular ethical values, were not objective, a denial which he took to mean that they were not 'part of the fabric
of the world' (p. 15; p. 58 of this volume). He stressed that this was to be
taken as an ontological thesis, as opposed to a 'linguistic or conceptual'
thesis, and to arrive at it was, for him, a matter of 'factual rather than
conceptual analysis' (p. 19; p. 61 of this volume). In this respect, he found
a parallel between value properties and secondary qualities, as he did more
generally, being prepared to say of both that they were 'projected' on to
the world. The idea of 'factual analysis', and the exact contrast that he
intended with conceptual analysis, are not entirely clear, and I suspect
that he put it in this way because he closely associated the conceptual and
the linguistic, and he wanted to stress—rightly—that the truth of what
he claimed was not going to be determined by an inquiry into the use of
ethical words. In any sense broader than that, it seems reasonable to hold,
as McGinn[2] has argued, that the question of the subjectivity of secondary
qualities is a conceptual question; and if that is, so will the same question
with respect to ethical qualities (as I shall, for the moment, vaguely call
them).

Mackie's own arguments for his conclusion make it unclear how this
could be a factual issue. One, the so-called 'argument from queerness',

From Ted Honderich (ed.), *Morality and Objectivity* (London: Routledge & Kegan Paul,
1985), 203–14. Reprinted by permission of Routledge Ltd.

[1] *Ethics: Inventing Right and Wrong* (Harmondsworth: Penguin, 1977); and first in 'A Refutation of Morals', *Australasian Journal of Psychology and Philosophy*, 24 (1964), 77–90. The
page references that I give in parentheses are to *Ethics*, or to Ch. V of this volume. I regret that
John Mackie and I never had an opportunity to discuss the kind of question raised here, though
we did talk about other issues in ethics, particularly utilitarianism. He would have certainly
brought to the discussion of our disagreements the clarity, honesty, and shrewd perception that
he so notably showed on all occasions, and he would also have recognized that on these
questions, the disagreements are rooted in a deeper agreement.
[2] *The Subjective View* (Oxford: Clarendon Press, 1983), to which I am indebted at several
points.

says in effect that the idea of ontologically objective values explains nothing and offends against parsimony: and the grounds of this criticism seem to be entirely a priori. The other, the 'argument from relativity', cites facts about the variation of ethical belief between cultures, and the plausible explanations of that variation that might be given by the social sciences. The facts about cultural variation can be accepted to be factual facts, even though, as is well known, their interpretation leaves a lot of room for disagreement. But that does not make the conclusion which Mackie draws from them into a factual rather than (in the broader sense) a conceptual conclusion. Even if mankind displayed more unanimity in its ethical reactions than it does—or unanimity, one might say, at a more specific level— that would not seem to make the reactions more objective, on Mackie's view, but simply more like perceptions of secondary qualities. We shall see later that cultural variation does play a part in the argument, but it is at a different level.

Mackie was prepared to call his position 'moral scepticism', though he made it clear that this was not meant to imply any first-order indifferentism, or the rejection of moral considerations as bearing on practical reason. He described his account as an 'error theory' of moral judgements. (The error in question seems, very roughly, to be that of taking moral values to be objective.) Mackie himself said that the name 'moral scepticism' was appropriate (p. 35; p. 73 of this volume) just because it was an error theory: presumably because the theory exposes as false something that common sense is disposed to believe. At the same time, however, he did not suppose that when this error was exposed, everyday moral convictions would properly be weakened or opened to doubt. I shall come back to the question of how these claims hang together. However, it is worth asking at this point why one should be more disposed, on the strength of the first of these claims (the error theory), to apply the name 'moral scepticism' to Mackie's view, than one is to withhold that name in virtue of the second claim—that everyday conviction is properly unshaken. That is not an obvious preference, and the fact that Mackie did choose to use 'moral scepticism' in this way reveals some assumptions. I take them to be, first, that scepticism is essentially concerned with knowledge or the lack of it, and, second, that in view of the error theory, there is no moral knowledge.

Particularly granted Mackie's own views, I do not think that this is the most helpful way to use this phrase. Scepticism is basically concerned with doubt, and not necessarily with (the denial of) knowledge. Where it is knowledge that is appropriately pursued in order to put an end to doubt, a denial that knowledge is possible will lead to a sceptical position; but in areas where, on a true view, there is no question of knowledge, and to seek it is inappropriate, this is not so. Scepticism will rather be whatever attacks conviction in those areas. On Mackie's view, which (as I take it) sees the moral as no candidate for knowledge at all, moral scepticism should rather be a position that upsets moral conviction, for instance by claiming that moral considerations have no place in practical reasoning. Of course, if the two claims, as I have called them, cannot after all be kept apart, there might be a good reason for thinking that the error theory was indeed a form of moral scepticism.

Mackie applied the error theory in ethics very widely. It is not simply a matter of those ethical perceptions that are nearest to certain aesthetic reactions, such as that certain people or actions are horrible. Many might agree that the perception of those characteristics can reasonably be assimilated in some degree to the perception of secondary qualities. Nor is it simply a matter of goodness. He says (p. 15; p. 58 of this volume) that in claiming moral values not to be objective, he intends to include, besides moral goodness, 'other things that could be more loosely called moral values or disvalues—rightness and wrongness, duty, obligation . . . and so on'.

In the same spirit, he connects (p. 29; p. 69 of this volume) the denial of objective values with the rejection of a categorical imperative: 'So far as ethics is concerned, my thesis that there are no objective values is specifically the denial that any such categorically imperative element is objectively valid. The objective values which I am denying would be action-directing absolutely, not contingently . . . upon the agent's desires and inclinations.'

This claim raises very sharply the question of what the objectivity is that Mackie is denying. It is not immediately clear what it could mean to say that a requirement or demand was 'part of the fabric of the world'. It might possibly mean that some agency which made the demand or imposed the requirement was part of the fabric, but, even if it were, that fact in itself would not be enough to make its demand categorical in the relevant sense. In purely logical or syntactic terms, of course, the demands of such an agent might be categorical, but so might the demands of any agent whatsoever. The person who peremptorily says 'get out of the way' speaks categorically. What he is telling you to do is to get out of the way, not to get out of the way unless you don't mind getting hurt: if you don't mind getting hurt, and stay in his way, you still prevent the state of affairs that he means to bring about. In this, his imperative is (logically) categorical, while the imperatives in the washing-machine instructions (or most of them) are logically hypothetical, even though their antecedent, which is very obvious, is usually suppressed. But this, the question whether an imperative is *intended* categorically, is not the point. The question is rather about the status of some logically categorical imperative, whether an agent in some sense goes wrong who does not recognize it as a demand on him. Whatever that may turn out to mean, it cannot be the same as the question whether there is an agent 'in the fabric of the world' who makes that demand. If there is an exceptional agent in, or perhaps outside, the world whose demands do have that character, that will be because of his nature, not simply because he is 'out there'.

Consider another picture of what it would be for a demand to be 'objectively valid'. It is Kant's own picture.[3] According to this, a demand will be inescapable in the required sense if it is one that a rational agent must accept if he is to be a rational agent. It is, to use one of Kant's favourite metaphors, *self-addressed* by any rational agent. Kant was wrong, in my view, in supposing that the fundamental demands of morality were objective in this sense, but that is not the immediate point, which is that the conception deploys an intelligible and adequate sense of objectivity. It seems to have little to do with those demands being part of the fabric of the world; or, at any rate, they will be no more or less so than the demands of logic—which was, of course, part of Kant's point.

Kant's theory offers an *objective grounding* of morality which is not (as one might say) realist. Moral claims are objectively correct or incorrect, but when one gives a general explanation of what makes them so, that explanation does not run through the relation between those statements and the world, but rather through the relation between *accepting* those statements, and practical reason. There are other candidates for a theory that is objective but not realist, such as a theory which suggests that one must have the desires appropriate to the ethical life if one is going to be in good shape as a human being, where the idea of 'being in good shape' is one that can be explained at least partly (it need not be wholly) prior to the ethical life. This again would be objectivity, and there would be ethical correctness, but it would be basically a correctness of desire, and arriving at it would be a feat of practical reasoning; or if of theoretical reasoning, then, to a significant degree, of a non-ethical kind (establishing, for instance, the appropriate psychological truths).

Even if no theory of these kinds is sound, the possibility of them is important for the present discussion. This is not because it shows Mackie

---

[3] Some of the immense confusion that surrounds this subject comes from the fact that Kant, who started it off, expressed himself in terms of a logical distinction between categorical and hypothetical. Readers of the *First Critique* should not be surprised to find him using what seems to be logical distinction to make a different level of point.

to have been looking for objectivity in the wrong place. The significant point is that under these possibilities we are *still* presented with the phenomenon that attracted Mackie's diagnosis, and they help one to understand what needs diagnosing. Suppose that the ethical life could be objectively grounded in one of these ways. One could come to know that it was so grounded, by developing or learning philosophical arguments which showed that ethical life satisfied the appropriate condition, of being related in the right way to practical reason or to well-being. But ethical life itself would continue to involve various experiences and judgements of the kind that present themselves as 'objective'—and what they present is not the objectivity which, on these theories, they would genuinely possess. They are not experienced as satisfying any such condition. This is notably clear in the Kantian case, and Kant saw the point himself. In acknowledging the categorical demand of obligation or recognizing a moral requirement (the kind of thing expressed in saying, for moral reasons, 'I must'), one does not experience it as an application of the demands of practical reason, but as something more immediate than that, something presented to one by the facts. That is one reason why Kant found an empirical psychological surrogate of one's rational relations to morality, in the emotional phenomenon of the sense of reverence for the Law. That feeling does, on Kant's theory, represent objectivity. But it also misrepresents it, by making it seem something different from what it is.

It is reasonable to think that no experience could adequately represent an objectivity that lay in the Kantian kind of argument. That argument is to the effect that the requirements of practical reason will be met only by leading a life in which moral considerations play a constitutive, in particular a motivational, role. Moreover, that life is understood to be one in which moral considerations can, in contrast to other motivations, present themselves as objective demands. It follows that what it is for a consideration to present itself as an objective demand could never consist merely in its presenting itself as so related to that very argument. So, in the Kantian version at least, there is no alternative to the experience being a misrepresentation of genuine objectivity. The really important question that is raised here is how far such an experience of being confronted by an objective demand, has to be the central experience of the ethical life—indeed, how far it has to be part of it at all.

There would be a certain misrepresentation, then, in that experience of objectivity even if there were genuine objectivity in the form of an objective grounding. What if there were acknowledged to be no such grounding? This covers two distinct possibilities. One is that this kind of grounding is an intelligible form of objectivity, but there is no convincing argument of this kind. (This is my own view.) This possibility raises much the same range of questions about the experience of objectivity as would be raised if the grounding argument were valid. If that argument is not valid, then we are to that extent the more deceived if we think that there is objectivity, but we are not any the more deceived *by the experience*; and whether the argument is valid or not, the same questions will arise about the necessity of that kind of experience to the ethical life.

The second possibility is to be found in the outlook of someone who agrees that there is no objective grounding, but nevertheless thinks that there is objectivity. Such a person (Prichard was one) will believe that it is mistaken to look for any argument of these kinds to yield objectivity; objectivity is, rather, something to be grasped through these experiences themselves. He thinks that objectivism gets its content just from the sense which these experiences embody, of confrontation with something independent. He construes objectivism as a kind of realism. This possibility is simply misconceived, and in relation to this idea, Mackie was right to detect error, since it takes the fact that an experience is demanding as sufficient evidence, indeed the only evidence, that it is the experience of a demand. It takes resonance to be reference, and that is certainly a mistake. The mistake, however, is not inherent simply in having that experience. It is not even inherent in having that experience and connecting it with objectivity. It lies in a theory which takes that experience to reveal all that one knows or needs to know about objectivity.

We can now go back to other kinds of what I earlier called 'ethical qualities', those that lie in the area of the good, the admirable, and so forth, and also the more affective characteristics—the outrageous, the contemptible, and the rest. In these last cases, at least, it is obvious to reflection that there is a relativity involved, and it is probable that there is some process of projection. It is tempting to see in this, as Mackie saw, some analogy to secondary qualities. However, there is a significant difference between the two cases; it lies in the conception that it is appropriate to have of 'the world' of which these various qualities are said not to be part. The fabric of the world from which the secondary qualities are absent (in their presented form) is the world of primary qualities, and (to take for granted the answers to several large and contentious questions) the claim that the secondary qualities, as presented, are not part of that world comes to much the same as the claim that they do not figure in an 'absolute conception' of the world on which scientific investigators, abstracting as much as possible from their various perceptual peculiarities, might converge.[4] There is nothing unnerving or subversive in the idea that ethical qualities are not part of the fabric of the world in this sense. They do not need to do better than secondary qualities.[5]

The subjective conception of secondary qualities rests on the notion that in principle the perception of (say) colours can be explained in terms of perceptual psychology, on the one hand, and the world as characterized in terms of primary qualities, on the other.[6] In the case of ethical qualities, however, if subjectivism holds that they are added to or projected on to the world, 'the world' has to be already construed in a psychologically and socially richer sense than 'the world' on to which secondary qualities are projected. Any conceivable explanations of variations in ethical reactions will have to include psychological and social elements in the cause. This would be so even if human beings as such converged in ethical reaction more than they do. However, the explanation of these variations can in fact be plausibly traced in many cases to cultural factors, and this is where we rejoin the 'argument from relativity' which earlier seemed not very relevant. It is not relevant, if (as I think Mackie had in mind) 'the world' is to be regarded in the same way for the two cases of secondary qualities and of ethics. But if this is not to be so, cultural variation and its explanations are relevant, because they help to make clear what kinds of convergence might appropriately be looked for in ethical thought, and how we might explain them.

The importance of those explanations comes out in the ways in which we might assess future processes of convergence in ethical thought. The mere fact that convergence occurred would not in itself be evidence of any kind of objectivity. What would matter would be the explanation of the

---

[4] See my *Descartes: The Project of Pure Enquiry* (Harmondsworth: Penguin, 1978), esp. chs. 1, 8, and 10; McGinn, *The Subjective View*, who well brings out how the absolute conception is not a perceptual one. For various formulations of the idea and assessments of their prospects, see N. Jardine, 'The Possibility of Absolutism', in D. H. Mellor (ed.), *Science, Belief and Behaviour: Essays in Honour of R. B. Braithwaite* (Cambridge: Cambridge University Press, 1980).

[5] The point is well brought out in David Wiggins, 'Truth, Invention, and the Meaning of Life', *Proceedings of the British Academy*, 62 (1976), 331–78 (Ch. IX of this volume). McGinn (p. 145–6) does think that ethical qualities, on our actual understanding of them, need to do better than secondary qualities: I shall come back to this point later.

[6] This is not to deny that variations in perceived colour may have psychological causes, as they do by juxtaposition and in many other cases. This is one area in which we invoke the difference between real and apparent colours: it is generally thought that a difference in the observer's expectations, for instance, cannot affect the colour a thing is. It is not the same with smells; and certainly not with affective qualities. Whether a substance is perceived as food can affect whether it *is* disgusting: the contrast with something's seeming disgusting is drawn at a different level.

convergence. Human beings might come to agree more on these matters than they do now just because of assimilation and a higher degree of interdependence, and that would tell us nothing about the status of ethical belief. It would be different if some argument for an objective grounding appeared to have gained increasing rational assent. Of course, what we think about the chances of finding an objective grounding will themselves affect and be affected by the ways in which we understand existing ethical variation: the relations, as one would expect, run in both directions.

None of these understandings, however, could make more plausible what I earlier called the *realist* version of objectivism. So, to summarize, the position seems to be the following. Realist objectivism, in that sense, is not an option and Mackie was right in rejecting it, though he was wrong in thinking that cultural variation was relevant to it. Cultural variation is relevant, but not at this point. It is so in virtue of the explanations that it requires us to give of ethical reactions, explanations which both affect our conception of 'the world' that elicits those reactions, and also are related to the prospects for objectivism in a different sense, that of an objective grounding of ethical beliefs and attitudes. The question of whether there could be such a grounding is not answered by Mackie's kind of critique, in terms of the fabric of the world; but that critique does nevertheless attack a feature of ethical experience, which, even if there were an objective grounding, would tend to misrepresent it—most starkly, as we have seen, in the Kantian case.

In referring here to the realist version of objectivism, I meant what I earlier called 'realism', the position which tries to conjure objectivity straight out of ethical experience. There are other positions that have been called 'realist', which involve the quite different idea that it is impossible to distinguish between 'the world' and what is supposedly projected on to it. They may deny this even for the supposedly absolute conception of the world in terms of primary qualities, or, alternatively, they may allow that conception, rightly point out that the fact that ethical qualities are not to be found in that is no great news, and then go on to say that when one tries to find a richer conception of 'the world' on to which values still need to be projected, one cannot find it. The first of these positions is, I think, that of John McDowell, while the second is perhaps taken by Wiggins. They raise wide issues that I cannot hope to pursue here.[7] In very bald summary, it seems to me that the approach makes a good point about certain substantive value concepts, in rejecting a prescriptivist or similar approach to them: that is to say, it discourages the idea that for each such concept, one

[7] I discuss them in *Ethics and the Limits of Philosophy* (London: Fontana, 1985), ch. 8.

could produce a value-free description of the world that corresponds to it. The point helps to put some basic questions of objectivity (for instance, the possibility of ethical knowledge) into a more helpful perspective, but as to answering those questions, I think that it only puts off the evil day, because it fails to consider, first, the fact that some substantive ethical concepts may be replaced by others, and what needs to be understood is the process by which that happens; and, second, that any given substantive ethical concept may be criticized without using another such concept, through the use of very general notions, such as 'good' or 'ought', with regard to which this 'realist' line does not give much help.

I come back now to what I called earlier the 'two claims', that our ethical experiences involve an error, and that ethical conviction need not be upset by recognizing that fact. It will be helpful to take the second claim first. In the case of secondary qualities, the discovery that they are subjective has very little, if any, effect on everyday practice, and it is obvious why that should be so. The psychological capacities that underly our perceiving the world in terms of certain secondary qualities have evolved so that the physical world can present itself to us in reliable and useful ways (it is an interesting question, discussed by McGinn, whether Kant was right in thinking that any world we could experience would have to present itself in terms of some secondary qualities). Coming to know that these secondary qualities constitute our form of perceptual engagement with the world, and how this mode of presentation works, will not unsettle the system. Indeed, in this case unreflective practice is so harmoniously related to theoretical understanding, that a good case can be made for rejecting Mackie's view that there is an *error* involved at all in everyday belief, though no doubt there is in naïve philosophical theory about it.[8]

If we ask similar questions about ethical qualities and our experience of them, it seems that it is the second claim that is harder to accept. If the general direction of Mackie's critique is right, then ethical qualities are felt to be in some sense independent of us and our motivations, whereas in truth they are dependent on us and our motivations. Moreover, and more damagingly, this can be plausibly explained by supposing that ethical constraints and objectives have to be internalized in such a way that they can serve to control and redirect potentially destructive and unco-operative desires, and that they can do this, or do it most effectively, only if they do not present themselves as one motivation or desire among others, nor as

---

[8] McGinn, *The Subjective View*, ch. 7. The issue involves the question of how the relativity of secondary-quality predicates shows up in their semantics. It is not wholly clear what McGinn's view is on this: cf. pp. 119–20 with pp. 9–10. See also Wiggins, 'Truth, Invention, and the Meaning of Life' (Ch. IX in this volume), and Williams, *Descartes*, 242–4.

offering one option among others. They thus present themselves as something given to the agent, but at the same time something from which he cannot feel himself entirely detached, as he could from some external, questionable, authority.

Similar experiences are involved when one's values come into conflict with other people's values. While one is involved in expressing one's own as against some other values, one cannot at the same time simply see those others as alternative ways of ordering society or of producing some very general kind of human good. One cannot, equally, simply think that, while as a matter of fact one sees the world from the perspective of one set of values, it might be more convenient if one could bring it about that one saw it from another; just as one cannot think it an acceptable way of dealing with some morally disagreeable phenomenon that one should stop being affected by it. It is for this kind of reason, indeed, that McGinn says that our moral consciousness is *not* like our experience of secondary qualities, since we readily accept that a way of changing the colours of the world could be to make a general enough psychological alteration. He may underestimate in this the momentum of our current conceptions of what colour things are: but, in any case, the consideration will not show that moral distinctions are not relative to our psychological and social constitution. It will only show how deeply entrenched they are.

If all this is so, then it is not easy to combine the two claims, and the consciousness of what the system is will not happily coexist with the system's working. In this respect, it is not like the example of secondary qualities. The fundamental difficulty is to combine the efficacy of a social system with consciousness of what it involves. Moreover, if one believes, as I think John Mackie did, that it is a desirable feature of a society that its practices could in principle become as far as possible transparent to it (though not all of them could do so at once), then one must ask whether, on anything like Mackie's view of it, ethical experience could itself pass that test.

Despite his second claim, Mackie did not think that things would go on exactly the same if subjectivism in his sense became known. He recognized that if subjectivism is true, then acquiring values is not the process it is supposed to be under objectivism (p. 22; p. 63 of this volume), and it must surely follow that if subjectivism were not just true but known to be true, those processes would be consciously conducted in some different way. Sometimes (e.g. p. 106) Mackie was disposed to conclude that if his views were right, 'morality is not to be discovered but made: we have to decide what moral views to adopt'. But, as so often when a conclusion of that kind is drawn from an ethical theory, it is unclear who 'we' are, and to what extent the process of decision is supposed to be individual or social or, indeed, concrete at all. It certainly cannot follow from Mackie's view that when we have come to realize what moral experience really is, we shall start to acquire our moral attitudes by self-consciously deciding on them, either individually or collectively. It is not clear that there could be such a process, and if there were, there is no reason at all to think, in the light of Mackie's theory itself, that it would be effective.

Mackie's theory, and any like it, leaves a real problem of what should happen when we know it to be true. I cannot try to take that problem further here. I shall offer just one speculation, that the first victim of this knowledge is likely to be the Kantian sense of presented duty. We have seen that it is the starkest example of objectification, and since there is virtually nothing to it except the sense of being given, it stands to suffer most if that sense is questioned. There are other ethical desires and perceptions which are better adapted to being seen for what they are. It is an important task for moral philosophy to consider what they may be, and into what coherent pictures of ethical life, philosophical, psychological, and social, they will fit.

XI

MORAL EXPLANATIONS

NICHOLAS L. STURGEON

There is one argument for moral scepticism that I respect even though I remain unconvinced. It has sometimes been called the argument from moral diversity or relativity, but that is somewhat misleading, for the problem arises not from the diversity of moral views, but from the apparent difficulty of *settling* moral disagreements, or even of knowing what would be required to settle them, a difficulty thought to be noticeably greater than any found in settling disagreements that arise in, for example, the sciences. This provides an argument for moral scepticism because one obviously possible explanation for our difficulty in settling moral disagreements is that they are really unsettlable, that there is no way of justifying one rather than another competing view on these issues; and a possible further explanation for the unsettlability of moral disagreements, in turn, is moral nihilism, the view that on these issues there just is no fact of the matter, that the impossibility of discovering and establishing moral truths is due to there not being any.

I am, as I say, unconvinced: partly because I think this argument exaggerates the difficulty we actually find in settling moral disagreements, partly because there are alternative explanations to be considered for the difficulty we do find. Under the latter heading, for example, it certainly matters to what extent moral disagreements depend on disagreements about other questions which, however disputed they may be, are neverthe-

From David Copp and David Zimmerman (eds.), *Morality, Reason and Truth* (Totowa, NJ: Rowman & Littlefield, 1985), 49–78. Copyright © 1984 by Rowman & Littlefield Publishers. Reprinted by permission.

This essay has benefited from helpful discussion of earlier versions read at the University of Virginia, Cornell University, Franklin and Marshall College, Wayne State University, and the University of Michigan. I have been aided by a useful correspondence with Gilbert Harman; and I am grateful also for specific comments from Richard Boyd, David Brink, David Copp, Stephen Darwall, Terence Irwin, Norman Kretzmann, Ronald Nash, Peter Railton, Bruce Russell, Sydney Shoemaker, and Judith Slein.

Only after this essay had appeared in print did I notice that several parallel points about *aesthetic* explanations had been made by Michael Slote in 'The Rationality of Aesthetic Value Judgments', *Journal of Philosophy*, 68 (1971), 821–39; interested readers should see that paper.

less regarded as having objective answers: questions such as which, if any, religion is true, which account of human psychology, which theory of human society. And it also matters to what extent consideration of moral questions is in practice skewed by distorting factors such as personal interest and social ideology. These are large issues. Although it is possible to say some useful things to put them in perspective,[1] it appears impossible to settle them quickly or in any a priori way. Consideration of them is likely to have to be piecemeal, and, in the short run at least, frustratingly indecisive.

These large issues are not my topic here. But I mention them, and the difficulty of settling them, to show why it is natural that moral sceptics have hoped to find some quicker way of establishing their thesis. I doubt that any exist, but some have of course been proposed. Verificationist attacks on ethics should no doubt be seen in this light, and J. L. Mackie's 'argument from queerness' is a clear instance.[2] The quicker argument on which I shall concentrate, however, is neither of these, but instead an argument by Gilbert Harman disigned to bring out the 'basic problem' about morality, which in his view is 'its apparent immunity from observational testing' and 'the seeming irrelevance of observational evidence'.[3] The argument is that reference to moral facts appears unnecessary for the *explanation* of our moral observations and beliefs.

Harman's view, I should say at once, is not in the end a sceptical one, and he does not view the argument I shall discuss as a decisive defence of moral scepticism or moral nihilism. Someone else might easily so regard it, however. For Harman himself regards it as creating a strong prima-facie case for scepticism and nihilism, strong enough to justify calling it 'the problem with ethics'.[4] And he believes it shows that the only recourse for someone who wishes to avoid moral scepticism is to find defensible reductive definitions for ethical terms; so scepticism would be the obvious conclusion for anyone to draw who doubted the possibility of such definitions. I believe, however, that Harman is mistaken on both counts. I shall show that his argument for scepticism either rests on claims that most people would find quite implausible (and so cannot be what constitutes, for *them*, the

[1] As, for example, in Alan Gewirth, 'Positive "Ethics" and Normative "Science"', *Philosophical Review*, 69 (1960), 311–30, in which there are some useful remarks about the first of them.

[2] Mackie, *Ethics: Inventing Right and Wrong* (Harmondsworth: Penguin, 1977), 38–42 (ch. V of this volume, pp. 76–9).

[3] Harman, *The Nature of Morality: An Introduction to Ethics* (New York: Oxford University Press, 1977), pp. vii, viii. Parenthetical page references are to this work, or to ch. VI of this volume.

[4] Harman's title for the entire first section of his book.

problem with ethics); or else it becomes just the application to ethics of a familiar *general* sceptical strategy, one which, if it works for ethics, will work equally well for unobservable theoretical entities, or for other minds, or for an external world (and so, again, can hardly be what constitutes the distinctive problem with *ethics*). In the course of my argument, moreover, I shall suggest that one can in any case be a moral realist, and indeed an ethical naturalist, without believing that we are now or ever will be in possession of reductive naturalistic definitions for ethical terms.

I. THE PROBLEM WITH ETHICS

Moral theories are often tested in thought experiments, against imagined examples; and, as Harman notes, trained researchers often test scientific theories in the same way. The problem, though, is that scientific theories can also be tested against the world, by observations or real experiments; and, Harman asks, 'can moral principles be tested in the same way, out in the world?' (p. 4; p. 86 of this volume).

This would not be a very interesting or impressive challenge, of course, if it were merely a resurrection of standard verificationist worries about whether moral assertions and theories have any testable empirical implications, implications statable in some relatively austere 'observational' vocabulary. One problem with that form of the challenge, as Harman points out, is that there are no 'pure' observations, and in consequence no purely observational vocabulary either. But there is also a deeper problem that Harman does not mention, one that remains even if we shelve worries about 'pure' observations and, at least for the sake of argument, grant the verificationist his observational language, pretty much as it was usually conceived: that is, as lacking at the very least any obviously theoretical terminology from any recognized science, and of course as lacking any moral terminology. For then the difficulty is that moral principles fare just as well (or just as badly) against the verificationist challenge as do typical scientific principles. For it is by now a familiar point about scientific principles—principles such as Newton's law of universal gravitation or Darwin's theory of evolution—that they are entirely devoid of empirical implications when considered in isolation.[5] We do of course base observa-

---

[5] This point is generally credited to Pierre Duhem, *The Aim and Structure of Physical Theory,* trs. Philip P. Wiener (Princeton: Princeton University Press, 1954). It is a prominent theme in the influential writings of W. V. O. Quine. For an especially clear application of it, see Hilary Putnam, 'The "Corroboration" of Theories', in *Mathematics, Matter, and Method, Philosophical Papers,* i, 2nd edn. (Cambridge: Cambridge University Press, 1977).

tional predictions on such theories and so test them against experience, but that is because we do *not* consider them in isolation. For we can derive these predictions only by relying at the same time on a large background of additional assumptions, many of which are equally theoretical and equally incapable of being tested in isolation. A less familiar point, because less often spelled out, is that the relation of moral principles to observation is similar in *both* these respects. Candidate moral principles—for example, that an action is wrong just in case there is something else the agent could have done that would have produced a greater net balance of pleasure over pain—lack empirical implications when considered in isolation. But it is easy to derive empirical consequences from them, and thus to test them against experience, if we allow ourselves, as we do in the scientific case, to rely on a background of other assumptions of comparable status. Thus, if we conjoin the act-utilitarian principle I just cited with the further view, also untestable in isolation, that it is always wrong deliberately to kill a human being, we can deduce from these two premises together the consequence that deliberately killing a human being always produces a lesser balance of pleasure over pain than some available alternative act; and this claim is one any positivist would have conceded we know, in principle at least, how to test. If we found it to be false, moreover, then we would be forced by this empirical test to abandon at least one of the moral claims from which we derived it.

It might be thought a worrisome feature of this example, however, and a further opening for scepticism, that there could be controversy about which moral premiss to abandon, and that we have not explained how our empirical test can provide an answer to *this* question. And this may be a problem. It should be a familiar problem, however, because the Duhemian commentary includes a precisely corresponding point about the scientific case: that if we are at all cautious in characterizing what we observe, then the requirement that our theories merely be *consistent* with observation is an astoundingly weak one. There are always many, perhaps indefinitely many, different mutually inconsistent ways to adjust our views to meet this constraint. Of course, in practice we are often confident to how to do it: If you are a freshman chemistry student, you do not conclude from your failure to obtain the predicted value in an experiment that it is all over for the atomic theory of gases. And the decision can be equally easy, one should note, in a moral case. Consider two examples. From the surprising moral thesis that Adolf Hitler was a morally admirable person, together with a modest piece of moral theory to the effect that no morally admirable person would, for example, instigate and oversee the degradation and death of millions of persons, one can derive the testable consequence that Hitler did not do this. But he did, so we must give up one of our premisses; and the choice of which to abandon is neither difficult nor controversial.

Or, to take a less monumental example, contrived around one of Harman's own, suppose you have been thinking yourself lucky enough to live in a neighbourhood in which no one would do anything wrong, at least not in public; and that the modest piece of theory you accept, this time, is that malicious cruelty, just for the hell of it, is wrong. Then, as in Harman's example, 'you round a corner and see a group of young hoodlums pour gasoline on a cat and ignite it'. At this point, either your confidence in the neighbourhood or your principle about cruelty has got to give way. But the choice is easy, if dispiriting, so easy as hardly to require thought. As Harman says, 'You do not need to *conclude* that what they are doing is wrong; you do not need to figure anything out; you can *see* that it is wrong (p. 4; p. 86 of this volume). But a sceptic can still wonder whether this practical confidence, or this 'seeing', rests in either sort of case on anything more than deeply ingrained conventions of thought—respect for scientific experts, say, and for certain moral traditions—as opposed to anything answerable to the facts of the matter, any reliable strategy for getting it right about the world.

Now, Harman's challenge is interesting partly because it does not rest on these verificationist doubts about whether moral beliefs have observational implications, but even more because what it does rest on is a partial answer to the kind of general scepticism to which, as we have seen, reflection on the verificationist picture can lead. Many of our beliefs are justified, in Harman's view, by their providing or helping to provide a reasonable *explanation* of our observing what we do. It would be consistent with your failure, as a beginning student, to obtain the experimental result predicted by the gas laws, that the laws are mistaken. That would even be one explanation of your failure. But a better explanation, in light of your inexperience and the general success experts have had in confirming and applying these laws, is that you made some mistake in running the experiment. So our scientific beliefs can be justified by their explanatory role; and so too, in Harman's view, can mathematical beliefs and many common-sense beliefs about the world.

Not so, however moral beliefs: They appear to have no such explanatory role. That is 'the problem with ethics'. Harman spells out his version of this contrast:

You need to make assumptions about certain physical facts to explain the occurrence of the observations that support a scientific theory, but you do not seem to need to make assumptions about any moral facts to explain the occurrence of the so-called moral observations I have been talking about. In the moral case, it would seem that you need only make assumptions about the psychology or moral sensibility of the person making the moral observation. (p. 6; pp. 87–8 of this volume)

More precisely, and applied to his own example, it might be reasonable, in order to explain your judging that the hoodlums are wrong to set the cat on fire, to assume 'that the children really are pouring gasoline on a cat and you are seeing them do it'. But there is no

obvious reason to assume anything about 'moral facts', such as that it is really wrong to set the cat on fire. . . . Indeed, an assumption about moral facts would seem to be totally irrelevant to the explanation of your making the judgement you make. It would seem that all we need assume is that you have certain more or less well articulated moral principles that are reflected in the judgements you make, based on your moral sensibility. (p. 7; pp. 88–9 of this volume)

And Harman thinks that if we accept this conclusion, suitably generalized, then, subject to a possible qualification I shall come to shortly, we must conclude that moral theories cannot be tested against the world as scientific theories can, and that we have no reason to believe that moral facts are part of the order of nature or that there is any moral knowledge (pp. 23, 35).

My own view is that Harman is quite wrong, not in thinking that the explanatory role of our beliefs is important to their justification, but in thinking that moral beliefs play no such role.[6] I shall have to say something about the initial plausibility of Harman's thesis as applied to his own example, but part of my reason for dissenting should be apparent from the other example I just gave. We find it easy (and so does Harman, p. 108) to conclude from the evidence not just that Hitler was not morally admirable, but that he was morally depraved. But isn't it plausible that Hitler's moral depravity—the fact of his really having been morally depraved—forms part of a reasonable explanation of why we believe he was depraved? I think so, and I shall argue concerning this and other examples that moral beliefs commonly play the explanatory role Harman denies them. Before I can press my case, however, I need to clear up several preliminary points about just what Harman is claiming and just how his argument is intended to work.

---

[6] Harman is careful always to say only that moral beliefs *appear* to play no such role; and since he eventually concludes that there *are* moral facts (p. 132), this caution may be more than stylistic. I shall argue that this more cautious claim, too, is mistaken (indeed, that is my central thesis). But to avoid issues about Harman's intent, I shall simply mean by 'Harman's argument' the sceptical argument of his first two chapters, whether or not he means to endorse all of it. This argument surely deserves discussion in its own right in either case, especially since Harman himself never explains what is wrong with it.

II. OBSERVATION, EXPLANATION, AND REDUCTION

1. For there are several ways in which Harman's argument invites misunderstanding. One results from his focusing at the start on the question of whether there can be moral *observations*.[7] But this question turns out to be a side issue, in no way central to his argument that moral principles cannot be tested against the world. There are a couple of reasons for this, of which the more important[8] by far is that Harman does not really require of moral facts, if belief in them is to be justified, that they figure in the explanation of moral observations. It would be enough, on the one hand, if they were needed for the explanation of moral beliefs that are not in any interesting sense observations. For example, Harman thinks belief in moral facts would be vindicated if they were needed to explain our drawing the moral conclusions we do when we reflect on hypothetical cases, but I think there is no illumination in calling these conclusions observations.[9] It would also be enough, on the other hand, if moral facts were needed for the explanation of what were clearly observations, but not moral observations. Harman thinks mathematical beliefs are justified, but he does not suggest that there are mathematical observations; it is rather that appeal to mathematical truths helps to explain why we make the physical observations we do (p. 10; p. 91 of this volume). Moral beliefs would surely be justified,

[7] He asks: 'Can moral principles be tested in the same way [as scientific hypotheses can], out in the world? You can observe someone do something, but can you ever perceive the rightness or wrongness of what he does?' (p. 4; p. 86 of this volume).

[8] The other is that Harman appears to use 'observe' and ('perceive' and 'see') in a surprising way. One would normally take observing (or perceiving, or seeing) something to involve knowing it was the case. But Harman apparently takes an observation to be *any* opinion arrived at as 'a direct result of perception' (p. 5; p. 87 of this volume) or, at any rate (see next footnote), 'immediately and without conscious reasoning' (p. 7; p. 88 of this volume). This means that observations need not even be true, much less known to be true. A consequence is that the existence of moral observations, in Harman's sense, would not be sufficient to show that moral theories can be tested against the world, or to show that there is moral knowledge, although this *would* be sufficient if 'observe' were being used in a more standard sense. What I argue in the text is that the existence of moral observations (in either Harman's or the standard sense) is not *necessary* for showing this about moral theories either.

[9] This sort of case does not meet Harman's characterization of an observation as an opinion that is 'a direct result of perception' (p. 5; p. 87 of this volume), but he is surely right that moral facts would be as well vindicated if they were needed to explain our drawing conclusions about hypothetical cases as they would be if they were needed to explain observations in the narrower sense. To be sure, Harman is still confining his attention to cases in which we draw the moral conclusion from our thought experiment 'immediately and without conscious reasoning', (p. 7; p. 88 of this volume), and it is no doubt the existence of such cases that gives purchase to talk of a 'moral sense'. But this feature, again, can hardly matter to the argument: Would belief in moral facts be less justified if they were needed only to explain the instances in which we draw the moral conclusion *slowly*? Nor can it make any difference for that matter whether the case we are reflecting on is hypothetical. So my example in which we, quickly or slowly, draw a moral conclusion about Hitler from what we know of him, is surely relevant.

too, if they played such a role, whether or not there are any moral observations.

So the claim is that moral facts are not needed to explain our having any of the moral beliefs we do, whether or not those beliefs are observations, and are equally unneeded to explain any of the observations we make, whether or not those observations are moral. In fact, Harman's view appears to be that moral facts aren't needed to explain anything at all: although it would perhaps be question-begging for him to begin with this strong a claim, since he grants that if there were any moral facts, then appeal to other moral facts, more general ones, for example, might be needed to explain *them* (p. 8; p. 89 of this volume). But he is certainly claiming, at the very least, that moral facts aren't needed to explain any non-moral facts we have any reason to believe in.

This claim has seemed plausible even to some philosophers who wish to defend the existence of moral facts and the possibility of moral knowledge. Thus, Thomas Nagel has recently retreated to the reply that 'it begs the question to assume that *explanatory* necessity is the test of reality in this area. . . . To assume that only what has to be included in the best explanatory picture of the world is real, is to assume that there are no irreducibly normative truths.'[10]

But this retreat will certainly make it more difficult to fit moral knowledge into anything like a causal theory of knowledge, which seems plausible for many other cases, or to follow Hilary Putnam's suggestion that we 'apply a generally causal account of reference . . . to moral terms.'[11] In addition, the concession is premature in any case, for I shall argue that moral facts do fit into our explanatory view of the world, and in particular into explanations of many moral observations and beliefs.

2. Other possible misunderstandings concern what is meant in asking whether reference to moral facts is *needed* to explain moral beliefs. One warning about this question I save for my comments on reduction below: but another, about what Harman is clearly *not* asking, and about what sort of answer I can attempt to defend to the question he is asking, can be spelled out first. For, to begin with, Harman's question is clearly not just whether there is *an* explanation of our moral beliefs that does not mention moral facts. Almost surely there is. Equally surely, however, there is *an*

---

[10] Thomas Nagel, 'The Limits of Objectivity', in Sterling M. McMurrin (ed.), *The Tanner Lectures on Human Values* (Salt Lake City and Cambridge: University of Utah Press and Cambridge University Press, 1980), 114 n. (Ch. VIII n. 2 of this volume). Nagel actually directs this reply to J. L. Mackie.

[11] Putnam, 'Language and Reality', in *Mind, Language, and Reality*, *Philosophical Papers*, ii (Cambridge: Cambridge University Press, 1975), 290.

explanation of our common-sense non-moral beliefs that does not mention an external world: one which cites only our sensory experience, for example, together with whatever needs to be said about our psychology to explain why with that history of experience we would form just the beliefs we do. Harman means to be asking a question that will lead to scepticism about moral facts, but not to scepticism about the existence of material bodies or about well-established scientific theories of the world.

Harman illustrates the kind of question he is asking, and the kind of answer he is seeking, with an example from physics which it will be useful to keep in mind. A physicist sees a vapour trail in a cloud chamber and thinks, 'There goes a proton'. What explains his thinking this? Partly, of course, his psychological set, which largely depends on his beliefs about the apparatus and all the theory he has learned; but partly also, perhaps, the hypothesis that 'there really was a proton going through the cloud chamber, causing the vapour trail, which he saw as a proton'. We will *not* need this latter assumption, however, 'if his having made that observation could have been equally well explained by his psychological set alone, without the need for any assumption about a proton' (p. 6; p. 88 of this volume).[12] So for reference to moral facts to be *needed* in the explanation of our beliefs and observations, is for this reference to be required for an explanation that is somehow *better* than competing explanations. Correspondingly, reference to moral facts will be unnecessary to an explanation, in Harman's view, not just because we can find some explanation that does not appeal to them, but because *no* explanation that appeals to them is any better than some competing explanation that does not.

Now, fine discriminations among competing explanations of almost anything are likely to be difficult, controversial, and provisional. Fortunately, however, my discussion of Harman's argument will not require any fine discriminations. This is because Harman's thesis, as we have seen, is *not* that moral explanations lose out by a small margin; nor is it that moral explanations, although sometimes initially promising, always turn out on further examination to be inferior to non-moral ones. It is, rather, that reference to moral facts always looks, right from the start, to be 'completely irrelevant' to the explanation of any of our observations and beliefs. And my argument will be that this is mistaken: that many moral

---

[12] It is surprising that Harman does not mention the obvious intermediate possibility, which would occur to any instrumentalist: to cite the physicist's psychological set *and* the vapour trail, but say nothing about protons or other unobservables. It is *this* explanation that is most closely parallel to an explanation of beliefs about an external world in terms of sensory experience and psychological make-up, or of moral beliefs in terms of non-moral facts together with our 'moral sensibility'.

explanations appear to be good explanations, or components in good explanations, that are not obviously undermined by anything else that we know. My suspicion, in fact, is that moral facts are needed in the sense explained, that they will turn out to belong in our best overall explanatory picture of the world, even in the long run, but I shall not attempt to establish that here. Indeed, it should be clear why I could not pretend to do so. For I have explicitly put to one side the issue (which I regard as incapable in any case of quick resolution) of whether and to what extent actual moral disagreements can be settled satisfactorily. But I assume it would count as a defect in any sort of explanation to rely on claims about which rational agreement proved unattainable. So I concede that it *could* turn out, for anything I say here, that moral explanations are all defective and should be discarded. What I shall try to show is merely that many moral explanations look reasonable enough to be in the running; and, more specifically, that nothing Harman says provides any reason for thinking they are not. This claim is surely strong enough (and controversial enough) to be worth defending.

3. It is implicit in this statement of my project, but worth noting separately, that I take Harman to be proposing an *independent* sceptical argument—independent not merely of the argument from the difficulty of settling disputed moral questions, but also of other standard arguments for moral scepticism. Otherwise his argument is not worth independent discussion. For *any* of these more familiar sceptical arguments will of course imply that moral explanations are defective, on the reasonable assumption that it would be a defect in any explanation to rely on claims as doubtful as these arguments attempt to show all moral claims to be. But if *that* is why there is a problem with moral explanations, one should surely just cite the relevant sceptical argument, rather than this derivative difficulty about moral explanations, as the basic 'problem with ethics', and it is that argument we should discuss. So I take Harman's interesting suggestion to be that there is a *different* difficulty that remains even if we put other arguments for moral scepticism aside and *assume*, for the sake of argument, that there are moral facts (for example, that what the children in his example are doing is really wrong): namely, that these assumed facts *still* seem to play no explanatory role.

This understanding of Harman's thesis crucially affects my argumentative strategy in a way to which I should alert the reader in advance. For it should be clear that assessment of this thesis not merely permits, but *requires*, that we provisionally assume the existence of moral facts. I can see no way of evaluating the claim that *even if* we assumed the existence of moral facts they would still appear explanatorily irrelevant, without assuming the existence of some, to see how they would look. So I do freely assume this in each of the examples I discuss in the next section. (I have tried to choose plausible examples, moreover, moral facts most of us would be inclined to believe in if we did believe in moral facts, since those are the easiest to think about: but the precise examples don't matter, and anyone who would prefer others should feel free to substitute his own.) I grant, furthermore, that if Harman were right about the outcome of this thought experiment—that even after we assumed these facts they still looked irrelevant to the explanation of our moral beliefs and of other non-moral facts—then we might conclude with him that there were, after all, no such facts. But I claim he is wrong: Once we have provisionally assumed the existence of moral facts, they *do* appear relevant, by perfectly ordinary standards, to the explanation of moral beliefs and of a good deal else besides. Does this prove that there *are* such facts? Well of course it helps support that view, but here I carefully make no claim to have shown so much. What I *show* is that any remaining reservations about the existence of moral facts must be based on those *other* sceptical arguments, of which Harman's argument is independent. In short, there may still be a 'problem with ethics', but it has *nothing* special to do with moral explanations.

4. A final preliminary point concerns a qualification Harman adds himself. As I have explained his argument so far, it assumes that we could have reason to believe in moral facts only if this helped us 'explain why we observe what we observe' (p. 13); but, he says, this assumption is too strong, for we can have evidence for the truth of some beliefs that play no such explanatory role. We might, for example, come to be able to explain colour perception without saying that objects have colours, by citing certain physical and psychological facts. But this would not show that there are no colours; it would show only that facts about colour are 'somehow reducible' to these physical and psychological facts. And this leaves the possibility that moral facts, too, even if they ultimately play no explanatory role themselves, might be 'reducible to certain other facts that can help explain our observations' (p. 14). So a crucial question is: What would justify a belief in reducibility? What makes us think colour facts might be reducible to physical (or physical and psychological) facts, and what would justify us in thinking moral facts reducible to explanatory natural facts of some kind?

Harman's answer is that it is still the *apparent* explanatory role of colour facts, or of moral facts, that matters; and hence that this qualification to his argument is not so great as it might seem. We know of no precise reduction for facts of either sort. We believe even so that reduction is possible for colour facts because even when we are able to explain colour perception without saying that objects are coloured, 'we will still *sometimes* refer to the actual colours of objects in explaining colour perception, if only for the sake of simplicity. . . . We will continue to believe that objects have colours because we will continue to refer to the actual colours of objects in the explanations that we will in practice give.' But Harman thinks that no comparable point holds for moral facts. 'There does not ever seem to be, even in practice, any point to explaining someone's moral observations by appeal to what is actually right or wrong, just or unjust, good or bad' (p. 22).

Now I shall argue shortly that this is just wrong: that sober people frequently offer such explanations of moral observations and beliefs, and that many of these explanations look plausible enough on the evidence to be worth taking seriously. So a quick reply to Harman, strictly adequate for my purpose, would be simply to accept his concession that this by itself should lead us to regard moral facts as (at worst) reducible to explanatory facts.[13] Concern about the need for, and the role of, reductive definitions has been so central to meta-ethical discussion in this century, however, and has also proved enough of a sticking-point in discussions I have had of the topic of this essay, that I should say a bit more.

As a philosophical naturalist, I take natural facts to be the only facts there are.[14] If I am prepared to recognize moral facts, therefore, I must take them, too, to be natural facts: But which natural facts? It is widely thought that an ethical naturalist must answer this question by providing reductive naturalistic definitions[15] for moral terms and, indeed, that until one has supplied such definitions one's credentials as a *naturalist* about any supposed moral facts must be in doubt. Once such definitions are in hand, however, it seems that moral explanations should be dispensable, since any such explanations can then be paraphrased in non-moral terms; so it is hard to see why an ethical naturalist should attach any importance to them. Now, there are several problems with this reasoning, but the main one is that the widely held view on which it is based is mistaken: mistaken about where a scheme of reductive naturalistic definitions would be found, if

[13] And it is hard to see how facts could be reducible to explanatory facts without being themselves explanatory. Opaque objects often look red to normally sighted observers in white light because they *are* red; it amplifies this explanation, but hardly undermines it, if their redness turns out to be an electronic property of the matter composing their surfaces.

[14] Some of what I say could no doubt be appropriated by believers in supernatural facts, but I leave the details to them. For an account I could largely accept, if I believed any of the theology, see R. M. Adams, 'Divine Command Metaethics as Necessary A Posteriori'. in Paul Helm (ed.), *Divine Commands and Morality* (Oxford: Oxford University Press, 1981), 109–18.

[15] Or, at any rate, a reductive scheme of translation. It surely needn't provide explicit term-by-term definitions. Since this qualification does not affect my argument, I shall henceforth ignore it.

there were to be one, but also about whether, on a naturalistic view of ethics, one should expect there to be such a thing at all. I shall take up these points in reverse order, arguing first (*a*) that it is a mistake to require of ethical naturalism that it even promise reductive definitions for moral terms, and then (*b*) that even if such definitions are to be forthcoming it is, at the very least, no special problem for ethical naturalism that we are not *now* in confident possession of them.

(*a*) Naturalism is in one clear sense a 'reductionist' doctrine of course, for it holds that moral facts are nothing but natural facts. What I deny, however, is that from this metaphysical doctrine about what sort of facts moral facts are, anything follows about the possibility of reduction in another sense (to which I shall henceforth confine the term) more familiar from the philosophical literature: that is, about whether moral expressions can be given reductive definitions in some distinctive non-moral vocabulary, in which any plausible moral explanations could then be recast. The difficulty with supposing naturalism to require this can be seen by pressing the question of just what this distinctive vocabulary is supposed to be. It is common to say merely that this reducing terminology must be 'factual' or 'descriptive' or must designate natural properties; but unless ethical naturalism has already been ruled out, this is no help, for what naturalists of course contend is that moral discourse is *itself* factual and descriptive (although it may be other things as well), and that moral terms themselves stand for natural properties. The idea, clearly, is supposed to be that the *test* of whether these naturalistic claims about moral discourse are correct is whether this discourse is reducible to some other; but what other? I consider two possibilities.

(i) Many would agree that it is too restrictive to understand ethical naturalism as requiring that moral terms be definable in the terminology of fundamental physics. One reason it is too restrictive is that philosophical naturalism might be true even if physicalism, the view that everything is physical, is not. Some form of emergent dualism might be correct, for example. A different reason, which I find more interesting (because I think physicalism *is* true), is that physicalism entails nothing in any case about whether even biology or psychology, let alone ethics, is reducible to physics. There are a number of reasons for this, but a cardinality problem noted by Richard Boyd is sufficient to secure the point.[16] If there are (as there appear to be) any continuous physical parameters, then there are continuum many physical states of the world, but there are at most countably

---

[16] In an unpublished paper, 'Materialism without Reductionism: Non-Humean Causation and the Evidence for Physicalism'.

many predicates in any language, including that of even ideal physics; so there are more physical properties than there are physical expressions to represent them. Thus, although physicalism certainly entails that biological and psychological properties (and ethical properties, too, if there are any) are physical, nothing follows about whether we have any but biological or psychological or ethical terminology for representing these particular physical properties.

(ii) Of course, not many discussions of ethical naturalism have focused on the possibility of reducing ethics to physics; social theory, psychology, and occasionally biology have appeared more promising possibilities. But that facts might be *physical* whether or not all the disciplines that deal with them are reducible to *physics*, helps give point to my question of why we should think that if all ethical facts are *natural* (or, for that matter, *social* or *psychological* or *biological*), it follows that they can equally well be expressed in some other, non-moral idiom; and it also returns us to the question of just what this alternative idiom is supposed to be. The answer to this latter question simply assumed in most discussions of ethical naturalism, I think, is that there are a number of disciplines that we pretty well know to deal with a single natural world, for example, physics, biology, psychology, and social theory; that it is a matter of no great concern whether any of *these* disciplines is reducible to some one of the others or to anything else; but that the test of whether ethical naturalism is true *is* whether ethics is reducible to some (non-moral) combination of *them*.[17]

But what rationale is there for holding ethics alone to this reductive test? Perhaps there would be one if ethics appeared in some salient respect strikingly dissimilar to these other disciplines: if, for example, Harman were right what whereas physics, biology, and the rest offer plausible explanations of many obviously natural facts, including facts about our beliefs and observations, ethics never does. Perhaps ethics could then plausibly be required to earn its place by some alternative route. But I shall of course argue that Harman is wrong about this alleged dissimilarity, and I take my argument to provide part of the defence required for a naturalistic but non-reductive view of ethics.

(*b*) A natualist, however, will certainly want (and a critic of naturalism will likely demand) a fuller account than this of just where moral facts are

---

[17] *Non-moral* because ethics (or large parts of it) will be trivially reducible to psychology and social theory if we take otherwise unreduced talk of moral character traits just to be *part* of psychology and take social theory to *include*, for example, a theory of justice. As an ethical naturalist, I see nothing objectionable or unscientific about conceiving of psychology and social theory in this way, but of course this is not usually how they are understood when questions about reduction are raised.

supposed to fit in the natural world. For all I have shown, moreover, this account might even provide a scheme of reduction for moral discourse: My argument has been not that ethical naturalism could not take this form, but only that it need not. So where should one look for such a fuller account or (if it is to be had) such a reduction? The answer is that the account will have to be derived from our best moral theory, together with our best theory of the rest of the natural world—exactly as, for example, any reductive account of colours will have to be based on all we know about colours, including our best optical theory together with other parts of physics and perhaps psychology. If hedonistic act-utilitarianism (and enough of its associated psychology) turns out to be true, for example, then we can define the good as pleasure and the absence of pain, and a right action as one that produces at least as much good as any other, and that will be where the moral facts fit. If, more plausible, some other moral theory turns out to be correct, we will get a different account and (if the theory takes the right form) different reductive definitions. It would of course be a serious objection to ethical *naturalism* if we discovered that the *only* plausible moral theories had to invoke supernatural facts of some kind, by making right and wrong depend on the will of a deity, for example, or by implying that only persons with immortal souls could have moral obligations. We would then have to choose between a naturalistic world view and a belief in moral facts. But an ethical naturalist can point out that there are familiar moral theories that lack implications of this sort and that appear defensible in the light of all we know about the natural world; and any of them, if correct, could provide a naturalistic account of moral facts and even (if one is to be had) a naturalistic reduction of moral discourse.

Many philosophers will balk at this confident talk of our discovering some moral theory to be correct. But their objection is just the familiar one whose importance I acknowledged at the outset, before putting it to one side: For I grant that the difficulty we experience in settling moral issues, including issues in moral theory, is a problem (although perhaps not an insuperable one) for any version of moral realism. All I contend here is that there is not, in addition to this acknowledged difficulty, any special further (or prior) problem of finding reductive definitions for moral terms or of figuring out where moral facts fit in the natural world. Our moral theory, if once we get it, will provide whatever reduction is to be had and will tell us where the moral facts fit. The suspicion that there must be more than this to the search for reductive definitions almost always rests, I believe, on the view that these definitions must be suited to a special epistemic role: for example, that they will have to be analytic or conceptual truths and so provide a privileged basis for the rest of our theory. But I am confident that moral reasoning, like reasoning in the sciences, is inevitably dialectical and lacks a priori foundations of this sort. I am also sure that no ethical naturalist need think otherwise.[18]

The relevance of these points is this: It is true that if we once obtained correct reductive definitions for moral terms, moral explanations would be in principle dispensable; so if ethical naturalism had to promise such definitions, it would also have to promise the eliminability in principle of explanations couched in moral terms. But note three points. First, it should be no surprise, and should be regarded as no special difficulty for naturalism even on a reductionist conception of it, that we are not now in possession of such definitions, and so not *now* in a position to dispense with any moral explanations that seem plausible. To be confident of such definitions we would need to know just which moral theory is correct; but ethics is an area of great controversy, and I am sure we do not yet know this. Second, if some moral explanations do seem plausible, as I shall argue, then one important step toward improving this situation in ethics will be to see what sort of theory emerges if we attempt to refine these explanations in the light both of empirical evidence and theoretical criticism. So it is easy to see, again even on a reductionist understanding of naturalism that promises the eliminability of moral explanations in the long run, why any naturalist will think that for the foreseeable short run such explanations should be taken seriously on their own terms.

The third and most important point, finally, is that the eliminability of moral explanations for *this* reason, if actually demonstrated, would of course not represent a triumph of ethical scepticism but would rather derive from its defeat. So we must add one further caution, as I promised, concerning Harman's thesis that no reference to moral facts is *needed* in the explanation of moral beliefs. For there are, as we can now see, two very different reasons one might have for thinking this. One—Harman's

---

[18] For more on this view of moral reasoning, see Nicholas L. Sturgeon, 'Brandt's Moral Empiricism', *Philosophical Review*, 91 (1982), 389–422. On scientific reasoning, see Richard N. Boyd, 'Realism and Scientific Epistemology'.

G. E. Moore, *Principia Ethica* (Cambridge: Cambridge University Press, 1903) thought that the *metaphysical* thesis that moral facts are natural facts entailed that moral theory would have a priori foundations. For he took the metaphysical thesis to require not merely that there be a reductive scheme of translation for moral terminology, but that this reduction include explicit property-identities (such as 'goodness = pleasure and the absence of pain'); and these he assumed could be true only if analytic. I of course reject the view that naturalism requires any sort of reductive definitions; but even if it required this sort, it is by now widely acknowledged that reductive property-identities (such as 'temperature = mean molecular kinetic energy') can be true without being analytic. See Hilary Putnam, 'On Properties', in *Mathematics, Matter and Method*.

reason, and my target in the remainder of this essay—is that no moral explanations even seem plausible, that reference to moral facts always strikes us as 'completely irrelevant' to the explanation of moral beliefs. This claim, if true, would tend to support moral scepticism. The other reason—which I have just been considering, and with which I also disagree—is that any moral explanations that *do* seem plausible can be paraphrased without explanatory loss in entirely non-moral terms. I have argued that it is a mistake to understand ethical naturalism as promising this kind of reduction even in principle; and I think it in any case absurd over-confidence to suppose that anyone can spell out an adequate reduction now. But any reader unconvinced by my arguments should note also that this *second* reason is no version of moral scepticism: For what anyone convinced by it must think, is that we either are or will be able to say, in entirely non-moral terms, exactly which natural properties moral terms refer to.[19] So Harman is right to present reductionism as an alternative to scepticism; part of what I have tried to show is just that it is neither the only nor the most plausible such alternative, and that no ethical naturalist need be committed to it.

III. MORAL EXPLANATIONS

With these preliminary points aside, I turn to my arguments against Harman's thesis. I shall first add to my example of Hitler's moral character several more in which it seems plausible to cite moral facts as part of an explanation of non-moral facts, and in particular of people's forming the moral opinions they do. I shall then argue that Harman gives us no plausible reason to reject or ignore these explanations; I shall claim, in fact, that the same is true for his own example of the children igniting the cat. I shall conclude, finally, by attempting to diagnose the source of the disagreement between Harman and me on these issues.

My Hitler example suggests a whole range of extremely common cases that appear not to have occurred to Harman, cases in which we cite someone's moral character as part of an explanation of his or her deeds, and in which that whole story is then available as a plausible further explanation of someone's arriving at a correct assessment of that moral character. Take just one other example. Bernard DeVoto, in *The Year of*

[19] Nor does this view really promise that we can do without reference to moral facts; it merely says that we can achieve this reference without using moral terms. For we would surely have as much reason to think that the facts expressed by *these* non-moral terms were moral facts as we would for thinking that our reductive definitions were correct.

Decision: 1846, describes the efforts of American emigrants already in California to rescue another party of emigrants, the Donner Party, trapped by snows in the High Sierras, once their plight became known. At a meeting in Yerba Buena (now San Francisco), the relief efforts were put under the direction of a recent arrival, Passed Midshipman Selim Woodworth, described by a previous acquaintance as 'a great busybody and ambitious of taking a command among the emigrants'.[20] But Woodworth not only failed to lead rescue parties into the mountains himself, where other rescuers were counting on him (leaving children to be picked up by him, for example), but had to be 'shamed, threatened, and bullied' even into organizing the efforts of others willing to take the risk; he spent time arranging comforts for himself in camp, preening himself on the importance of his position; and as a predictable result of his cowardice and his exercises in vainglory, many died who might have been saved, including four known still to be alive when he turned back for the last time in mid-March. DeVoto concludes: 'Passed Midshipman Woodworth was just no damned good' (p. 442). I cite this case partly because it has so clearly the structure of an inference to a reasonable explanation. One can think of competing explanations, but the evidence points against them. It isn't, for example, that Woodworth was a basically decent person who simply proved too weak when thrust into a situation that placed heroic demands on him. He volunteered, he put no serious effort even into tasks that required no heroism, and it seems clear that concern for his own position and reputation played a much larger role in his motivation than did any concern for the people he was expected to save. If DeVoto is right about this evidence, moreover, it seems reasonable that part of the explanation of his believing that Woodworth was no damned good is just that Woodworth *was* no damned good.

DeVoto writes of course with more moral intensity (and with more of a flourish) than academic historians usually permit themselves, but it would be difficult to find a serious work of biography, for example, in which actions are not explained by appeal to moral character: sometimes by appeal to specific virtues and vices, but often enough also by appeal to a more general assessment. A different question, and perhaps a more difficult one, concerns the sort of example on which Harman concentrates, the explanation of judgements of right and wrong. Here again Harman appears just to have overlooked explanations in terms of moral character: A judge's thinking that it would be wrong to sentence a particular offender to

---

[20] DeVoto, *The Year of Decision: 1846* (Boston: Little, Brown, 1942), 426; a quotation from the notebooks of Francis Parkman. The account of the entire rescue effort is on pp. 424–44.

the maximum prison term the law allows, for example, may be due in part to her decency and fair-mindedness, which I take to be moral facts if any are. But do moral features of the action or institution being judged ever play an explanatory role? Here is an example in which they appear to. An interesting historical question is why vigorous and reasonably widespread moral opposition to slavery arose for the first time in the eighteenth and nineteenth centuries, even though slavery was a very old institution; and why this opposition arose primarily in Britain, France, and in French- and English-speaking North America, even though slavery existed throughout the New World.[21] There is a standard answer to this question. It is that chattel slavery in British and French America, and then in the United States, was much *worse* than previous forms of slavery, and much worse than slavery in Latin America. This is, I should add, a controversial explanation. But as is often the case with historical explanations, its proponents do not claim it is the whole story, and many of its opponents grant that there may be some truth in these comparisons, and that they may after all form a small part of a larger explanation.[22] This latter concession is all I require for my example. Equally good for my purpose would be the more limited thesis that explains the growth of anti-slavery sentiment in the United States, between the Revolution and the Civil War, in part by saying that slavery in the united States became a more oppressive institution during that time. The appeal in these standard explanations is straightforwardly to moral facts.

What is supposed to be wrong with all these explanations? Harman says that assumptions about moral facts seem 'completely irrelevant' in explaining moral observations and moral beliefs (p. 7; p. 89 of this volume), but on its more natural reading that claim seems pretty obviously mistaken about these examples. For it is natural to think that if a particular assumption is completely irrelevant to the explanation of a certain fact, then the fact would have obtained, and we could have explained it just as well, even if the assumption had been false.[23] But I do not believe that Hitler would

---

[21] What is being explained, of course, is not just why people came to think slavery wrong, but why people who were not themselves slaves or in danger of being enslaved came to think it so seriously wrong as to be intolerable. There is a much larger and longer history of people who thought it wrong but tolerable, and an even longer one of people who appear not to have got past the thought that the world would be a better place without it. See David Brion Davis, *The Problem of Slavery in Western Culture* (Ithaca, NY: Cornell University Press, 1966).

[22] For a version of what I am calling the standard view about slavery in the Americas, see Frank Tannenbaum, *Slave and Citizen* (New York: Alfred Knopf, 1947). For an argument against both halves of the standard view, see Davis, *The Problem of Slavery in Western Culture* esp. pp. 60–1, 223–5, 262–3.

[23] This counterfactual test no doubt requires qualification. When there are concomitant effects that in the circumstances could each only have been brought about by their single cause,

have done all he did if he had not been morally depraved, nor, on the assumption that he was not depraved, can I think of any plausible alternative explanation for his doing those things. Nor is it plausible that we would all have believed he was morally depraved even if he hadn't been. Granted, there is a tendency for writers who do not attach much weight to fascism as a social movement to want to blame its evils on a single maniacal leader, so perhaps some of them would have painted Hitler as a moral monster even if he had not been one. But this is only a tendency, and one for which many people know how to discount, so I doubt that our moral belief really is overdetermined in this way. Nor, similarly, do I believe that Woodworth's actions were overdetermined, so that he would have done just as he did even if he had been a more admirable person. I suppose one could have doubts about DeVoto's objectivity and reliability; it is obvious he dislikes Woodworth, so perhaps he would have thought him a moral loss and convinced his readers of this no matter what the man was really like. But it is more plausible that the dislike is mostly based on the same evidence that supports DeVoto's moral view of him, and that very different evidence, at any rate, would have produced a different verdict. If so, then Woodworth's moral character is part of the explanation of DeVoto's belief about his moral character.

It is more plausible of course that serious moral opposition to slavery would have emerged in Britain, France, and the United States even if slavery hadn't been worse in the modern period than before, and worse in the United States than in Latin America, and that the American antislavery movement would have grown even if slavery had not become more oppressive as the nineteenth century progressed. But that is because these moral facts are offered as at best a partial explanation of these developments in moral opinion. And if they really *are* part of the explanation, as seems plausible, then it is also plausible that whatever effect they produced was not entirely overdetermined; that, for example, the growth of the antislavery movement in the United States would at least have been somewhat slower if slavery had been and remained less bad an institution. Here again it hardly seems 'completely irrelevant' to the explanation whether or not these moral facts obtained.

it may be true that if the one effect had not occurred, then neither would the other, but the occurrence of the one is not relevant to the explanation of the other. The test will also be unreliable if it employs backtracking or 'that-would-have-had-to-be-because' counterfactuals. (I take these to include ones in which what is tracked back to is not so much a cause as a condition that partly constitutes another: as when someone's winning a race is part of what constitutes her winning five events in one day, and it is true that if she hadn't won five events, that would have had to be because she didn't win that particular race.) So it should not be relied on in cases of either of these sorts. But none of my examples falls into either of these categories.

It is more puzzling, I grant, to consider Harman's own example in which you see the children igniting a cat and react immediately with the thought that this is wrong. Is it true, as Harman claims, that the assumption that the children are really doing something wrong is 'totally irrelevant' to any reasonable explanation of your making that judgement? Would you, for example, have reacted in just the same way, with the thought that the action is wrong, even if what they were doing *hadn't* been wrong, and could we explain your reaction equally well on this assumption? Now, there is more than one way to understand this counterfactual question, and I shall return below to a reading of it that might appear favourable to Harman's view. What I wish to point out for now is merely that there is a natural way of taking it, parallel to the way in which I have been understanding similar counterfactual questions about my own examples, on which the answer to it has to be simply: It depends. For to answer the question, I take it, we must consider a situation in which what the children are doing is not wrong, but which is otherwise as much like the actual situation as possible, and then decide what your reaction would be in that situation. But since what makes their action wrong, what its wrongness *consists* in, is presumably something like its being an act of gratuitous cruelty (or, perhaps we should add, of intense cruelty, and to a helpless victim), to imagine them not doing something wrong we are going to have to imagine their action different in this respect. More cautiously and more generally, if what they are actually doing is wrong, and if moral properties are, as many writers have held, supervenient on natural ones,[24] then in order to imagine them not doing something wrong we are going to have to suppose their action different from the actual one in some of its natural features as well. So our question becomes: Even if the children had been doing something else, something just different enough not to be wrong, would you have taken them even so to be doing something wrong?

Surely there is no one answer to this question: It depends on a lot about you, including your moral views and how good you are at seeing at a glance

[24] What would be generally granted is just that *if* there are moral properties they supervene on natural properties. But, remember, we are assuming for the sake of argument that there are.

From my view that moral properties *are* natural properties, it of course follows trivially that they supervene on natural properties: that, necessarily, nothing could differ in its moral properties without differing in some natural respect. But I also accept the more interesting thesis usually intended by the claim about supervenience—that there are more basic natural features such that, necessarily, once they are fixed, so are the moral properties. (In supervening on more basic facts of some sort, moral facts are like *most* natural facts. Social facts like unemployment, for example, supervene on complex histories of many individuals and their relations; and facts about the existence and properties of macroscopic physical objects—colliding billiard-balls, say—clearly supervene on the microphysical constitution of the situations that include them.)

what some children are doing. It probably depends also on a debatable moral issue; namely, just *how* different the children's action would have to be in order not to be wrong. (Is unkindness to animals, for example, also wrong?) I believe we can see how, in a case in which the answer was clearly affirmative, we might be tempted to agree with Harman that the wrongness of the action was no part of the explanation of your reaction. For suppose you are like this. You hate children. What you especially hate, moreover, is the sight of children enjoying themselves; so much so that whenever you see children having fun, you immediately assume they are up to no good. The more they seem to be enjoying themselves, furthermore, the readier you are to fasten on any pretext for thinking them engaged in real wickedness. Then it is true that even if the children had been engaged in some robust but innocent fun, you would have thought they were doing something wrong; and Harman is perhaps right[25] about you that the actual wrongness of the action you see is irrelevant to your thinking it wrong. This is because your reaction is due to a feature of the action that coincides only very accidentally with the ones that make it wrong.[26] But, of course, and fortunately, many people aren't like this (nor does Harman argue that they are). It isn't true of them that, in general, if the children had been doing something similar, although different enough not to be wrong, they would still have thought the children were doing something wrong. And it isn't true either, therefore, that the wrongness of the action is irrelevant to the explanation of why they think it wrong.

Now, one might have the sense from my discussion of all these examples—but perhaps especially from my discussion of this last one, Harman's own—that I have perversely been refusing to understand his claim about the explanatory irrelevance of moral facts in the way he intends. And perhaps I have not been understanding it as he wishes. In any

[25] Not *certainly* right, because there is still the possibility that your reaction is to some extent overdetermined and is to be explained partly by your sympathy for the cat and your dislike of cruelty, as well as by your hatred for children (although this last alone would have been sufficient to produce it).

We could of course rule out this possibility by making you an even less attractive character, indifferent to the suffering of animals and not offended by cruelty. But it may then be hard to imagine that such a person (whom I shall cease calling 'you') could retain enough of a grip on moral thought for us to be willing to say he thought the action wrong, as opposed to saying that he merely pretended to do so. This difficulty is perhaps not insuperable, but it is revealing. Harman says that the actual wrongness of the action is 'completely irrelevant' to the explanation of the observer's reaction. Notice that what is in fact true, however, is that it is *very hard* to imagine someone who reacts in the way Harman describes, but whose reaction is *not* due, at least in part, to the actual wrongness of the action.

[26] Perhaps deliberate cruelty is worse the more one enjoys it (a standard counter-example to hedonism). If so, the fact that the children are enjoying themselves makes their action worse, but presumably isn't what makes it wrong to begin with.

case, I agree, I have certainly not been understanding the crucial counter-factual question, of whether we would have drawn the same moral conclusion even if the moral facts had been different, in the way he must intend. But I am not being perverse. I believe, as I said, that my way of taking the question is the more natural one. And more important, although there is, I grant, a reading of that question on which it will always yield the answer Harman wants—namely, that a difference in the moral facts would *not* have made a difference in our judgement—I do not believe this can support his argument. I must now explain why.

It will help if I contrast my general approach with his. I am addressing questions about the justification of belief in the spirit of what Quine has called 'epistemology naturalized'.[27] I take this to mean that we have in general no a priori way of knowing which strategies for forming and refining our beliefs are likely to take us closer to the truth. The only way we have of proceeding is to assume the approximate truth of what seems to us the best overall theory we already have of what we are like and what the world is like, and to decide in the light of *that* what strategies of research and reasoning are likely to be reliable in producing a more nearly true overall theory. One result of applying these procedures, in turn, is likely to be the refinement or perhaps even the abandonment of parts of the tentative theory with which we began.

I take Harman's approach, too, to be an instance of this one. He says we are justified in believing in those facts that we need to assume to explain why we observe what we do. But he does not think that our knowledge of this principle about justification is a priori. Furthermore, as he knows, we cannot decide whether one explanation is better than another without relying on beliefs we already have about the world. Is it really a better explanation of the vapour trail the physicist sees in the cloud chamber to suppose that a proton caused it, as Harman suggests in his example, rather than some other charged particle? Would there, for example, have been no vapour trail in the absence of that proton? There is obviously no hope of answering such questions without assuming at least the approximate truth of some quite far-reaching microphysical theory, and our knowledge of such theories is not a priori.

But my approach differs from Harman's in one crucial way. For among the beliefs in which I have enough confidence to rely on in evaluating explanations, at least at the outset, are some moral beliefs. And I have

[27] W. V. O. Quine, 'Epistemology Naturalized', in *Ontological Relativity and Other Essays* (New York: Columbia University Press, 1969), 69–90. See also Quine, 'Natural Kinds', in the same volume.

been relying on them in the following way.[28] Harman's thesis implies that
the supposed moral fact of Hitler's being morally depraved is irrelevant to
the explanation of Hitler's doing what he did. (For we may suppose that if
it explains his doing what he did, it also helps explain, at greater remove,
Harman's belief and mine in his moral depravity.) To assess this claim, we
need to conceive a situation in which Hitler was *not* morally depraved and
consider the question whether in that situation he would still have done
what he did. My answer is that he would not, and this answer relies on a
(not very controversial) moral view: that in any world at all like the actual
one, only a morally depraved person could have initiated a world war,
ordered the 'final solution', and done any number of other things Hitler
did. That is why I believe that, if Hitler hadn't been morally depraved, he
wouldn't have done those things, and hence that the fact of his moral
depravity is relevant to an explanation of what he did.

Harman, however, cannot want us to rely on any such moral views in
answering this counterfactual question. This comes out most clearly if we
return to his example of the children igniting the cat. He claims that the
wrongness of this act is irrelevant to an explanation of your thinking it
wrong, that you would have *thought* it wrong even if it wasn't. My reply was
that in order for the action not to be wrong it would have had to lack the
feature of deliberate, intense, pointless cruelty, and that if it had differed in
this way you might very well *not* have thought it wrong. I also suggested a
more cautious version of this reply: that since the action is in fact wrong,
and since moral properties supervene on more basic natural ones, it would
have had to be different in *some* further natural respect in order not to be
wrong; and that we do not know whether if it had so differed you would still
have thought it wrong. Both of these replies, again, rely on moral views, the
latter merely on the view that there is *something* about the natural features
of the action in Harman's example that makes it wrong, the former on a
more specific view as to which of these features do this.

But Harman, it is fairly clear, intends for us *not* to rely on any such moral
views in evaluating his counterfactual claim. His claim is not that if the
action had not been one of deliberate cruelty (or had otherwise differed in
whatever way would be required to remove its wrongness), you would
still have thought it wrong. It is, instead, that if the action were one of

---

[28] Harman of course allows us to assume the moral facts whose explanatory relevance is being
assessed: that Hitler was depraved, or that what the children in his example are doing is wrong.
But I have been assuming something more—something about what depravity *is*, and about what
makes the children's action wrong. (At a minimum, in the more cautious version of my argument, I have been assuming that *something* about its more basic features makes it wrong, so that
it could not have differed in its moral quality without differing in those other features as well.)

deliberate, pointless cruelty, but this *did not make it wrong*, you would still have thought it was wrong. And to return to the example of Hitler's moral character, the counterfactual claim that Harman will need in order to defend a comparable conclusion about that case is not that if Hitler had been, for example, humane and fair-minded, free of nationalistic pride and racial hatred, he would still have done exactly as he did. It is, rather, that if Hitler's psychology, and anything else about his situation that could strike us as morally relevant, had been exactly as it in fact was, but this had *not constituted moral depravity*, he would still have done exactly what he did.

Now the antecedents of these two conditionals are puzzling. For one thing, both are, I believe, necessarily false. I am fairly confident, for example, that Hitler really was morally depraved,[29] and since I also accept the view that moral features supervene on more basic natural properties,[30] I take this to imply that there is no possible world in which Hitler has just the personality he in fact did, in just the situation he was in, but is not morally depraved. Any attempt to describe such a situation, moreover, will surely run up against the limits of our moral concepts—what Harman calls our 'moral sensibility'—and this is no accident. For what Harman is asking us

---

[29]   And anyway, remember, this is the sort of fact Harman allows us to assume in order to see whether, if we assume it, it will look explanatory.

[30]   It is about here that I have several times encountered the objection: but surely *supervenient* properties aren't needed to explain anything. It is a little hard, however, to see just what this objection is supposed to come to. If it includes endorsement of the conditional I here attribute to Harman, then I believe the remainder of my discussion is an adequate reply to it. If it is the claim that, because moral properties are supervenient, we can always exploit the insights in any moral explanations, however plausible they may seem, without resort to moral *language*, then I have already dealt with it in my discussion of reduction: The claim is probably false, but even if it is true, it is no support for Harman's view, which is not that moral explanations are plausible but reducible, but that they are totally implausible. And doubts about the causal efficacy of supervenient facts seem misplaced in any case, as attention to my earlier examples (n. 24) illustrates. High unemployment causes widespread hardship, and can also bring down the rate of inflation. The masses and velocities of two colliding billiard-balls causally influence the subsequent trajectories of the two balls. There is no doubt some sense in which these facts are causally efficacious *in virtue of* the way they supervene on—that is, are constituted out of, or causally realized by—more basic facts, but this hardly shows them *in*efficacious. (Nor does Harman appear to think it does: for his *favoured* explanation of your moral belief about the burning cat, recall, appeals to psychological facts (about your moral sensibility), a biological fact (that it's a cat), and macrophysical facts (that it's on fire)—supervenient facts all, on his physicalist view and mine.) If anyone does hold to a general suspicion of causation by supervenient facts and properties, however, as Jaegwon Kim appears to ('Causality, Identity and Supervenience in the Mind Body Problem', in *Midwest Studies*, 4 (Morris: University of Minnesota Press, 1979), 47–8), it is enough here to note that this suspicion cannot diagnose any special difficulty with *moral* explanations, any distinctive 'problem with ethics'. The 'problem', arguably, will be with every discipline but fundamental physics. On this point, see Richard W. Miller, 'Reason and Commitment in the Social Sciences', *Philosophy and Public Affairs*, 8 (1979), esp. 252–5.

to do, in general, is to consider cases in which absolutely *everything* about the non-moral facts that could seem morally relevant to us, in light of whatever moral theory we accept and of the concepts required for our understanding of that theory, is held fixed, but in which the moral judgement that our theory yields about the case is nevertheless mistaken. So it is hardly surprising that, using that theory and those concepts, we should find it difficult to conceive in any detail what such a situation would be like. It is especially not surprising when the cases in question are as paradigmatic in light of the moral outlook we in fact have as is Harman's example or as is, even more so, mine of Hitler's moral character. The only way we could be wrong about this latter case (assuming we have the non-moral facts right) would be for our whole moral theory to be hopelessly wrong, so radically mistaken that there could be no hope of straightening it out through adjustments from within.

But I do not believe we should conclude, as we might be tempted to,[31] that we therefore know a priori that this is not so, or that we cannot understand these conditionals that are crucial to Harman's argument. Rather, now that we have seen how we have to understand them, we should grant that they are true: that if our moral theory were somehow hopelessly mistaken, but all the non-moral facts remained exactly as they in fact are, then, since we do *accept* that moral theory, we would still draw exactly the moral conclusions we in fact do. But we should deny that any sceptical conclusion follows from this. In particular, we should deny that it follows that moral facts play no role in explaining our moral judgements.

For consider what follows from the parallel claim about microphysics, in particular about Harman's example in which a physicist concludes from his observation of a vapour trail in a cloud chamber, and from the microphysical theory he accepts, that a free proton has passed through the chamber. The parallel claim, notice, is *not* just that if the proton had not been there the physicist would have thought it was. This claim is implausible, for we may assume that the physicist's theory is generally correct, and it follows from that theory that if there hadn't been a proton there, then there wouldn't have been a vapour trail. But in a perfectly similar way it is implausible that if Hitler hadn't been morally depraved we would still have thought he was: for we may assume that our moral theory also is at least roughly correct, and it follows from the most central features of that theory that if Hitler hadn't been morally depraved, he wouldn't have done what he did. The *parallel* claim about the microphysical example is, instead, that

---

[31] And as I take it Philippa Foot, in *Moral Relativism*, Lindley Lectures (Lawrence: University of Kansas Press, 1978), for example, is still prepared to do, at least about paradigmatic cases.

if there hadn't been a proton there, but there *had* been a vapour trail, the physicist would still have concluded that a proton was present. More precisely, to maintain a perfect parallel with Harman's claims about the moral cases, the antecedent must specify that although no proton is present, absolutely *all* the non-microphysical facts that the physicist, in light of his theory, might take to be relevant to the question of whether or not a proton is present, are exactly as in the actual case. (These macrophysical facts, as I shall for convenience call them, surely include everything one would normally think of as an observable fact.) Of course, we shall be unable to imagine this without imagining that the physicist's theory is pretty badly mistaken,[32] but I believe we should grant that, *if* the physicist's theory were somehow this badly mistaken, but all the macrophysical facts (including all the observable facts) were held fixed, then the physicist, since he does accept that theory, would still draw all the same conclusions that he actually does. That is, this conditional claim, like Harman's parallel claims about the moral cases, is true.

But no sceptical conclusions follow; nor can Harman, since he does not intend to be a sceptic about physics, think that they do. It does not follow, in the first place, that we have any reason to think the physicist's theory *is* generally mistaken. Nor does it follow, furthermore, that the hypothesis that a proton really did pass through the cloud chamber is not part of a good explanation of the vapour trail, and hence of the physicist's thinking this has happened. This looks like a reasonable explanation, of course,

---

[32] If we imagine the physicist *regularly* mistaken in this way, moreover, we will have to imagine his theory not just mistaken but hopelessly so. And we can easily reproduce the other notable feature of Harman's claims about the moral cases, that what we are imagining is *necessarily* false, if we suppose that one of the physicist's (or better, chemist's) conclusions is about the microstructure of some common substance, such as water. For I agree with Saul Kripke that whatever microstructure water actually has is essential to it, that it has this structure in every possible world in which it exists. (S. A. Kripke, *Naming and Necessity* (Cambridge, Mass.: Harvard University Press, 1980), 115–44.) If we are right (as we have every reason to suppose) in thinking that water is actually H_2O, therefore, the conditional 'If water were not H_2O, but all the observable, macrophysical facts were just as they actually are, chemists would still have come to *think* it was H_2O' has a necessarily false antecedent; just as, if we are right (as we also have good reason to suppose) in thinking that Hitler was actually morally depraved, the conditional 'If Hitler were just as he was in all natural respects, but not morally depraved, we would still have *thought* he was depraved' has a necessarily false antecedent. Of course, I am not suggesting that in either case our knowledge that the antecedent is false is a priori.

These counterfactuals, because of their impossible antecedents, will have to be interpreted over worlds that are (at best) only 'epistemically' possible; and, as Richard Boyd has pointed out to me, this helps to explain why anyone who accepts a causal theory of knowledge (or any theory according to which the justification of our beliefs depends on what explains our holding them) will find their truth irrelevant to the question of how much we know, either in chemistry or in morals. For although there certainly are counterfactuals that are relevant to questions about what causes what (and, hence, about what explains what), these have to be counterfactuals about real possibilities, not merely epistemic ones.

only on the assumption that the physicist's theory is at least roughly true, for it is this theory that tells us, for example, what happens when charged particles pass through a supersaturated atmosphere, what other causes (if any) there might be for a similar phenomenon, and so on. But, as I say, we have not been provided with any reason for not trusting the theory to this extent.

Similarly, I conclude, we should draw no sceptical conclusions from Harman's claims about the moral cases. It is true, I grant, that if our moral theory were seriously mistaken, but we still believed it, and the non-moral facts were held fixed, we would still make just the moral judgements we do. But *this* fact by itself provides us with no reason for thinking that our moral theory *is* generally mistaken. Nor, again, does it imply that the fact of Hitler's really having been morally depraved forms no part of a good explanation of his doing what he did and hence, at greater remove, of our thinking him depraved. This explanation will appear reasonable, of course, only on the assumption that our accepted moral theory is at least roughly correct, for it is this theory that assures us that only a depraved person could have thought, felt, and acted as Hitler did. But, as I say, Harman's argument has provided us with no reason for not trusting our moral views to this extent, and hence with no reason for doubting that it is sometimes moral facts that explain our moral judgements.

I conclude with three comments about my argument.

1. I have tried to show that Harman's claim—that we would have held the particular moral beliefs we do even if those beliefs were untrue—admits of two readings, one of which makes it implausible, and the other of which reduces it to an application of a general sceptical strategy, which could as easily be used to produce doubt about microphysical as about moral facts. The general strategy is this. Consider any conclusion C we arrive at by relying both on some distinguishable 'theory' T and on some body of evidence not being challenged, and ask whether we would have believed C even if it had been false. The plausible answer, *if* we are allowed to rely on T, will often be no: for if C had been false, then (according to T) the evidence would have had to be different, and in that case we wouldn't have believed C. (I have illustrated the plausibility of this sort of reply for all my moral examples, as well as for the microphysical one.) But the sceptic intends us *not* to rely on T in this way, and so rephrases the question: Would we have believed C even if it were false *but* all the evidence had been exactly as it in fact was? Now the answer has to be yes, and the sceptic concludes that C is doubtful. (It should be obvious how to extend this strategy to belief in other minds, or in an external world.) I am

of course not convinced: I do not think answers to the rephrased question show anything interesting about what we know or justifiably believe. But it is enough for my purposes here that no such *general* sceptical strategy could pretend to reveal any problems peculiar to belief in *moral* facts.

2. My conclusion about Harman's argument, although it is not exactly the same as, is nevertheless similar to and very much in the spirit of the Duhemian point I invoked earlier against verificationism. There the question was whether typical moral assertions have testable implications, and the answer was that they do, so long as you include additional moral assumptions of the right sort among the background theories on which you rely in evaluating these assertions. Harman's more important question is whether we should ever regard moral facts as relevant to the explanation of non-moral facts, and in particular of our having the moral beliefs we do. But the answer, again, is that we should, so long as we are willing to hold the right sorts of *other* moral assumptions fixed in answering counterfactual questions. Neither answer shows morality to be on any shakier ground than, say, physics: for typical microphysical hypotheses, too, have testable implications, and appear relevant to explanations, only if we are willing to assume at least the approximate truth of an elaborate microphysical theory and to hold this assumption fixed in answering counterfactual questions.

3. Of course, this picture of how explanations depend on background theories, and moral explanations in particular on moral background theories, does show why someone already tempted toward moral scepticism on other grounds (such as those mentioned at the beginning of this essay) might find Harman's claim about moral explanations plausible. To the extent that you already have pervasive doubts about moral theories, you will also find moral facts non-explanatory. So I grant that Harman may have located a natural symptom of moral scepticism; but I am sure he has neither traced this scepticism to its roots nor provided any independent argument for it. His claim that we do not *in fact* cite moral facts in explanation of moral beliefs and observations cannot provide such an argument, for that claim is false. So, too, is the claim that assumptions about moral facts seem irrelevant to such explanations, for many do not. The claim that we *should* not rely on such assumptions because they *are* irrelevant, on the other hand, unless it is supported by some independent argument for moral scepticism, will just be question-begging: for the principal test of whether they are relevant, in any situation in which it appears they might be, is a counterfactual question about what would have happened if the moral fact had not obtained, and how we answer that question depends precisely upon whether we *do* rely on moral assumptions in answering it.

A different concern, to which Harman only alludes in the passages I have discussed, is that belief in moral facts may be difficult to render consistent with a naturalistic world view. Since I share a naturalistic viewpoint, I agree that it is important to show that belief in moral facts need not be belief in anything supernatural or 'non-natural'. I have of course not dealt with every argument from this direction, but I *have* argued for the important point that naturalism in ethics does not require commitment to reductive definitions for moral terms, any more than physicalism about psychology and biology requires a commitment to reductive definitions for the terminology of those sciences.

My own view I stated at the outset: that the only argument for moral scepticism with any independent weight is the argument from the difficulty of settling disputed moral questions. I have shown that anyone who finds Harman's claim about moral explanations plausible must already have been tempted toward scepticism by some other considerations, and I suspect that the other considerations will always just be the ones I sketched. So that is where discussion should focus. I also suggested that those considerations may provide less support for moral scepticism than is sometimes supposed, but I must reserve a thorough defence of that thesis for another occasion.

XII

VALUES AND SECONDARY QUALITIES

JOHN MCDOWELL

1

J. L. Mackie insists that ordinary evaluative thought presents itself as a matter of sensitivity to aspects of the world.[1] And this phenomenological thesis seems correct. When one or another variety of philosophical non-cognitivism claims to capture the truth about what the experience of value is like, or (in a familiar surrogate for phenomenology[2]), about what we mean by our evaluative language, the claim is never based on careful attention to the lived character of evaluative thought or discourse. The idea is, rather, that the very concept of the cognitive or factual rules out the possibility of an undiluted representation of how things are, enjoying, nevertheless, the internal relation to 'attitudes' or the will that would be needed for it to count as evaluative.[3] On this view the phenomenology of value would involve a mere incoherence, if it were—as Mackie says—a

From Ted Honderich (ed.), *Morality and Objectivity* (London: Routledge & Kegan Paul, 1985), 110–29. Reprinted by permission of Routledge Ltd.

This paper grew out of my contributions to a seminar on J. L. Mackie's *Ethics: Inventing Right and Wrong* (Harmondsworth: Penguin, 1977), hereafter referred to as *E*, which I had the privilege of sharing with Mackie and R. M. Hare in 1978. I do not believe John Mackie would have found it strange that I should pay tribute to a sadly missed colleague by continuing a strenuous disagreement with him.

[1] See *E* 31–5; pp. 69–74 in this volume. I shall also abbreviate references to the following other books by Mackie: *Problems from Locke* (Oxford: Clarendon Press, 1976), hereafter *PFL*; and *Hume's Moral Theory* (London: Routledge & Kegan Paul, 1980), hereater *HMT*.

[2] An inferior surrogate: it leads us to exaggerate the extent to which expressions of our sensitivity to values are signalled by the use of a special vocabulary. See my 'Aesthetic Value, Objectivity, and the Fabric of the World', in Eva Schaper (ed.), *Pleasure, Preference, and Value* (Cambridge: Cambridge University Press, 1983), 1–2.

[3] I am trying here to soften a sharpness of focus that Mackie introduces by stressing the notion of prescriptivity. Mackie's singleness of vision here has the perhaps unfortunate effect of discouraging a distinction such as David Wiggins has drawn between 'valuations' and 'directives or deliberative (or practical) judgements' (see 'Truth, Invention, and the Meaning of Life', *Proceedings of the British Academy*, 62 (1976), 338–9 (Ch. ix of this volume, pp. 125–68). My topic here is really the former of these. (It may be that the distinction does not matter in the way Wiggins suggests: see n. 35 below.)

possibility that then tends (naturally enough) not to be so much as enter-
tained. But, as Mackie sees, there is no satisfactory justification for supposing that the factual is, by definition, attitudinally and motivationally
neutral. This clears away the only obstacle to accepting his phenomenological claim; and the upshot is that non-cognitivism must offer to correct
the phenomenology of value, rather than to give an account of it.[4]

In Mackie's view the correction is called for. In this paper I want to
suggest that he attributes an unmerited plausibility to this thesis, by giving
a false picture of what one is committed to if one resists it.

2

Given that Mackie is right about the phenomenology of value, an attempt
to accept the appearances makes it virtually irresistible to appeal to a
perceptual model. Now Mackie holds that the model must be perceptual
awareness of *primary* qualities (see *HMT* 32, 60–1, 73–4). And this makes
it comparatively easy to argue that the appearances are misleading. For it
seems impossible—at least on reflection—to take seriously the idea of
something that is like a primary quality in being simply *there*, independently of human sensibility, but is nevertheless intrinsically (not condition-
ally on contingencies about human sensibility) such as to elicit some
'attitude' or state of will from someone who becomes aware of it. Moreover, the primary-quality model turns the epistemology of value into mere
mystification. The perceptual model is no more than a model: perception,
strictly so called, does not mirror the role of reason in evaluative thinking,
which seems to require us to regard the apprehension of value as an
intellectual rather than a merely sensory matter. But if we are to take
account of this, while preserving the model's picture of values as brutely
and absolutely *there*, it seems that we need to postulate a faculty—'intuition'—about which all that can be said is that it makes us aware of objective rational connections: the model itself ensures that there is nothing
helpful to say about how such a faculty might work, or why its deliverances
might deserve to count as knowledge.

---

[4] I do not believe that the 'quasi-realism' that Simon Blackburn has elaborated is a real
alternative to this. (See p. 358 of his 'Truth, Realism, and the Regulation of Theory', in Peter A.
French, Theodore E. Uehling, Jr., and Howard Wettstein, (eds.), *Studies in Epistemology,
Midwest Studies in Philosophy*, 5 (Minneapolis: University of Minnesota Press, 1980). In so far
as the quasi-realist holds that the values, in his thought and speech about which he imitates the
practices supposedly characteristic of realism, are *really* products of projecting 'attitudes' into
the world, he must have a conception of genuine reality—that which the values lack and the
things on to which they are projected have. And the phenomenological claim ought to be that
that is what the appearances entice us to attribute to values.

But why is it supposed that the model must be awareness of primary qualities rather than secondary qualities? The answer is that Mackie, following Locke, takes secondary-quality perceptions, as conceived by a pre-philosophical consciousness, to involve a projective error: one analogous to the error he finds in ordinary evaluative thought. He holds that we are prone to conceive secondary-quality experience in a way that would be appropriate for experience of primary qualities. So a pre-philosophical secondary-quality model for awareness of value would in effect be, after all, a primary-quality model. And to accept a philosophically corrected secondary-quality model for the awareness of value would be simply to give up trying to go along with the appearances.

I believe, however, that this conception of secondary-quality experience is seriously mistaken.

3

A secondary quality is a property the ascription of which to an object is not adequately understood except as true, if it is true, in virtue of the object's disposition to present a certain sort of perceptual appearance: specifically, an appearance characterizable by using a word for the property itself to say how the object perceptually appears. Thus an object's being red is understood as obtaining in virtue of the object's being such as (in certain circumstances) to look, precisely, red.

This account of secondary qualities is faithful to one key Lockean doctrine, namely the identification of secondary qualities with 'powers to produce various sensations in us'.[5] (The phrase 'perceptual appearance', with its gloss, goes beyond Locke's unspecific 'sensations', but harmlessly; it serves simply to restrict our attention, as Locke's word may not, to properties that are in a certain obvious sense perceptible.[6])

I have written of what property-ascriptions are understood to be true in virtue of, rather than of what they are true in virtue of. No doubt it is true that a given thing is red in virtue of some microscopic textural property of its surface; but a predication understood only in such terms—not in terms

---

[5] *An Essay Concerning Human Understanding*. II. viii, 10.

[6] Being stung by a nettle is an actualization of a power in the nettle that conforms to Locke's description, but it seems wrong to regard it as a perception of that power; the experience lacks an intrinsically representational character which that would require. (It is implausible that looking red is intelligible independently of being red; combined with the account of secondary qualities that I am giving, this sets up a circle. But it is quite unclear that we ought to have the sort of analytic or definitional aspirations that would make the circle problematic. See Colin McGinn, *The Subjective View* (Oxford: Clarendon Press, 1983), 6–8.)

of how the object would look—would not be an ascription of the secondary quality of redness.[7]

Secondary-quality experience presents itself as perceptual awareness of properties genuinely possessed by the objects that confront one. And there is no general obstacle to taking that appearance at face value.[8] An object's being such as to look red is independent of its actually looking red to anyone on any particular occasion; so, notwithstanding the conceptual connection between being red and being experienced as red, an experience of something as red can count as a case of being presented with a property that is there anyway—there independently of the experience itself.[9] And there is no evident ground for accusing the appearance of being misleading. What would one expect it to be like to experience something's being such as to look red, if not to experience the thing in question (in the right circumstances) as looking, precisely, red?

On Mackie's account, by contrast, to take experiencing something as red at face value, as a non-misleading awareness of a property that really confronts one, is to attribute to the object a property which is 'thoroughly objective' (*PFL* 18), in the sense that it does not need to be understood in terms of experiences that the object is disposed to give rise to; but which nevertheless resembles redness as it figures in our experience—this to ensure that the phenomenal character of the experience need not stand accused of misleadingness, as it would if the 'thoroughly objective' property of which it consituted an awareness were conceived as a microscopic textural basis for the object's disposition to look red. This use of the notion of resemblance corresponds to one key element in Locke's exposition of the concept of a primary quality.[10] In these Lockean terms Mackie's view amounts to accusing a naïve perceptual consciousness of taking secondary qualities for primary qualities (see *PFL* 16).

According to Mackie, this conception of primary qualities that resemble colours as we see them is coherent: that nothing is characterized by such qualities is established by merely empirical argument (see *PFL* 17–20). But is the idea coherent? This would require two things: first, that colours

---

[7] See ibid. 12–14.

[8] Of course there is room for the concept of illusion, not only because the senses can malfunction but also because of the need for a modifier like my '(in certain circumstances)', in an account of what it is for something to have a secondary quality. (The latter has no counterpart with primary qualities.)

[9] See the discussion of (one interpretation of the notion of) objectivity at pp. 77–8 of Gareth Evans, 'Things without the Mind', in Zak van Straaten (ed.), *Philosophical Subjects: Essays Presented to P. F. Strawson* (Oxford: Clarendon Press, 1980). Throughout the present section I am heavily indebted to this most important paper.

[10] See *Essay*, II. viii. 15.

figure in perceptual experience neutrally, so to speak, rather than as essentially phenomenal qualities of objects, qualities that could not be adequately conceived except in terms of how their possessors would look; and, second, that we command a concept of resemblance that would enable us to construct notions of possible primary qualities out of the idea of resemblance to such neutral elements of experience. The first of these requirements is quite dubious. (I shall return to this.) But even if we try to let it pass, the second requirement seems impossible. Starting with, say, redness as it (putatively neutrally) figures in our experience, we are asked to form the notion of a feature of objects which resembles that, but which is adequately conceivable otherwise than in terms of how its possessors would look (since if it were adequately conceivable only in those terms it would simply be secondary). But the second part of these instructions leaves it wholly mysterious what to make of the first: it precludes the required resemblance being in phenomenal respects, but it is quite unclear what other sense we could make of the notion of resemblance to redness as it figures in our experience. (If we find no other, we have failed to let the first requirement pass; redness as it figures in our experience proves stubbornly phenomenal.[11]) I have indicated how we can make error-free sense of the thought that colours are authentic objects of perceptual awareness; in face of that, it seems a gratuitous slur on perceptual 'common sense' to accuse it of this wildly problematic understanding of itself.

Why is Mackie resolved, nevertheless, to convict 'common sense' of error? Secondary qualities are qualities not adequately conceivable except in terms of certain subjective states, and thus subjective themselves in a sense that that characterization defines. In the natural contrast, a primary quality would be objective in the sense that what it is for something to have it can be adequately understood otherwise than in terms of dispositions to give rise to subjective states. Now this contrast between objective and subjective is not a contrast between veridical and illusory experience. But it is easily confused with a different contrast, in which to call a putative object of awareness 'objective' is to say that it is there to be experienced, as opposed to being a mere figment of the subjective state that purports to be an experience of it. If secondary qualities were subjective in the sense that naturally contrasts with this, naïve consciousness would indeed be wrong about them, and we would need something like Mackie's Lockean picture of the error it commits. What is acceptable, though, is only that

---

[11] Cf. pp. 56–7 of P. F. Strawson, 'Perceptin and its Objects', in G. F. Macdonald (ed.), *Perception and Identity: Essays Presented to A. J. Ayer* (London: Macmillan, 1979).

secondary qualities are subjective in the first sense, and it would be simply wrong to suppose that this gives any support to the idea that they are subjective in the second.[12]

More specifically, Mackie seems insufficiently whole-hearted in an insight of his about perceptual experiences. In the case of 'realistic' depiction, it makes sense to think of veridicality as a matter of resemblance between aspects of a picture and aspects of what it depicts.[13] Mackie's insight is that the best hope of a philosophically hygienic interpretation for Locke's talk of 'ideas', in a perceptual context, is in terms of 'intentional objects': that is, aspects of representational content—aspects of how things seem to one in the enjoyment of a perceptual experience. (See *PFL* 47–50). Now it is an illusion to suppose, as Mackie does, that this warrants thinking of the relation between a quality and an 'idea' of it on the model of the relation between a property of a picture's subject and an aspect of the picture. Explaining 'ideas' as 'intentional objects' should direct our attention to the relation between how things are and how an experience represents them as being—in fact, identity, not resemblance, if the representation is veridical.[14] Mackie's Lockean appeal to resemblance fits something quite different: a relation borne to aspects of how things are by intrinsic aspects of a bearer of representational content—not how things are represented to be, but features of an item that does the representing, with particular aspects of its content carried by particular aspects of what it is intrinsically (non-representationally) like.[15] Perceptual experiences have representational content; but nothing in Mackie's defence of the

[12] This is a different way of formulating a point made by McGinn, *The Subjective View*, 121. Mackie's phrase 'the fabric of the world' belongs with the second sense of 'objective', but I think his arguments really address only the first. *Pace* p. 103 of A. W. Price, 'Varieties of Objectivity and Values', *Proceedings of the Aristotelian Society*, 82 (1982–3), 103–19, I do not think the phrase can be passed over as unhelpful, in favour of what the arguments do succeed in establishing, without missing something that Mackie wanted to say. (A gloss on 'objective' as 'there to be experienced' does not figure in Price's inventory, p. 104. It seems to be the obvious response to his challenge at pp. 118–19.)

[13] I do not say it is correct: scepticism about this is very much in point. (See Nelson Goodman, *Languages of Art* (London: Oxford University Press, 1969), ch. 1.)

[14] When resemblance is in play, it functions as a palliative to lack of veridicality, not as what veridicality consists in.

[15] Intrinsic features of experience, functioning as vehicles for aspects of content, seem to be taken for granted in Mackie's discussion of Molyneux's problem (*PFL* 28–32). The slide from talk of content to talk that fits only bearers of content seems to happen also in Mackie's discussion of truth, in *Truth, Probability, and Paradox* (Oxford: Clarendon Press, 1973), with the idea that a formulation like 'A true statement is one such that the way things are is the way it represents things as being' makes truth consist in a relation of correspondence (rather than identity) between how things are and how things are represented as being; pp. 56–7 come too late to undo the damage done by the earlier talk of 'comparison', e.g. at pp. 50, 51. (A subject-matter for the talk that fits bearers is unproblematically available in this case; but Mackie does not mean to be discussing truth as a property of sentences or utterances.)

'intentional objects' gloss on 'ideas' would force us to suppose that they have it in that sort of way.[16]

The temptation to which Mackie succumbs, to suppose that intrinsic features of experience function as vehicles for particular aspects of representational content, is indifferent to any distinction between primary and secondary qualities in the representational significance that these features supposedly carry. What it is for a colour to figure in experience and what it is for a shape to figure in experience would be alike, on this view, in so far as both are a matter of an experience's having a certain intrinsic feature. If one wants, within this framework, to preserve Locke's intuition that primary-quality experience is distinctive in potentially disclosing the objective properties of things, one will be naturally led to Locke's use of the notion of resemblance. But no notion of resemblance could get us from an essentially experiential state of affairs to the concept of a feature of objects intelligible otherwise than in terms of how its possessors would strike us. (A version of this point told against Mackie's idea of possible primary qualities answering to 'colours as we see them'; it tells equally against the Lockean conception of shapes.)

If one gives up the Lockean use of resemblance, but retains the idea that primary and secondary qualities are experientially on a par, one will be led to suppose that the properties attributed to objects in the 'manifest image' are all equally phenomenal—intelligible, that is, only in terms of how their possessors are disposed to appear. Properties that are objective, in the contrasting sense, can then figure only in the 'scientific image'.[17] On these lines one altogether loses hold of Locke's intuition that primary qualities are distinctive in being both objective and perceptible.[18]

If we want to preserve the intuition, as I believe we should, then we need to exorcize the idea that what it is for a quality to figure in experience is for an experience to have a certain intrinsic feature; in fact I believe that we need to reject these supposed vehicles of content altogether. Then we can

---

[16] Indeed, this goes against the spirit of a passage about the word 'content' at *PFL* 43. Mackie's failure to profit by his insight emerges particularly strikingly in his remarkable claim (*PFL* 50) that the 'intentional object' conception of the content of experience yields an account of perception that is within the target area of 'the stock objections against an argument from an effect to a supposed cause of a type which is never directly observed'. (Part of the trouble here is a misconception of direct realism as a surely forlorn attempt to make perceptual knowledge unproblematic; *PFL* 43.)

[17] The phrases 'manifest image' and 'scientific image' are due to Wilfrid Sellars; see 'Philosophy and the Scientific Image of Man', in *Science, Perception and Reality* (London: Routledge & Kegan Paul, 1963).

[18] This is the position of Strawson, 'Perception and its Objects' (and see also his 'Reply to Evans', in van Straaten (ed.), *Philosophical Subjects*. I am suggesting a diagnosis, to back up McGinn's complaint, *The Subjective View*, 124 n.

say that colours and shapes figure in experience, not as the representational significance carried by features that are—being intrinsic features of experience—indifferently subjective (which makes it hard to see how a difference in respect of objectivity could show up in their representational significance); but simply as properties that objects are represented as having, distinctively phenomenal in the one case and not so in the other. (Without the supposed intrinsic features, we would be immune to the illusion that experiences cannot represent objects as having properties that are not phenomenal—properties that are adequately conceivable otherwise than in terms of dispositions to produce suitable experiences.[19]) What Locke unfelicitously tried to yoke together, with his picture of real resemblances of our 'ideas', can now divide into two notions that we must insist on keeping separate: first, the possible veridicality of experience (the objectivity of its object, in the second of the two senses I distinguished), in respect of which primary and secondary qualities are on all fours; and second, the not essentially phenomenal character of some properties that experience represents objects as having (their objectivity in the first sense), which marks off the primary perceptible qualities from the secondary ones.

In order to deny that a quality's figuring in experience consists in an experience's having a certain intrinsic feature, we do not need to reject the intrinsic features altogether; it would suffice to insist that a quality's figuring in experience consists in an experience's having a certain intrinsic feature *together with* the quality's being the representational significance carried by that feature. But I do not believe that this yields a position in which acceptance of the supposed vehicles of content coheres with a satisfactory account of perception. This position would have it that the fact that an experience represents things as being one way rather than another is strictly additional to the experience's intrinsic nature, and so extrinsic to the experience itself (it seems natural to say 'read into it'). There is a phenomenological falsification here. (This brings out a third role for Locke's resemblance, namely to obviate the threat of such a falsification by constituting a sort of instrinsic representationality: Locke's 'ideas' carry the representational significance they do by virtue of what they are like, and this can be glossed both as 'how they are intrinsically' and as 'what

---

[19] Notice Strawson's sleight of hand with phrases like 'shapes-as-seen', at p. 286 of 'Reply to Evans'. Strawson's understanding of what Evans is trying to say fails altogether to accommodate Evans's remark ('Things without the Mind', 96) that 'to deny that . . . primary properties are *sensory* is not at all to deny that they are *sensible* or *observable*'. Shapes as seen are *shapes*—that is, non-sensory properties: it is one thing to deny, as Evans does, that experience can furnish us with the concepts of such properties, but quite another to deny that experience can disclose instantiations of them to us.

they resemble'.) In any case, given that we cannot project ourselves from features of experience to non-phenomenal properties of objects by means of an appeal to resemblance, it is doubtful that the metaphor of representational significance being 'read into' intrinsic features can be spelled out in such a way as to avoid the second horn of our dilemma. How could representational significance be 'read into' intrinsic features of experience in such a way that what was signified did not need to be understood in terms of them? How could a not intrinsically representational feature of experience become imbued with objective significance in such a way that an experience could count, by virtue of having that feature, as a direct awareness of a not essentially phenomenal property of objects?[20]

How things strike someone as being is, in a clear sense, a subjective matter: there is no conceiving it in abstraction from the subject of the experience. Now a motive for insisting on the supposed vehicles of aspects of content might lie in an aspiration, familiar in philosophy, to bring subjectivity within the compass of a fundamentally objective conception of reality.[21] If aspects of content are not carried by elements in an intrinsic structure, their subjectivity is irreducible. By contrast, one might hope to objectivize any 'essential subjectivity' that needs to be attributed to not intrinsically representational features of experience, by exploiting a picture involving special access on a subject's part to something conceived in a broadly objective way—its presence in the world not conceived as constituted by the subject's special access to it.[22] Given this move, it becomes natural to suppose that the phenomenal character of the 'manifest image' can be explained in terms of a certain familiar picture: one in which a confronted 'external' reality, conceived as having only an objective nature, is processed through a structured 'subjectivity', conceived in this objectivistic manner. This picture seems to capture the essence of Mackie's approach to the secondary qualities.[23] What I have tried to suggest it that

---

[20] Features of physiologically specified states are not to the point here. Such features are not apparent in experience; whereas the supposed features that I am concerned with would have to be aspects of what experience is like for us, in order to function intelligibly as carriers for aspects of the content that experience presents to us. There may be an inclination to ask why it should be any harder for a feature of experience to acquire an objective singificance than it is for a word to do so. But the case of language affords no counterpart to the fact that the objective significance in the case we are concerned with is a matter of how things (e.g.) *look* to be: the special problem is how to stop that 'look' having the effect that a supposed intrinsic feature of experience gets taken up into its own representational significance, thus ensuring that the significance is phenomenal and not primary.

[21] See Thomas Nagel, 'Subjective and Objective', in *Mortal Questions* (Cambridge: Cambridge University Press, 1979).

[22] Cf. Bernard Williams, *Descartes: The Project of Pure Enquiry* (Harmondsworth: Penguin, 1978), 295.

[23] Although McGinn, *The Subjective View*, is not taken in by the idea that 'external' reality has only objective characteristics, I am not sure that he sufficiently avoids the picture that

the picture is suspect in threatening to cut us off from the *primary* (not essentially phenomenal) qualities of the objects that we perceive: either (with the appeal to resemblance) making it impossible, after all, to keep an essentially phenomenal character out of our conception of the qualities in question, or else making them merely hypothetical, not accessible to perception. If we are to achieve a satisfactory understanding of experience's openness to objective reality, we must put a more radical construction on experience's essential subjectivity. And this removes an insidious obstacle—one whose foundation is summarily captured in Mackie's idea that it is not simply wrong to count 'colours as we see them' as items in our minds (see the diagram at *PEL* 17)—that stands in the way of understanding how secondary-quality experience can be awareness, with nothing misleading about its phenomenal character, of properties genuinely possessed by elements in a not exclusively phenomenal reality.

4

The empirical ground that Mackie thinks we have for not postulating 'thoroughly objective features which resemble our ideas of secondary qualities' (*PFL* 18–19) is that attributing such features to objects is surplus to the requirements of explaining our experience of secondary qualities (see *PFL* 17–18). If it would be incoherent to attribute such features to objects, as I believe, this empirical argument falls away as unnecessary. But it is worth considering how an argument from explanatory superfluity might fare against the less extravagant construal I have suggested for the thought that secondary qualities genuinely characterize objects: not because the question is difficult or contentious, but because of the light it casts on how an explanatory test for reality—which is commonly thought to undermine the claims of values—should be applied.

A '*virtus dormitiva*' objection would tell against the idea that one might mount a satisfying explanation of an object's looking red on its being such as to look red. The weight of the explanation would fall through the disposition to its structural ground.[24] Still, however optimistic we are about the prospects for explaining colour experience on the basis of surface

underlies that idea: see pp. 106–9. (This connects with a suspicion that at pp. 9–10 he partly succumbs to a temptation to objectivize the subjective properties of objects that he countenances: it is not as clear as he seems to suppose that, say, redness can be, so to speak, abstracted from the way things strike *us* by an appeal to relativity. His worry at pp. 132–6, that secondary-quality experience may after all be phenomenologically misleading, seems to betray the influence of the idea of content-bearing intrinsic features of experience.)

[24] See ibid. 14.

textures,[25] it would be obviously wrong to suppose that someone who gave such an explanation could in consistency deny that the object was such as to look red. The right explanatory test is not whether something pulls its own weight in the favoured explanation (it may fail to do so without thereby being explained away), but whether the explainer can consistently deny its reality.[26]

Given Mackie's view about secondary qualities, the thought that values fail an explanatory test for reality is implicit in a parallel that he commonly draws between them (see, for instance, *HMT* 51–2; E 19–20. It is nearer the surface in his 'argument from queerness' (*E* 38–42; pp. 76–9 in this volume), and explicit in his citing 'patterns of objectification' to explain the distinctive phenomenology of value experience (*E* 42–6; pp. 79–82 in this volume).[27] Now it is, if anything, even more obvious with values than with essentially phenomenal qualities that they cannot be credited with causal efficacy: values would not pull their weight in any explanation of value experience even remotely analogous to the standard explanations of primary-quality experience. But reflection on the case of secondary qualities has already opened a gap between that admission and any concession that values are not genuine aspects of reality. And the point is reinforced by a crucial disanalogy between values and secondary qualities. To press the analogy is to stress that evaluative 'attitudes', or states of will, are like (say) colour experience in being unintelligible except as modifications of a sensibility like ours. The idea of value experience involves taking admiration, say, to represent its object as having a property which (although there in the object) is essentially subjective in much the same way as the property that an object is represented as having by an experience of redness—that is, understood adequately only in terms of the appropriate modification of human (or similar) sensibility. The disanalogy, now, is that a virtue (say) is conceived to be not merely such as to elicit the appropriate 'attitude' (as a colour is merely such as to cause the appropriate experiences), but rather such as to *merit* it. And this makes it doubtful whether merely causal

---

[25] There are difficulties over how complete such explanations could aspire to be: see Price, 'Varieties of Objectivity and Values', 114–15; and my 'Aesthetic Value, Objectivity, and the Fabric of the World', 10–12.

[26] Cf. pp. 206–8, esp. p. 208, of David Wiggins, 'What would be a Substantial Theory of Truth?' in van Straaten (ed.), *Philosophical Subjects*. The test of whether the explanations in question are consistent with rejecting the item in contention is something that Wiggins once mooted, in the course of a continuing attempt to improve that formulation; I am indebted to discussions with him.

[27] See also Simon Blackburn, 'Rule-Following and Moral Realism', in Steven Holtzman and Christopher Leich (eds.). *Wittgenstein: To Follow a Rule* (London: Routledge & Kegan Paul, 1981); and the first chapter of Gilbert Harman, *The Nature of Morality* (New York: Oxford University Press, 1977) (Ch. VI in this volume).

explanations of value experience are relevant to the explanatory test, even to the extent that the question to ask is whether someone could consistently give such explanations while denying that the values involved are real. It looks as if we should be raising that question about explanations of a different kind.

For simplicity's sake, I shall elaborate this point in connection with something that is not a value, though it shares the crucial feature: namely danger or the fearful. On the face of it, this might seem a promising subject for a projectivist treatment (a treatment that appeals to what Hume called the mind's 'propensity to spread itself on external objects'[28]). At any rate the response that, according to such a treatment, is projected into the world can be characterized, without phenomenological falsification, otherwise than in terms of seeming to find the supposed product of projection already there.[29] And it would be obviously grotesque to fancy that a case of fear might be explained as the upshot of a mechanical (or perhaps paramechanical) process initiated by an instance of 'objective fearfulness'. But if what we are engaged in is an 'attempt to understand ourselves',[30] then merely causal explanations of responses like fear will not be satisfying anyway.[31] What we want here is a style of explanation that makes sense of what is explained (in so far as sense can be made of it). This means that a technique for giving satisfying explanations of cases of fear—which would perhaps amount to a satisfying explanatory theory of danger, though the label is possibly too grand—must allow for the possibility of criticism; we make sense of fear by seeing it as a response to objects that *merit* such a response, or as the intelligibly defective product of a propensity towards responses that would be intelligible in that way.[32] For an object to merit fear just is for it to be fearful. So explanations of fear that manifest our capacity to understand ourselves in this region of our lives will simply not

[28] *A Treatise of Human Nature*. I. iii. 14. 'Projectivist' is Blackburn's useful label: see 'Rule-Following and Moral Realism'; and 'Opinions and Chances', in D. H. Mellor (ed.), *Prospects for Pragmatism* (Cambridge: Cambridge University Press, 1980).

[29] At pp. 180–1 of 'Opinions and Chances', Blackburn suggests that a projectivist need not mind whether or not this is so; but I think he trades on a slide between 'can . . . only be understood in terms of' and 'our best vocabulary for identifying' (which allows that there may be an admittedly inferior alternative).

[30] The phrase is from p. 165 of Blackburn, 'Rule-Following and Moral Realism'.

[31] I do not mean that satisfying explanations will not be causal. But they will not be *merely* causal.

[32] I am assuming that we are not in the presence of a theory according to which no responses of the kind in question *could* be well-placed. That would have a quite unintended effect. (See *E* 16; p. 59 in this volume.) Notice that it will not meet my point to suggest that calling a response 'well-placed' is to be understood only quasi-realistically. Explanatory indispensability is supposed to be the test for the *genuine* reality supposedly lacked by what warrants only quasi-realistic treatment.

cohere with the claim that reality contains nothing in the way of fearful-ness.[33] Any such claim would undermine the intelligibility that the explana-tions confer on our responses.

The shared crucial features suggest that this disarming of a supposed explanatory argument for unreality should carry over to the case of values. There is, of course, a striking disanalogy in the contentiousness that is typical of values; but I think it would be a mistake to suppose that this spoils the point. In so far as we succeed in achieving the sort of understand-ing of our responses that is in question, we do so on the basis of prepared-ness to attribute, to at least some possible objects of the responses, properties that would validate the responses. What the disanalogy makes especially clear is that the explanations that preclude our denying the reality of the special properties that are putatively discernible from some (broadly) evaluative point of view are themselves constructed from that point of view. (We already had this in the case of the fearful, but the point is brought home when the validation of the responses is controversial.) However, the critical dimension of the explanations that we want means that there is no question of just any actual response pulling itself up by its own bootstraps into counting as an undistorted perception of the relevant special aspect of reality.[34] Indeed, awareness that values are contentious tells against an unreflective contentment with the current state of one's critical outlook, and in favour of a readiness to suppose that there may be something to be learned from people with whom one's first inclination is to disagree. The aspiration to understand oneself is an aspiration to change one's responses, if that is necessary for them to become intelligible other-wise than as defective. But although a sensible person will never be confi-dent that his evaluative outlook is incapable of improvement, that need not stop him supposing, of some of his evaluative responses, that their objects really do merit them. He will be able to back up this supposition with explanations that show how the responses are well placed; the expla-nations will share the contentiousness of the values whose reality they certify, but that should not stop him accepting the explanations any more than (what nobody thinks) it should stop him endorsing the values.[35] There

[33] Cf. Blackburn, 'Rule-Following and Moral Realism', 164.

[34] This will be so even in areas in which there are no materials for constructing standards of criticism except actual responses: something that is not so with fearfulness, although given a not implausible holism it will be so with values.

[35] I can see no reason why we should not regard the contentiousness as ineliminabe. The effect of this would be to detach the explanatory test of reality from a requirement of conver-gence (cf. the passage by Wiggins cited in n. 26 above). As far as I can see, this separation would be a good thing. It would enable resistance to projectivism to free itself, with a good conscience, of some unnecessary worries about relativism. It might also discourage a misconception of the appeal to Wittgenstein that comes naturally to such a position. (Blackburn, 'Rule-Following and

is perhaps an air of bootstrapping about this. But if we restrict ourselves to explanations from a more external standpoint, at which values are not in our field of view, we deprive ourselves of a kind of intelligibility that we aspire to; and projectivists have given no reason whatever to suppose that there would be anything better about whatever different kind of self-understanding the restriction would permit.

5

It will be obvious how these considerations undermine the damaging effect of the primary-quality model. Shifting to a secondary-quality analogy renders irrelevant any worry about how something that is brutely *there* could nevertheless stand in an internal relation to some exercise of human sensibility. Values are not brutely there—not there independently of our sensibility—any more than colours are; though, as with colours, this does not stop us supposing that they are there independently of any particular apparent experience of them. As for the epistemology of value, the epistemology of danger is a good model. (Fearfulness is not a secondary quality, although the model is available only after the primary-quality model has been dislodged. A secondary-quality analogy for value experience gives out at certain points, no less than the primary-quality analogy that Mackie attacks.) To drop the primary-quality model in this case is to give up the idea that fearfulness itself, were it real, would need to be intelligible from a standpoint independent of the propensity to fear; the same must go for the relations of rational consequentiality in which fearfulness stands to more straightforward properties of things.[36] Explanations of fear of the sort I envisaged would not only establish, from a different standpoint, that some of its objects are really fearful, but also make plain, case by case, what it is about that that makes them so; this should leave it quite unmysterious how a fear response rationally grounded in awareness (unproblematic, at least for present purposes) of these 'fearful-making characteristics' can be counted as being, or

Moral Realism', 170–4, reads into my 'Non-Cognitivism and Rule-Following', in Holtzman and Leich, (eds.), *Wittgenstein*, an interpretation of Wittgenstein as, in effect, making truth a matter of consensus, and has no difficulty in arguing that this will not make room for hard cases; but the interpretation is not mine.) With the requirement of convergence dropped, or at least radically relativized to a point of view, the question of the claim to truth of directives may come closer to the question of the truth status of evaluations than Wiggins suggests, at least in 'Truth, Invention, and the Meaning of Life' (Ch. ix in this volume).

[36] Mackie's question (*E* 41; p. 78 in this volume) 'Just what *in the world* is signified by this "because"?' involves a tendentious notion of 'the world'.

yielding, knowledge that one is confronted by an instance of real fearfulness.[37]

Simon Blackburn has written, on behalf of a projectivist sentimentalism in ethics, that 'we profit . . . by realizing that a training of the feelings rather than a cultivation of a mysterious ability to spot the immutable fitnesses of things is the foundation of how to live'.[38] This picture of what an opponent of projectivism must hold is of a piece with Mackie's primary-quality model; it simply fails to fit the position I have described.[39] Perhaps with Aristotle's notion of practical wisdom in mind, one might ask why a training of the feelings (as long as the notion of feeling is comprehensive enough) cannot *be* the cultivation of an ability—utterly unmysterious just because of its connections with feelings—to spot (if you like) the fitnesses of things; even 'immutable' may be all right, so long as it is not understood (as I take it Blackburn intends) to suggest a 'platonistic' conception of the fitnesses of things, which would reimport the characteristic ideas of the primary-quality model.[40]

Mackie's response to this suggestion used to be, in effect, that it simply conceded his point.[41] Can a projectivist claim that the position I have outlined is at best a notational variant, perhaps an inferior notational variant, of his own position?

It would be inferior if, in eschewing the projectivist metaphysical framework, it obscured some important truth. But what truth would this be? It will not do at this point to answer 'the truth of projectivism'. I have disarmed the explanatory argument for the projectivist's thin conception of genuine reality. What remains is rhetoric expressing what amounts to a now unargued primary-quality model for genuine reality.[42] The picture that this suggests for value experience—objective (value-free) reality processed through a moulded subjectivity—is no less questionable than the

---

[37] See Price, Varieties of Objectivity and Values', 106–7, 115.

[38] 'Rule-Following and Moral Realism', 186.

[39] Blackburn's realist evades the explanatory burdens that sentimentalism discharges, by making the world rich (cf. p. 181) and then picturing it as simply setting its print on us. Cf. *E* 22 (p. 63 in this volume): 'If there were something in the fabric of the world that validated certain kinds of concern, then it would be possible to acquire these merely by finding something out, by letting one's thinking be controlled by how things were.' This saddles an opponent of projectivism with a picture of awareness of value as an exercise of pure receptivity, preventing him from deriving any profit from an analogy with secondary-quality perception.

[40] On 'platonism', see my 'Non-Cognitivism and Rule-Following', 156–7. On Aristotle, see M. F. Burnyeat, 'Aristotle on Learning to be Good', in Amelie O. Rorty (ed.), *Essays on Aristotle's Ethics* (Berkeley and Los Angeles: University of California Press, 1980).

[41] Price, 'Varieties of Objectivity and Values', 107, cites Mackie's response to one of my contributions to the 1978 seminar.

[42] We must not let the confusion between the two notions of objectivity distinguished in Sect. 3 above seem to support this conception of reality.

picture of secondary-quality experience on which, in Mackie at any rate, it is explicitly modelled. In fact I should be inclined to argue that it is projectivism that is inferior. Deprived of the specious explanatory argument, projectivism has nothing to sustain its thin conception of reality (that on to which the projections are effected) but a contentiously substantial version of the correspondence theory of truth, with the associated picture of genuinely true judgement as something to which the judge makes no contribution at all.[43]

I do not want to argue this now. The point I want to make is that even if projectivism were not actually worse, metaphysically speaking, than the alternative I have described, it would be wrong to regard the issue between them as nothing but a question of metaphysical preference.[44] In the projectivist picture, having one's ethical or aesthetic responses rationally suited to their objects would be a matter of having the relevant processing mechanism functioning acceptably. Now projectivism can of course perfectly well accommodate the idea of assessing one's processing mechanism. But it pictures the mechanism as something that one can contemplate as an object in itself. It would be appropriate to say 'something one can step back from', were it not for the fact that one needs to use the mechanism itself in assessing it; at any rate one is supposed to be able to step back from any naïvely realistic acceptance of the values that the first-level employment of the mechanism has one attribute to items in the world. How, then, are we to understand this pictured availability of the processing mechanism as an object for contemplation, separated off from the world of value? Is there any alternative to thinking of it as capable of being captured, at least in theory, by a set of principles for superimposing values onto a value-free reality? The upshot is that the search for an evaluative outlook that one can endorse as rational becomes, virtually irresistibly, a search for such a set of principles: a search for a *theory* of beauty or goodness. One comes to count 'intuitions' respectable only in so far as they can be validated by an approximation to that ideal.[45] (This is the shape that the attempt to objectivize subjectivity takes here.) I have a hunch that

[43] Blackburn uses the correspondence theorist's pictures for rhetorical effect, but he is properly sceptical about whether this sort of realism makes sense (see 'Truth, Realism, and the Regulation of Theory'). His idea is that the explanatory argument makes a counterpart to its metaphysical favouritism safely available to a projectivist about values in particular. Deprived of the explanatory argument, this projectivism should simply wither away. (See 'Rule-Following and Moral Realism', 165.) Of course I am not saying that the thin conception of reality that Blackburn's projectivism needs is unattainable, in the sense of being unformulable. What we lack are reasons of a respectable kind to recognize it as a complete conception of *reality*.

[44] Something like this seems to be suggested by Price, 'Varieties of Objectivity and Values', 107–8.

[45] It is hard to see how a rational *inventing* of values could take a more piecemeal form.

such efforts are misguided; not that we should rest content with an 'anything goes' irrationalism, but that we need a conception of rationality in evaluation that will cohere with the possibility that particular cases may stubbornly resist capture in any general net. Such a conception is straightforwardly available within the alternative to projectivism that I have described. I allowed that being able to explain cases of fear in the right way might amount to having a theory of danger, but there is no need to generalize that feature of the case; the explanatory capacity that certifies the special objects of an evaluative outlook as real, and certifies its responses to them as rational, would need to be exactly as creative and case-specific as the capacity to discern those objects itself. (It would be the same capacity: the picture of 'stepping back' does not fit here.[46]) I take it that my hunch poses a question of moral and aesthetic taste, which—like other questions of taste—should be capable of being argued about. The trouble with projectivism is that it threatens to bypass that argument, on the basis of a metaphysical picture whose purported justification falls well short of making it compulsory. We should not let the question seem to be settled by what stands revealed, in the absence of compelling argument, as a prejudice claiming the honour due to metaphysical good taste.

---

[46] Why do I suggest that a particularistic conception of evaluative rationality is unavailable to a projectivist? (See Blackburn, 'Rule-Following and Moral Reaslism', 167–70.) In the terms of that discussion, the point is that (with no good explanatory argument for his metaphysical favouritism) a projectivist has no alternative to being 'a real realist' about the world on which he thinks values are superimposed. He cannot stop this from generating a quite un-Wittgensteinian picture of what *really* going on in the same way would be; which means that *he* cannot appeal to Wittgenstein in order to avert, as Blackburn puts it, 'the threat which shapelessness poses to a respectable notion of consistency' (p. 169). So, at any rate, I meant to argue in my 'Non-Cognitivism and Rule-Following', to which Blackburn's paper is a reply. Blackburn thinks his projectivism is untouched by the argument, because he thinks he can sustain its metaphysical favouritism without appealing to *real* realism', on the basis of the explanatory argument. But I have argued that this is an illusion. (At p. 181, Blackburn writes: 'Of course, it is true that our reactions are "simply felt" and, in a sense, not rationally explicable.' He thinks he can comfortably say this because our conception of reason will go along with the quasi-realist truth that his projectivism confers on some evaluations. But how can one restrain the metaphysical favouritism that a projectivist must show from generating some such thought as 'This is not *real* reason'? If that is allowed to happen, a remark like the one I have quoted will merely threaten—like an ordinary nihilism—to dislodge from our ethical and aesthetic convictions.)

XIII

TWO CONCEPTIONS OF MORAL REALISM

JONATHAN DANCY

I

In this paper I distinguish two conceptions of moral realism, strong and weak, and argue the merits of the former. In fact, I argue that the weak conception is not a form of moral realism at all. I take moral realism to be a view about the nature of moral properties; the realist holds that moral properties are real properties of objects. The two conceptions differ on the sense they give to the notion of a real property. According to the weaker conception, a property is a real property of an object if it is a property which is there anyway, independent of any particular experience of it. A popular (but not the only nor necessarily the best) way of capturing this notion of independence is to require that real properties persist when unperceived. As Hume held, continuity entails independence. On this approach, real properties are real (i.e. are there to be experienced) because they persist (i.e. are there *waiting* to be experienced). Another way of capturing this notion of independence is to turn our attention away from continuity in our world, and consider instead characterizations which turn on the nature of other worlds. Thus we might require the real properties to be ones which objects can have in certain counterfactual circumstances. On the first approach, then, subjunctive conditionals about what would be experienced if one were to look are sustained by statements about the actual continuity of the objects of experience. On the second, the subjunctive conditionals are grounded in statements about the properties that objects can bear in worlds very different from ours, typically worlds which lack perceiving minds. Such worlds are unfortunately not much use in ethical theory, not because it is so obvious that moral properties have no

From *Proceedings of the Aristotelian Society*, suppl. vol. 60 (1986), 167–87. Reprinted by courtesy of the Editor of the Aristotelian Society, © 1986.

I acknowledge with gratitude the helpful comments I have received on earlier drafts from David Bakhurst, Robert Gay, Harry Lewis, Richard Swinburne, and particularly David McNaughton and Michael Smith.

place in worlds devoid of minds to perceive them, but because the only possible objects of moral approval and disapproval are necessarily absent in such worlds. There are no actions and no agents there. Whether or not a suitable version of the relevant notion of independence can be constructed by some similar appeal to possible worlds, I do not here presume to judge. For present purposes, it will be sufficient to work with the simpler notion of continuity. Real properties, then, on the weaker conception, are those that are there waiting to be experienced.

There is, however, a stronger account of what it is for a property to be a real property of objects, which offers a stronger sense in which the moral properties of actions exist independent of our awareness of them and so generates a stronger conception of moral realism. On this account, real properties are those which are not constituted by the availability or possibility of a characteristic human response. This differs from its predecessor because properties which are real on the weaker conception may still count as unreal on the stronger. Neither sense of 'real' is in itself better than the other, of course. But in deciding what the moral realist can and should claim we need to hold the two apart. The question is whether the realist should and can restrict himself to holding that moral properties are real in the weaker sense.

We should distinguish questions about the real from questions about the objective and subjective. In my terms this last is a distinction between two types of concepts, the question in ethics being 'Are moral concepts subjective?' A concept of ours is subjective if it could not be grasped by a being that did not share in characteristic human concerns. Our moral concepts are subjective if beings that do not share in those concerns could not make any sense of the way of carving up the world that our moral vocabulary represents. I take John McDowell to have provided an effective argument that moral concepts are subjective.[1] This is what is sometimes called the disentangling argument, which holds that there is only one way in which beings who do not share our concerns could hope to come to understand the distinctions we draw between right and wrong, good and bad (and all the 'thick' distinctions between the generous, tactless, rude, kind etc.). This would be for them to substitute for our way of drawing these distinctions, which naturally depends upon their relation to our concerns, a different way which latches onto *natural* similarities between objects, similarities which fit and act as ground for our regular responses to them. But we have no reason to suppose there to be any such natural similarities. Why should

---

[1] See his 'Non-Cognitivism and Rule-Following', in Steven Holtzman and Christopher Leich (eds.), *Wittgenstein: To Follow a Rule* (London: Routledge & Kegan Paul, 1981), esp. pp. 144–5.

there be only one way of getting to be rude, a natural similarity between rude actions (or people) to which our perception of them as rude can be seen as a response? And if there are many ways of being rude, our aliens will have no way of catching onto the shape we give to our concept of rudeness. Our moral concepts will for them be shapeless because their natural grounds are shapeless. The natural properties from which rudeness results in particular cases will differ in ways whose irrelevance the aliens will have no hope of understanding, and if they cannot understand this they will be unable to predict our uses of the concept, and thus unable to find any substitute way of joining in with (or at least appearing to join in with) our moral thought.

Moral concepts, then, are subjective, and this claim is one, but only one, sense of the idea that moral properties are anthropocentric. They are anthropocentric because the concepts of those properties could not be grasped by beings who did not share in characteristic human concerns.

There is however another sense we could give to the idea that moral properties are anthropocentric, which has already emerged in discussion of the two acounts of what it is for a property to be a real property of objects. We might say that moral properties are anthropocentric because they are constituted by the possibility or availability of a characteristic human response. And this would give anyone who, though tempted by moral realism, was also convinced by the disentangling argument that moral concepts are subjective a strong incentive to stick to the weaker conception of real properties. For such a person ends up in the apparently comfortable position of maintaining that moral properties are anthropocentric in both senses, but still real properties of objects.

I see no reason in advance, however, to suppose that the two notions of the anthropocentric necessarily go together. There still remains the possibility, for all that has been said so far, of maintaining that moral properties are anthropocentric in the first sense (because moral concepts are subjective), but not anthropocentric in the second sense (because they are not constituted by the possibility of or availability of a characteristic human response). Someone attracted by the stronger form of moral realism would find himself in this position; for such a person, moral properties, *qua* real, are not anthropocentric in the second sense.

I do not see any argument which is going to show it straightforwardly inconsistent to hold both that moral concepts are subjective and that moral properties are, in the strong sense, real properties of objects. There seem to be plenty of examples where we want to adopt this combination of strong realism and subjectivity. For instance, I take the pain of another to be a real property which she has unfortunately got, but I want to hold that the concept of such a pain is subjective. But there is no doubt that this is an uncomfortable position in ethics; though there seem to me to be good reasons for getting into it, it is difficult to be entirely happy when one is there. This sense of tension in the position, which I share, is probably what has led some to accept the weaker sense of realism, one which claims less and suffers from correspondingly fewer threats of lurking inconsistency. It is this search which has led some of those sympathetic with the claims of moral realism to take seriously an analogy between moral properties and secondary qualities.

Secondary qualities of objects, conceived of in Locke's way, are unreal properties of objects on the strong conception of what it is for a property to be a real property. As dispositions to cause certain effects, they are permanent properties of the objects that have them, but their nature is constituted by the nature of the characteristic effect which they are dispositions to cause. The effect is a characteristic human response, and so this leaves the secondary properties as unreal properties. But if we adopted instead the weaker conception of what it is for a property to be real, colour, viewed in Locke's way as a disposition to cause a characteristic effect in us, is a real because persisting property of objects. It is real because the disposition persists even when not being triggered by events, as commentators on Locke have been so rightly fond of emphasizing.

The point now is, of course, that we can easily conceive of moral properties as real in the weaker sense, while agreeing that moral concepts are subjective, without even the appearance of inconsistency. All we need to do is to conceive of moral properties in a way analogous to colours as Locke conceives them, i.e. as dispositions in the object to cause or elicit certain characteristic human responses in us; and then the analogy with secondary qualities does the work for us. This is the approach of John McDowell's 'Values and Secondary Qualities'[2] (henceforth VASQ), to which the present paper is intended as a reply. And for his purposes there we do not need to drive the analogy very far. All that we need it to do is to show that it is possible for moral concepts to be subjective although moral properties are real properties of objects. The analogy relies on our agreement that colour is a distinctively phenomenal property and a real property at the same time, i.e. that phenomenal aspects of objects can be real aspects of the world. And we then simply say that this is how moral properties are too. But the analogy pretends to achieve no more than this, and respects in which colour is disanalogous with moral properties, which

---

[2] In Ted Honderich (ed.), *Morality and Objectivity* (London: Routledge & Kegan Paul, 1985). I have also been very much helped by Michael Smith's unpublished paper 'An Argument for Moral Realism'.

are admitted to be numerous, are irrelevant; they do not impugn its limited use for this one purpose, as McDowell insists.

Despite the attractions of this weaker conception of moral realism, I want to argue that it should be viewed as satisfactory by nobody, and that realists have got to be brave. The only possible form of moral realism lies in the stronger conception. This is because the weaker conception is inconsistent with the main argument for moral realism, and hence has no possible provenance. It is not a form of moral realism at all. I shall also argue that the weaker conception collapses into the stronger one at the end of the day.

It is not necessary for this purpose that I say more in defence of the stronger conception, for which I have offered no defence beyond a non-ethical example, that of another's pain. But I shall need to deal at some point with one direct argument in favour of the weaker conception, given by John McDowell (VASQ 110). This is that only by adopting some such view can we achieve a conception of an objective circumstance which is internally related to the will. Now it may be that not all realists are committed to or even attracted to such a conception; not all may or need share his idea of a cognitive state all the possessors of which see exactly the same reasons to act. Indeed, it is not clear exactly how McDowell pictures the content of such a state. But even for those who do share this idea, I do not believe that the weaker conception succeeds in making good sense of objective circumstances internally related to the will. Reasons for this will emerge later, after suitable preparation.

II

The first step must be an expression of the main argument for moral realism. This is the argument from moral phenomenology; it is beginning to acquire its own history and bibliography.[3] I take there to be two forms of the argument, one simple and one more complex.

The simple form can be found in Mackie's view that we take moral value to be part of the fabric of the world; taking our experience at face value, we judge it to be experience of the moral properties of actions and agents in

---

[3] See J. L. Mackie, *Ethics: Inventing Right and Wrong* (Harmondsworth: Penguin, 1977), ch. 1 (Ch. V of this volume); David Wiggins, 'Truth, Invention, and the Meaning of Life', *Proceedings of the British Academy*, 62 (1976), 331–78 (Ch. IX of this volume); S. Lovibond, *Realism and Imagination in Ethics* (Oxford: Basil Blackwell, 1989); Thomas Nagel, 'The Limits of Objectivity', in Sterling McMurrin (ed.), *The Tanner Lectures on Human Values*, i (Salt Lake City and Cambridge: University of Utah Press and Cambridge University Press, 1980), esp. pp. 100–1 (Ch. VIII of this volume, esp. pp. 109–24).

the world. And if we are to work with the presumption that the world is the way our experience represents it to us as being, we should take it in the absence of contrary considerations that actions and agents do have the sorts of moral properties we experience in them. This is an argument about the nature of moral experience, which moves from that nature to the probable nature of the world.

We shall return to the question whether the weaker conception is consistent with this simple form of the phenomenology argument. But before doing so it is worth spelling out the more complex form. This starts from Wiggins's suggestion that non-cognitivism distorts the phenomenology of moral choice. In moral choice we struggle to find, not any answer that we can bring ourselves to accept, nor any answer that we can accept in consistency with previous answers, but the right answer. We present our search to ourselves as one governed by a criterion which does not lie in ourselves; our fear is that we may make the wrong choice, a fear not allayed by the thought that we might make that choice quite happily and/or consistently with previous choices. Why otherwise should moral choice be so dodgy? Why otherwise should I agonize about what is the right thing to do in the circumstances? Non-cognitivism leaves moral life too easy, and is inconsistent with the phenomenology. It distorts our sense of the authority that the action which we choose as right has over us. That authority is one to which our choice must conform, and cannot itself depend on our choice; our choice is a recognition of an authority which it could not itself create. We can express this in another way by saying that in this area at least desire is impossible without desirability. Moral desire and commitment does not appear as a free inclination of the will, but as a response demanded by the desirability of the object–action. We recognize that desirability, and our choice begins to be constrained by that recognition. The criterion for choice then is the desirability of the action, rather than the criterion for desirability being our choice (desire).

It is the simple form of the argument that will concern us for the remainder of this paper, for only the simple form is concerned with our experience of the moral properties of actions we perform or see performed in front of us. The complex form is more to do with the phenomenology of moral *choice* than that of moral experience, and this means that the sense in which it combines with the simple to make a single case is not perfectly clear. However they do combine, I do not want to say that the two arguments are conclusive, though they do seem to me in combination to be very strong; at the limit, they aim to show that we abandon moral realism at the cost of making our moral experience unintelligible. The point here is that anything that presents itself as a form of realism needs to be consistent with their general thrust. I hold that the weaker conception fails just at this point.

There are two ways to make this out. The first is to raise general doubts about the compatibility of the sort of primary–secondary distinction to which the weaker conception appeals with any serious use of the phenomenology argument. Perhaps the best way to do this is to move away from ethics for a moment and look at a distinction between two sorts of direct realism in the theory of perception. The direct realist holds that we are not aware of physical objects in virtue of a more direct awareness of some intermediary objects, sensa perhaps. One of the arguments for this position is a feeling that we cannot make good enough sense of the intermediary objects, in particular that they do not seem to have sufficient properties of the right sort to sustain the role here assigned to them. But another argument starts from the phenomenology of perception. The sort of double awareness of which indirect realists speak so warmly is not one of which we are aware; for us there only seems to be a single awareness, which when we are lucky is an awareness of the world around us. This phenomenology argument is far from conclusive, but it represents perhaps the first reason for taking direct realism seriously (just as in ethics the phenomenology of moral experience is the first and perhaps the only argument for realism, remaining thoughts being used for defence–offence). And the point of all this is that it is not clear that the primary–secondary-quality distinction is compatible with the realist's attitude to the phenomenology. For that distinction amounts to taking the phenomenology seriously only some of the time; the more we draw the secondary qualities away from the objects and nearer to ourselves, the more we step away from the direct realist's feeling that in perception we are open to the world as it is before us. For some of the way the world presents itself to us is abstracted from it by the distinction between primary and secondary qualities, becoming instead more an aspect of our response than an aspect of that to which perception is a response.

It might still be objected to this that the weaker conception does not draw the secondary qualities away from the objects and nearer to ourselves, since it places those qualities firmly in the objects as dispositions to cause characteristic responses in us. This leads me to the second and more powerful argument that the weaker position is not consistent with the phenomenology argument(s): it is hard to make good sense, within that position, of the idea that moral properties can be experienced. For the experiences we have, as effects of a disposition in the objects to cause those experiences in us, do not seem to be experiences *of* that disposition. More is required for an experience that is caused by a dispositional property to be an experience *of* that property, and that more is lacking in the case we are now considering. Our moral experiences, on this approach, seem to be more like manifestations of the disposition than experiences of it.

So far this complaint has only the status of a suspicion. But if it is sound it will be fatal to the weaker conception's claim to be a form of moral realism, for in undermining the idea of moral experience it removes all possibility of reliance on the phenomenology argument. In the next section I attempt to make the best sense of this thought. One difficulty will be that it threatens to prove too much, for if sound it bids fair to have the same consequences for colour perception, on the Lockean primary–secondary model. Can we really accept that Locke was unable to make good sense of the idea that we experience the colour of objects? There is some reason to believe that he was, but we will return to this question later and our rejection of the weaker conception will not initially depend upon our answer to it. I shall however end up suggesting that current versions of the primary–secondary-quality distinction leave the secondary qualities beyond the reach of experience.

III

What more is required for an experience caused by a dispositional property to be an experience of that property? One suggestion, firmly within the Lockean tradition, requires our experience of the property to *resemble* that property 'as it is in the object'. But this fails to provide what we want, for two reasons. First, our experience of moral properties on the weaker view does not resemble them as they are in the object, for there they are only dispositions which our experience can hardly be said to resemble at all. Second, the classic Lockean account of the primary–secondary-quality distinction in terms of ideas of properties that do and do not resemble those properties as they are in the object is completely flawed, and must be rejected if that distinction is to survive. The reason why it is flawed is that Locke requires us to make sense of an instruction to distinguish between primary qualities which resemble purely phenomenal objects (ideas) and secondary qualities which don't. But this is a hopeless muddle, worse in its account of primary qualities than of secondary ones. Primary qualities, viewed in this light, will be impossible because we can make no sense of properties which are objective and able to exist independent of perception but yet resemble our experience in purely phenomenal respects. (This is the main thrust of Berkeley's objections to Locke, based on his claim that an idea can be like nothing but another idea.[4]) So the primary–secondary distinction would collapse in favour of the secondary. We need, therefore, a new account of the distinction before we can really judge the strength of the analogy between moral properties and secondary qualities.

The only way in which a distinctively different account can be constructed is to abandon the hope of running the distinction in terms of an intrinsic resemblance, or the lack of one, between external object and internal subjective state. Instead we should drop talk of resemblance in favour of talking of an identity between how the objects are and how our experience represents them as being.[5] Here there is no suggestion that experiences act as intermediaries between ourselves and the world, having representational properties only in virtue of their intrinsic ones. Instead we should think of experience as intrinsically representational (cf. VASQ 115–16). This makes room for us to think of the content of experience as being in favourable cases identical with the way the world is; the world can be the way it seems to be. And with this we can recover the primary–secondary distinction as the difference between those properties that are represented to us in experience as distinctively phenomenal (the secondary ones) and those that are not.

One of the purposes of the shift from talk of resemblance between perceptual state and object to talk of identity between representation and property represented is to avoid the insidious attractions of a question which looks very like the one I asked at the beginning of this section. Representative (or indirect) realists tend to ask 'What more is required for a perceptual state that resembles an object to count as a perception of that object?', and then to try causal answers. If the question is well conceived, and in particular if the concept of a perceptual state which it requires is sound, some causal answer must be right; though this faith has hardly been borne out by any conspicuous success in the answers offered.[6] But the attempt to buttress resemblance with causation in order to arrive at an account of perception is rendered void by the shift from talk of resemblance to talk of identity, and with it falls the 'What more' question mentioned above (as well as a traditional ground for the argument from illusion). But this does not mean that *our* 'What more' question is no longer applicable, for ours can be asked within the new approach. In asking what more is required for an experience caused by a dispositional

<hr />

[4] The objection is used also by McDowell at VASQ 113–17.

[5] Here I follow McDowell and Gareth Evans, 'Things without the Mind', in Zak van Straaten (ed.), *Philosophical Subjects: Essays Presented to P. F. Strawson* (Oxford: Clarendon Press, 1980), esp. pp. 94–9.

[6] See P. Snowdon, 'Perception, Vision and Causation', *Proceedings of the Aristotelian Society*, 81 (1980–1), 175–92.

property to be an experience of that property, we are asking under what conditions a dispositional property can be the content of an experience which it causes, or under what conditions an experience caused by a dispositional property can represent that property to us and be an experience *of* that property.

My strategy will be as follows: first I shall pretend that we can make good sense of colour experience as the experience of something which is in the object only a disposition, and argue that even then we cannot make similar sense of moral experience. This will mean that colour experience is secure and moral experience is not. But I will then turn to suggest more strongly that the experiences caused by the disposition which is what colour is in the object are not experiences of that disposition, on our present understanding. So if you find the first part of the argument unconvincing, you should remember that it is succeeded by a stronger and more general one.

So let us suppose for a moment that there is some answer to this question, which persuades us that we can make good sense of the experience caused by the colour of an object being an experience of that colour, even though colour is to be conceived dispositionally. Can our moral experience similarly represent objects (actions) to us as having the dispositions which are moral properties in the objects?

Now there seem to be two ways in which our experience can represent dispositions to us. The first is what one would think is the normal one, that of actually having the sort of perceptual experience which the disposition is a disposition to elicit. (We are supposing for the moment that this works at least in the case of colours.) The second is perhaps rather rarer, but none the less interesting for that; it is when we experience the disposition unactualized. A good example of this is our ability to experience the sharpness of a knife by running a thumb across the blade, so that we experience its ability to cut without experiencing any actual cutting. Which of these models is most suitable for our present purpose? The second model looks initially unpromising. If we are trying to conceive of a moral property as a disposition to elicit certain responses from us, are we not to take it that the standard way to experience that disposition is when we find ourselves approving or disapproving? If so, the first model has first claim on our attention.

To discern the difficulties presented by the first model we need to notice one respect in which moral properties are disanalogous with the secondary quality of colour (and other secondary qualities too). We can consider the experience of colour either determinately or determinably, either as the experience of some particular colour or as the experience simply of some colour or other. Considering the matter determinably, a coloured object is one which has a disposition to cause a distinctive sort of perceptual experience, colour experience. What is it for an object to be red? Analogously, it is for the object to have a disposition to cause a distinctive sort of colour experience. But all objects have a disposition to cause that sort of experience in *some* conditions; a red object is one which has a disposition to cause that sort of experience in standard or normal conditions. Turning now to ethics, we might hope for a reasonable analogy for the determinable; an object that has some moral property is one with a disposition to elicit a certain sort of response, let us say approval and disapproval (stones can't do this, perhaps). But when we turn to the determinate, we cannot suppose that a determinate moral property is a disposition to cause a certain moral response in normal circumstances. Normal situations are precisely not very good ones for discerning the moral properties of the choices we face. We have to deal with distractions, contrary influences, prejudices, lack of time and similar problems. More promising, it seems, is to conceive of the moral property of rightness, for example, as a disposition to cause a certain response (approval) in *ideal* circumstances. (I allow this notion of ideal circumstances to package together what are really two requirements, that the perceiver be 'ideal' and that the situation be 'ideal' too.)

Our question now is whether it is possible for our moral experience, which never occurs in ideal circumstances, to represent to us moral properties conceived now as dispositions to cause certain responses in us in ideal situations, which we never experience. In such a case, though our experience may be indistinguishable from the experience which the relevant disposition is a disposition to elicit, it is not that experience itself. And this means that our first model turns out to be inapplicable. For the model is written around the notion of an *identity*; we experience a disposition if we have the experience which the disposition is a disposition to cause. Our normal moral experience may be indistinguishable from the experience which the moral property is a disposition to cause, but it will not be identical with it, for the phrase 'in ideal circumstances' is an ineliminable part of the specification of that disposition.[7]

But this is not yet the end of the matter. After all, we are able to tell from an experience of colour in an abnormal situation what colour the object would look in a normal situation; at least we can do this with a bit of gathered knowledge about the relevant relations between normal and abnormal situations. Can't we hope to do the same in ethics? I don't see how we can. The problem is not that the sort of response we are here

---

[7] I find a slightly different use of the ideal–normal distinction in Colin McGinn, *The Subjective View* (Oxford: Clarendon Press, 1983), 150–3.

talking about is one of which we cannot conceive; as far as the response goes we can conceive of it because we have experienced it, or responses indistinguishable from it, in more normal, less ideal circumstances. Nor do I think that the right way to express the problem is by claiming that we are in such cases involved in inference from what we perceive rather than in perception itself; this would matter because of the constant need to remain consistent with the general thrust of the phenomenology argument, but I am not confident enough about the distinction between perception and inference to rely on it for the present purpose. The real point is that though we might be said, in the case of colour, to see what colour the object really is in seeing what colour it appears in this light, this is because we have sufficient independent experience of the normal and of the abnormal in this case. But in the ethical case, we lack the independent experience which would, if it existed, enable our present non-ideal moral experience to count as experience of the real moral properties of the object. We cannot be said to experience here the object's disposition to elicit a certain response in ideal circumstances.

Nor will it help to return to the second model, which we initially ruled out as unpromising. To do so would now amount in this case to saying, by analogy, that our only way of telling that a knife is sharp is by running our thumb along its edge. But surely, though running one's thumb along in that way may perfectly well be a way of perceiving the sharpness (rather than inferring that the knife is sharp from something else that we perceive), still this can only be so because we have established a way of correlating the way the knife now feels with an ability to cut. But in the ethical case no such correlation is available, because of the unavailability (and indeed the redundancy) of experiences of those moral properties which are dispositions to elicit characteristic responses in ideal circumstances.

This argument, and the distinction which it uses between the normal and ideal, is what undermines McDowell's main independent argument in favour of the weaker conception of moral realism, referred to at the end of Section I. The crucial consideration is that a moral property, conceived as a disposition to elicit a certain response in ideal circumstances, is not for that reason internally related to the will of a perceiver who is not himself in those circumstances.[8] If, for instance, I am drunk or overcome by greed, or even surrounded by and distracted by ordinary concerns, why should I care about the disposition an action may have to cause certain responses in me in situations in which I do not at present find myself? We may for these purposes admit that if I were in such a situation, the objective circum-

---

[8] I owe this thought to David McNaughton.

stances with which I take myself to be faced would be internally related to my will. But I am never in such circumstances, and this means that the sort of internal relation that McDowell is seeking to establish is never (or at least not normally) present. So the weaker conception succumbs itself to his objection to the stronger, if that objection is valid at all.

It is beginning to look, then, as if there is a real difficulty in the idea that moral properties, conceived as analogous to secondary qualities, are genuinely experienceable. And the argument to this conclusion does not have the unfortunate consequence of ruling out any experience of secondary qualities. For it traded first on a distinction between moral properties and ideal circumstances, on the one hand, and secondary qualities and normal circumstances on the other; and second on the resulting availability of independent background knowledge to extend the bounds of the perceivable in the case of colour but not in the ethical case. We have not yet argued that on the revised account of secondary qualities colour cannot be experienced. Of course on the faulty account derived from Locke, which we rejected, there is such an argument, for Locke cannot make good sense of there being an idea in our mind *resembling* colour as it is in the object, as he admits (indeed insists). And this seems to entail that though we can have experiences caused by the disposition which is colour as it is in the object, and in this extensional sense have experiences of colour, still our experience in this case is not *of* colour any more than an experience caused by a dangerous object, and caused by the disposition which is its dangerousness, is for that reason an experience *of* danger. But the revised account of secondary qualities, as distinctively phenomenal properties which our experience represents objects as having, does not admit this sort of attack. Our objects are, on this account, represented to us as having certain dispositions to elicit responses from us in certain circumstances; this relation is irreducibly intensional.

This does not mean that no doubts can be raised about the account of experience of secondary qualities given here. We may well wonder whether our experience really does represent objects to us as having these dispositions, and suppose instead that however dispositional our understanding of them may be, still our experience of them is as non-dispositional. Can we take seriously the way in which colour appears to us, which seems to me at least to be stubbornly non-dispositional, if we insist that the right account of the 'distinctively phenomenal' nature which colour is represented as having is to be understood as its being (or existing in virtue of) a disposition to present a certain sort of appearance? It may turn out that real realists will eventually be able to think of moral properties as analogous to secondary qualities, but only at the cost of abandoning the dispositional account of both which is the core of the weaker conception of moral realism, for on it hangs the argument that moral properties are real properties of objects. The central questions here are 'Can dispositions appear, and how do they do it?'. Two important matters depend on our answers. First is the question whether the revised account of the primary–secondary-quality distinction is in the end any improvement; it may seem that whereas Locke's account fails to make good sense of the primary qualities, as McDowell argues, McDowell's own account fails to make sense of the secondary ones as possible objects of experience. Second is the question whether the sense, if any, in which moral properties are distinctively phenomenal bears any relation to the sense (or senses) in which colour is distinctively phenomenal.

So far we have been discussing the question whether the weaker conception of moral realism is really a form of moral realism at all, and arguing that it is not because it does not make satisfactory sense of the experience of moral properties of objects, and therefore is eventually inconsistent with the phenomenology argument, which is the main incentive to moral realism in the first place. But we have now reached a point at which our considerations take a rather different tack, tending to show that the weaker conception collapses eventually into the stronger. The difference between the two conceptions lies in a dispute about whether to introduce a richer conception of moral properties as they are in objects than that of a disposition to cause or elicit a certain response, or to present a certain perceptual appearance. McDowell's formulation of the position (VASQ 111), which speaks of ascriptions of secondary qualities as only able to be understood as true, if true, in virtue of the object's disposition to present a certain sort of perceptual appearance pretends to leave it open whether the moral property is to be seen as the disposition itself, or whether the moral property is something which results from the disposition. But perhaps the main competing view is that the disposition itself results from the moral property: this not merely causally, of course, just as it is not possible that red objects should not have a disposition to look red. Speaking in general of secondary qualities, a possible position is that though we continue to see them as distinctively phenomenal, we understand the disposition to present certain sorts of perceptual appearance as lying between the secondary quality as it is in the object and ourselves as perceivers. This position involves giving an account of what it is to be distinctively phenomenal other than the McDowell one in terms of a disposition or of that which exists in virtue of a disposition. But with a new account, the question will be whether colour is distinctively phenomenal in any sense in which moral properties are. There must be some such sense for McDowell's purposes, for otherwise the reality of the phenomenal, established in the case of colour, will not spread over to establish the reality of the moral.

The present point, however, is that an account of moral properties as dispositions to elicit certain responses in ideal circumstances seems itself to introduce a more substantial conception of those properties than the dispositional one. This emerges when we ask what is ideal about the ideal circumstances? What are the ideal circumstances ideal for? Presumably for the elicitation of moral attitudes. But the question is what is better about the attitudes elicited in ideal circumstances. They, like other attitudes formed in more normal situations, are responses to a disposition—a disposition which shows no need to be understood in terms of its effect in certain very special circumstances. It is only if we smuggle in the idea that the disposition cannot reveal itself as it really is except in those special circumstances that those circumstances come to play an important role. But this idea is uncongenial to the weaker conception of moral realism (whether it is consistent with the phenomenology argument or not), for it comes naturally only to someone who says that as well as the disposition to elicit attitudes of certain kinds, there is something further in the objects–actions which the attitudes caused by the disposition only fit, or can only be guaranteed to fit (whatever sort of fit is in play here), in ideal conditions. The conditions are ideal because they are the ones in which our response fits the moral property, which cannot therefore be conceived of as a disposition. So the conclusion seems to be that the weaker conception collapses into the stronger one, because the attempt to see moral properties as dispositions to elicit certain responses in ideal circumstances depends covertly on the richer conception to which it was supposed to be an alternative, if it is to be able to explain why the ideal circumstances are ideal.

IV

This concludes my argument against the weaker conception and in favour of a stronger alternative. But it may seem that even if my arguments succeed in demolishing the target at which they are aimed, there remains a further and better version of the attempt to use an analogy between secondary qualities and moral properties, which escapes what has been said so far. For towards the end of his paper, John McDowell himself begins to stress a feature of disanalogy between the two (VASQ 118–20). This is that while a secondary quality like colour is adequately conceived as a disposition to cause certain responses in us, a moral property should be seen rather as a way in which an object *merits* some distinctive responses.

McDowell has his reasons for this shift, of course; they concern the way
in which he thinks we should seek to avoid Mackie's charge[9] that we have
empirical reason to avoid taking the deliverances of experience seriously in
certain cases, because the properties which our experience represents
objects as having are explanatorily redundant. But this shift seems to make
the use of a secondary-quality model harder to sustain, at least at first sight.
Admittedly the model was never intended as more than a model. There
was no intention of holding that moral properties are secondary qualities
in just the sort of way that colour is. As I have already suggested, moral
properties may not be perceptual in just the way that colour is; they are not
in the same way 'distinctively phenomenal'. This may mean that McDowell
is wrong to insist on the notion of a perceptual appearance as central to the
distinction between primary and secondary qualities; there seem to be
some properties such as those of being dangerous (to which McDowell
refers at VASQ 120) and interesting (to which he doesn't) for which a
secondary-quality model looks promising but which do not seem to fit
a centrally perceptual version of that model. (Even if dangerousness is a
quality of Locke's third sort, interestingness should, as a power in objects
to cause ideas in us, count as secondary.) But talk of meriting a response
rather than causing it seems to make the perceptual model harder to cash
for ethics, and thus to distance it from what we are still maintaining to be
analogous. It strengthens the sense in which the distinctive phenomenality
of colours differs from that of moral properties. So the purpose of the
analogy begins to become mysterious.

I said that the use of the notion of meriting seems at first sight to have
the effect of undermining the secondary-quality analogy. But in fact my
opinion is that is it not in the end distinct from a notion we have already
considered and found wanting, that of a disposition to elicit a certain sort
of response in ideal circumstances. It is not as if we have here two differences between moral properties and colour, the first lying in the distinction
between normal and ideal circumstances and the second in that between
eliciting and meriting a response. The only way to understand the notion of
meriting a response is to see a merited response as the one which would be
elicited in ideal conditions. We can give no good sense to the thought that
an object should merit a response which it would never receive, even in
ideal circumstances; that there should be something about a good or a right
action which lies beyond any possibility of recognition; that an action
might be right even though there are no circumstances in which we could
hope or be expected to notice the fact; or that the rightness of an action

---

[9] See Mackie's *Ethics*, 19–20 (pp. 61–2 of this volume).

might only be revealed to us in less than ideal circumstances. So it seems to me that the notion of a response which an action merits is identical with the notion of the response which it would elicit (has a disposition to elicit) in ideal circumstances. And this means that we are left with our two original thoughts, that there is something odd about the experienceability of dispositions, and that the distinction between the normal and the ideal undermines the weaker conception of moral realism. The detour through merit is in the end no improvement.

V

What then remains of the primary–secondary distinction? Abandoning the attempt to run this distinction in terms of those properties which in the object are merely dispositions to cause certain perceptual states in us, what importance can we attach to the idea that the distinction can or must survive as part of an attempt to separate properties that are distinctively phenomenal from those that are not? This separation must rest on a difference which is not merely a matter of degree.

What we are looking for as direct realists is a distinction between two types of property which is not mirrored in the epistemology. (This is because any attempt to mirror it in the epistemology is likely to open the door to indirect realism.) McDowell's idea is that secondary qualities are something distinctively, even essentially, to do with the way things look. There is a contrast in this idea, but it must not be that between appearance and reality; we are not separating properties which concern the way things look from those which concern the way they are—not at least if we intend to wind up with some form of realism about the secondary qualities. Nor can we be here contrasting ways things can look with ways they can't look. There is no future in denying that things can look square. Perhaps instead the distinction is between the secondary qualities, which are essentially to do with how things look, and the primary qualities as other ways things can be but which they don't need to look. Primary qualities, on this account, can get by without the looks.

But don't square things need to look square? On the Lockean resemblance theory, now rejected, they perhaps don't. It might be a contingent question whether our ideas of square objects really resemble those objects in respect of squareness. (Actually we have already decided on Berkeleian grounds that they can't; this feature of Lockean theory is not a strength.) But on the identity-based theory which we have substituted for the resemblance theory, it is surely not a contingent question whether our perceptual states do or don't *represent* objects to us as square, or whether objects that are square are or are not as our perceptual states represent them to be. This gives one sense in which both primary and secondary qualities are essentially phenomenal. Is there another sense in which the essential phenomenality of the secondary is distinctive?

We earlier considered the suggestion that to be red is to look red in normal conditions; to be coloured is to (be able to) present a certain kind of perceptual appearance. And we suggested that it is not possible for red objects not to have a disposition to look red. But this takes us no further forward; on the identity-based theory it is not possible for square objects not to have a disposition to look square, although the conditions in which they will look the shape they are (i.e. those that are to count as normal for shape perception) will be of a different style from those in which they will look the colour they are. In a way, the identity theory makes it impossible for us to ask which leads here—whether our conception of what it is to look *F* is derived from our conception of what it is to be *F*, or vice versa. It collapses this contrast, and with it should fall our trust in any recognizable version of the primary–secondary distinction. With this collapse moral realists are in no danger of suggesting ludicrously that moral properties are or are like primary qualities. But neither will they derive much sustenance from an analogy with secondary qualities. Real realists don't need the distinction at all.

NOTES ON THE CONTRIBUTORS

JONATHAN DANCY, Professor of Philosophy at the University of Reading, works in the area between moral theory and epistemology. He is the author of *An Introduction to Contemporary Epistemology* and *Moral Reasons*.

DAVID GAUTHIER is Distinguished Service Professor of Philosophy at the University of Pittsburgh. His most recent books are *Morals by Agreement*, and a collection of his essays, *Moral Dealing: Contract, Ethics, and Reason*.

R. M. HARE, a Fellow of the British Academy, retired as White's Professor of Moral Philosophy at Oxford and then became Research Professor of Philosophy at the University of Florida. Among his many influential books are *The Language of Morals*, *Freedom and Reason*, and *Moral Thinking*.

GILBERT HARMAN is Professor of Philosophy at Princeton University, where he is also Faculty Associate of the University Center for Human Values and Co-Director of the Cognitive Science Laboratory. His most recent book is *Moral Relativism and Moral Objectivity* (with Judith Jarvis Thomson), in which he defends relativism while Thomson defends objectivity.

JOHN MCDOWELL is University Professor of Philosophy at the University of Pittsburgh. He is the author of *Mind and World* and numerous articles; he also translated Plato's *Theaetetus* in the Clarendon Plato series. Professor McDowell is a Fellow of the British Academy and of the American Academy of Arts and Sciences.

J. L. MACKIE was an Australian philosopher who moved to England and taught at Oxford. He was known for his work on various philosophical topics, including his book on causality, *The Cement of the Universe*, and his book *Ethics: Inventing Right and Wrong*. *The Miracle of Theism* was published posthumously.

G. E. MOORE's association with Cambridge University began in 1898; he was named Professor of Philosophy there in 1925. An enormously respected thinker, Moore was a defender of common sense against the idealists. His book *Principia Ethica*, published in 1903, marked the beginning of twentieth-century moral philosophy.

THOMAS NAGEL is Professor of Philosophy and Law at New York University. His books include *The Possibility of Altruism*, *The View from Nowhere*, and *The Last Word*.

JAMES RACHELS is University Professor at the University of Alabama at Birmingham. He is the author of *The End of Life* (1986), *Created from Animals: The Moral Implications of Darwinism* (1991), *The Elements of Moral Philosophy* (1993), and *Can Ethics Provide Answers?* (1997).

BERTRAND RUSSELL was one of the leading figures of twentieth-century thought. The *Bibliography of Bertrand Russell* lists over 3,000 items.

CHARLES L. STEVENSON, who taught for most of his career at the University of Michigan, was the chief proponent of the ethical theory of emotivism. His books are *Ethics and Language* and *Facts and Values*.

NICHOLAS L. STURGEON is Professor of Philosophy at Cornell University. He has written about the foundations of ethics and the interpretation of the eighteenth-century philosophers Joseph Butler and David Hume.

DAVID WIGGINS is Professor of Philosophy at Oxford University. He writes about metaphysics (especially identity), philosophical logic, and ethics. He wrote *Sameness and Substance* and *Needs, Values, Truth: Essays in the Philosophy of Value*, among other works.

BERNARD WILLIAMS is Deutsche Professor of Philosophy at the University of California, Berkeley; he is retired from being White's Professor of Moral Philosophy at Oxford. He is a Fellow of the British Academy. His books include *Moral Luck*, *Ethics and the Limits of Philosophy*, *Shame and Necessity*, and *Making Sense of Humanity*.

SELECT BIBLIOGRAPHY

BAIER, KURT, *The Rational and the Moral Order* (Chicago and La Salle, Ill.: Open Court, 1995).

BAMBROUGH, RENFORD, *Moral Skepticism and Moral Knowledge* (Atlantic Heights, NJ: Humanities Press, 1979).

BECKER, LAWRENCE, *On Justifying Moral Judgments* (New York: Humanities Press, 1973).

BLACKBURN, SIMON, *Essays in Quasi-Realism* (New York: Oxford University Press, 1993).

BRINK, DAVID O., *Moral Realism and the Foundations of Ethics* (Cambridge: Cambridge University Press, 1989).

COBURN, ROBERT, 'Morality, Truth and Relativism', *Ethics*, 92 (1982), 661–9.

——— 'Relativism and the Basis of Morality', *Philosophical Review*, 85 (1976), 87–93.

COOPER, DAVID E., 'Moral Relativism', *Midwest Studies in Philosophy*, 3 (Morris: University of Minnesota Press, 1978), 97–108.

COPP, DAVID, *Morality, Normativity, and Society* (New York: Oxford University Press, 1995).

——— and DAVID ZIMMERMAN (eds.), *Morality, Reason and Truth* (Totowa, NJ: Rowman & Allanheld, 1985).

COUTURE, JOCELYNE, and KAI NIELSEN (eds.), *On the Relevance of Metaethics: New Essays on Metaethics* (Calgary: University of Calgary Press, 1995).

DANCY, JONATHAN, *Moral Reasons* (Oxford: Basil Blackwell, 1993).

DARWALL, STEPHEN, *Impartial Reason* (Ithaca, NY: Cornell University Press, 1983).

——— ALLAN GIBBARD, and PETER RAILTON (eds.), *Moral Discourse and Practice* (New York: Oxford University Press, 1997).

——— ——— ——— 'Toward *Fin de siècle* Ethics: Some Trends', *Philosophical Review*, 101 (1992), 115–89.

EWING, A. C., *The Definition of Good* (New York: Macmillan, 1947).

FALK, W. D., *Ought, Reasons, and Morality* (Ithaca, NY: Cornell University Press, 1986).

FOOT, PHILIPPA, *Virtues and Vices* (Los Angeles: University of California Press, 1978).

GIBBARD, ALAN, *Wise Choices, Apt Feelings* (Cambridge, Mass.: Harvard University Press, 1990).

GILLESPIE, NORMAN (ed.), *Spindel Conference 1986: Moral Realism*, Southern Journal of Philosophy, suppl. vol. 24 (1986).

GOLDMAN, ALAN H., *Moral Knowledge* (London: Routledge, 1988).

HALDANE, JOHN, and CRISPIN WRIGHT, *Reality, Representation and Projection* (New York: Oxford University Press, 1993).

HARE, R. M., *Freedom and Reason* (Oxford: Oxford University Press, 1963).

——— *The Language of Morals* (New York: Oxford University Press, 1952).

——— *Moral Thinking* (New York: Oxford University Press, 1981).

HARMAN, GILBERT, *The Nature of Morality: An Introduction to Ethics* (New York: Oxford University Press, 1977).

248 SELECT BIBLIOGRAPHY

HARMAN, GILBERT, and JUDITH JARVIS THOMSON, *Moral Relativism and Moral Objectivity* (Oxford: Basil Blackwell, 1996).

HONDERICH, TED (ed.), *Morality and Objectivity* (London: Routledge & Kegan Paul, 1985).

HORGAN, TERENCE, and MARK TIMMONS, 'Troubles on Moral Twin Earth: Moral Queerness Revived', *Synthèse*, 92 (1992), 221–60.

HUDSON, W. D. (ed.), *The Is–Ought Question* (London: Macmillan, 1969).

KORSGAARD, CHRISTINE, G. A. COHEN, RAYMOND GEUSS, THOMAS NAGEL, and BERNARD WILLIAMS, *The Sources of Normativity* (Cambridge: Cambridge University Press, 1996).

LEWIS, DAVID K., 'Dispositional Theories of Value', *Proceedings of the Aristotelian Society*, suppl. vol. 63 (1989), 113–37.

McDOWELL, JOHN, 'Are Moral Requirements Hypothetical Imperatives?' *Proceedings of the Aristotelian Society*, suppl. vol. 52 (1978), 13–29.

MACKIE, J. L., *Ethics: Inventing Right and Wrong* (Harmondsworth: Penguin, 1977).
——*Persons and Values* (New York: Oxford University Press, 1985).

MOORE, G. E., *Principia Ethica* (Cambridge: Cambridge University Press, 1903).

NAGEL, THOMAS, *The View from Nowhere* (New York: Oxford University Press, 1987).

PRICHARD, H. A., *Moral Obligation* (New York: Oxford University Press, 1949).

PUTNAM, HILARY, *Realism with a Human Face* (Cambridge, Mass.: Harvard University Press, 1990).

QUINN, WARREN, *Morality and Action* (New York: Cambridge University Press, 1993).

RAILTON, PETER, 'Moral Realism', *Philosophical Review*, 95 (1986), 163–207.

ROSS, W. D., *Foundations of Ethics* (Oxford: Oxford University Press, 1939).
——*The Right and the Good* (Oxford: Oxford University Press, 1930).

SAYRE-McCORD, GEOFFREY (ed.), *Essays on Moral Realism* (Ithaca, NY: Cornell University Press, 1988).

SINOTT-ARMSTRONG, WALTER, and MARK TIMMONS (eds.), *Moral Knowledge: New Readings in Moral Epistemology* (New York: Oxford University Press, 1996).

SMITH, MICHAEL, *The Moral Problem* (Oxford: Basil Blackwell, 1994).

STEVENSON, C. L., *Ethics and Language* (New Haven: Yale University Press, 1944).
——*Facts and Values* (New Haven: Yale University Press, 1963).

STURGEON, NICHOLAS, 'Moral Disagreement and Moral Relativism', *Social Philosophy and Policy*, 11 (1994), 80–115.
——'What Difference does it Make whether Moral Realism is True?' *Southern Journal of Philosophy*, suppl. vol. 24 (1986), 115–42.

TIMMONS, MARK (ed.), *Spindel Conference 1990: Moral Epistemology Southern Journal of Philosophy*, suppl. vol. 29 (1990).

URMSON, J. O., *The Emotive Theory of Ethics* (Oxford: Oxford University Press, 1968).

WIGGINS, D., *Needs, Values, Truth: Essays in the Philosophy of Value* (Oxford: Basil Blackwell, 1987).

INDEX